Fading Past

Foreword

Sandwiched between mushrooming metro Denver and Colorado Springs, Douglas became the fastest-growing county in the United States during the 1990s. Highlands Ranch and other fabled spreads faded into residential subdivisions and shopping paradises.

Despite Colorado's greatest growth rate, Douglas County maintains its picturesque eastern prairies and ponderosa forest, its central tablelands and western foothills guarded by gnarly old Devils Head. The devil has been at work in this county, destroying pioneer homes, churches, schools, general stores, and ranches.

Thank heaven for angels like Susan Appleby, who herein attempts to record, preserve, and celebrate a vanishing heritage. Susan has been expanding and polishing this work, which began in 1993 as her master's degree thesis at the University of Colorado at Denver. I and her other advisors thought this was too good and too needed not to publish.

While exploring Douglas County's Native American and Euro-American relics, Susan grew alarmed about their disappearance. Subsequently she joined and became a board member of the Douglas County Historic Preservation Board, the Castle Rock Historic Preservation Board, and the Highlands Ranch Historical Society. With husband Don, son Jacob, and daughter Lauren, she has prowled every inch of the county to put together this book.

Fading Past: The Story of Douglas County, Colorado is now in your hands. May you enjoy touring and celebrating these places, which give Douglas County a sense of perspective, a sense of place and roots. Thanks to concerned citizens, Douglas County can celebrate in recent years the preservation of one of the county's largest ranches, Greenland, and the most picturesque one, Cherokee. Castle Rock's fabulous pink, purple, and gray railroad depot is now a crackerjack museum; the town's old St. Francis of Assisi Church is reborn as a delicious restaurant and Colorado's only saloon with stained glass saints.

The buffalo grazing in Daniels Park and the lonely churchyard tombstones guarding St. Philip-in-the-Field have stories to tell. So do landmarks such as the Pike's Peak Grange Hall, the American Federation of Human Rights Headquarters, and the Spring Valley School. Citizens of Louviers, a dynamite town, obtained a National Register Historic District listing in 1999. Castle Rock, with its fabulous and unique rhyolite buildings, should pursue a similar celebration of its pioneer builders.

Fading Past in hand, Douglas Countians today and tomorrow are well armed to preserve and even reconstruct a fascinating heritage of Indians and cowboys, of stage drivers and railroaders, of quarries and lumbermen, of one-room school teachers and women ranchers, of saloonkeepers and general store tenders. Such a past should not keep fading away, but be there to comfort the old-timers and to greet thousands of new families rushing to Colorado's fast-growing twenty-first century frontier.

Thomas J. Noel
Professor of History
University of Colorado at Denver

Acknowledgments

Although this book has only one author, its production and eventual fruition was made possible by the collective efforts of many people and institutions. While I have accumulated a large, possibly unpayable debt, I appreciate this opportunity to thank those whose help, encouragement, and recommendations facilitated the completion of this book.

My debt to Johanna Harden, archivist for the Local History Collection of the Douglas Public Library District, is beyond words. By opening up her archives and allowing me to rummage endlessly through every cavity of the collection, Johanna truly introduced me to the many facets of Douglas County history. I will forever appreciate and cherish her trust and faith in me.

Members of the Douglas County Historic Preservation Board, particularly Clyde Jones and Kent Brandebery, showed untiring support for my work as well as admirable patience with my endless questions. Karen Kievit and Joni Jones of the Parker Area Historical Society, Elaine Frasher and Chris Eppers of the Highlands Ranch Historical Society, and Lionel and Starr Oberlin of the Castle Rock Historical Society offered helpful suggestions and advice.

I thoroughly enjoyed the opportunity to work with Doris Baker of Filter Press, whose enthusiasm was positively contagious and inspiring. The invaluable tips, knowledge, and encouragement of Professor Thomas J. Noel of the University of Colorado at Denver always proved timely and useful. Judy Matthews of Libraries Unlimited spent a considerable amount of her off-hours time with me. Robert Barten of the Douglas County Planning Department helped decipher maps and modern residential development files. Jess Stainbrook, Dave Wruck, and David Schler of Douglas County Television graciously allowed me to view their library of video interviews. Talented artist Mary Elliott provided her beautiful drawing of the Highlands Ranch windmill. Jamie LaRue, director of the Douglas Public Library District, maintained a steadfast confidence in this book's future and his support will always be appreciated.

I am extremely thankful to the people who allowed me to interview them. While all generously granted me their time and contributed greatly to my understanding of Douglas County's past and present, I want to thank especially the following: Sally Maguire, Micki Clark, Richard and Iola Geiger, Myrna Been, Lester and Florence Burch, Loyd Glasier, Bob Lowenberg, Fran Snyder, and Susie Trumble.

This book had many proofreaders. I am thankful to the following people for their time and suggestions: William Kirby, Jennifer Drybread, Marlene Thomas, Jan Herman, Penny Burdick, Cheryl Haflich, and Susan Hindman.

Other, more indirect, contributors to the completion of this work were Cindy Murphy, Keith Schrum, Shaun Boyd, Ida May Noe, Pam Cress, Norman Tuinstra, Professor James Fell, Kristyn Pye, Christine Smith, Joan Fingerle, Mike and Larisa Stassi, Kristi Aukamp, Donna Bardallis, Dick and Dodie Guntren, and Mary Biskner, who listened to my grumbling, and Brian Smith, who preserved an enormous amount of my time with his computer expertise.

Most importantly, my family deserves the utmost praise for countering my continual preoccupation and many mood swings with immutable patience and support. My parents, James and Cynthia Consola, who always encouraged my love of books, sacrificed an unspeakable amount of their personal time to help their daughter fulfill her dream. The inquisitiveness and genuine interest expressed by Amy, Max, Robert, and Lucy Consola and by Douglas, Maribelle, and Dana Appleby in the progress of this book proved especially motivating. Lastly, I want to thank my husband, Don Appleby, for his sagacious editing, good humor, and revitalizing support; and my son, Jacob, and daughter, Lauren, for giving my life perspective and always greeting me with a smile when I emerged from my work.

To the historic preservationists of Douglas County,
whose devotion to saving the past has been an inspiration to me.

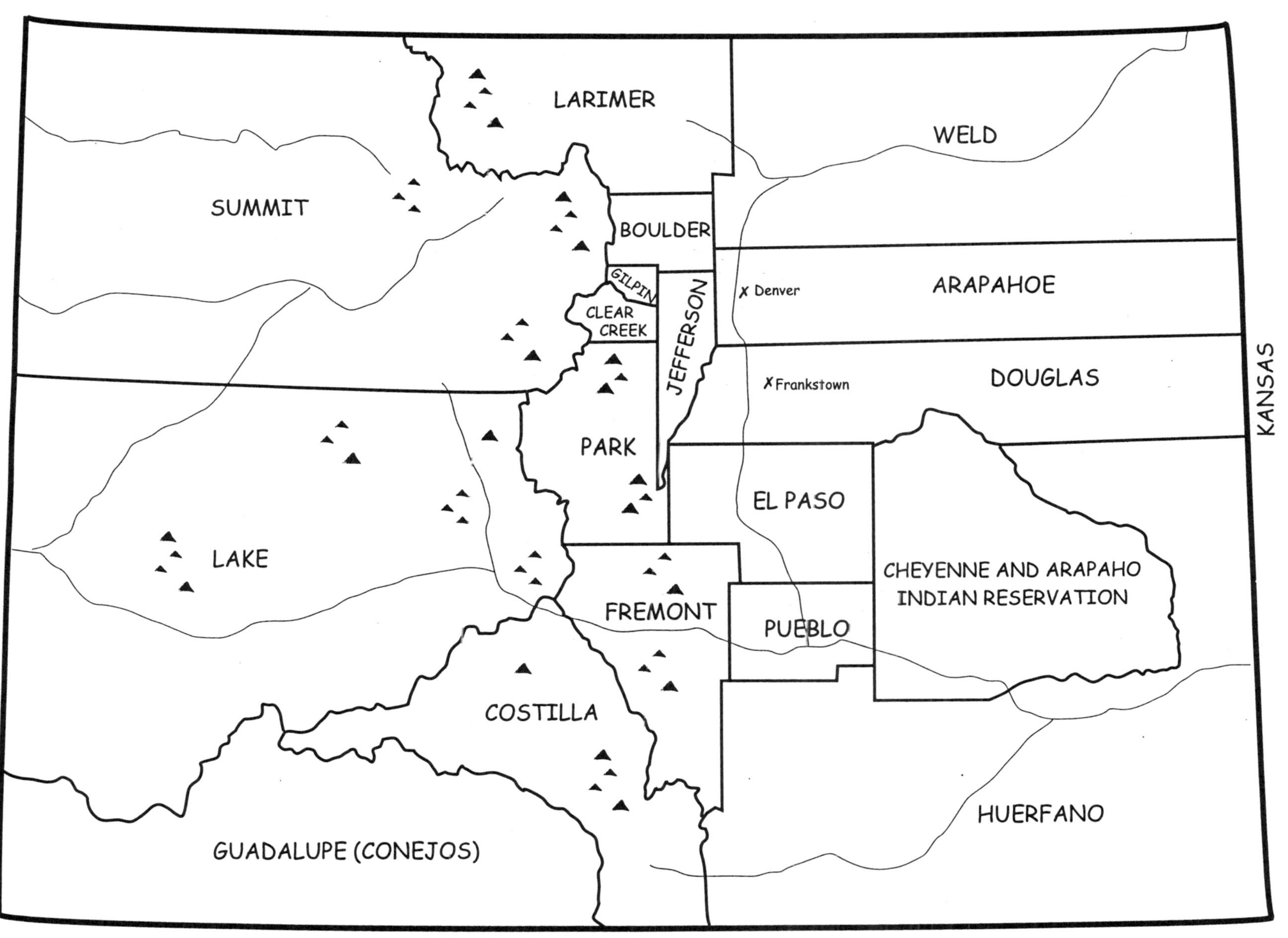

Douglas County boundaries until 1874 when Elbert County was created from the eastern half of the county and the county seat moved from Frankstown to Castle Rock.

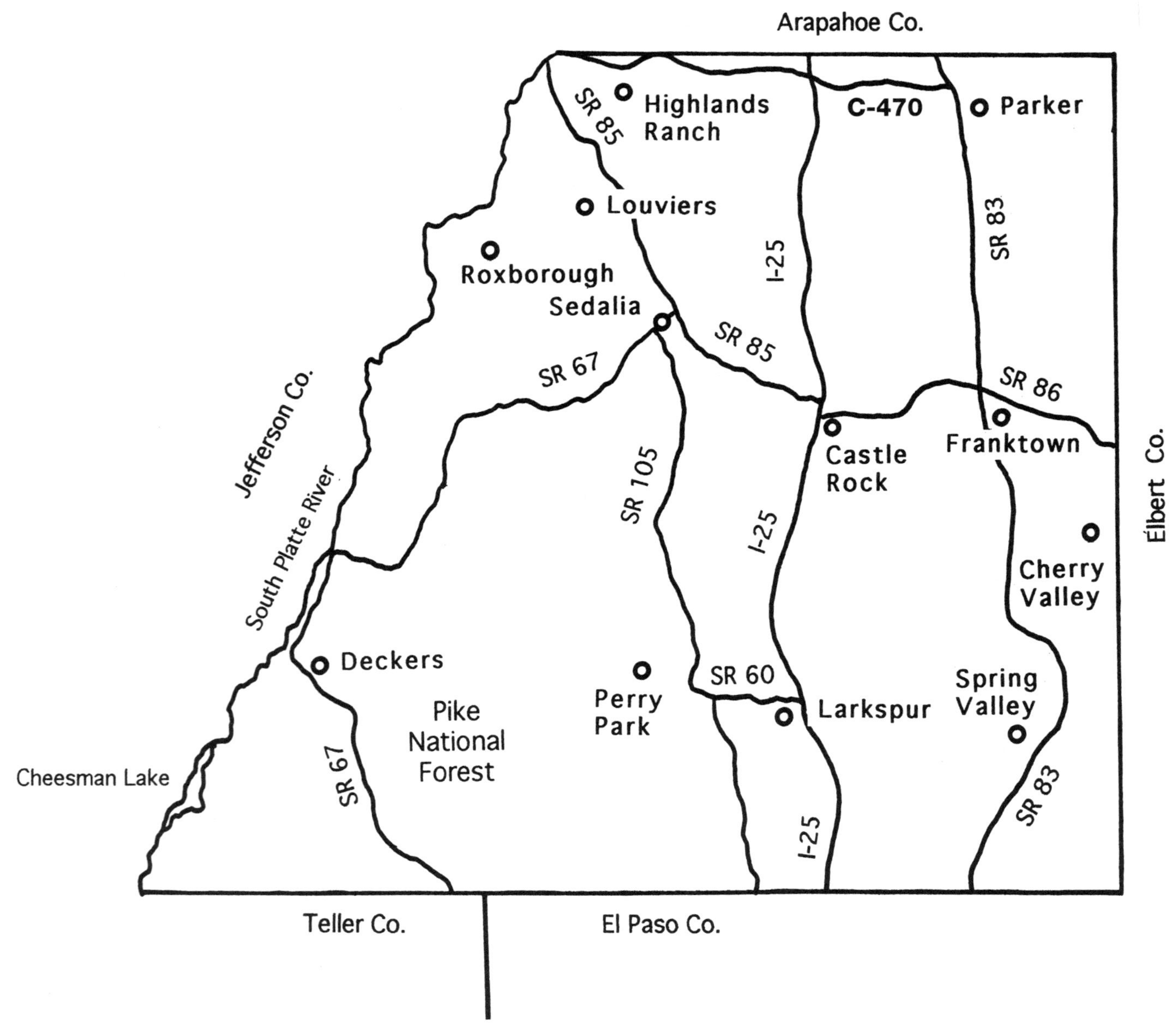

Douglas County's major towns and communities.

Introduction

Early pioneers ventured into the vast, mysterious western United States for a myriad of reasons. Some were led by enticing visions of dazzling gold fields; for others, the concept of Manifest Destiny and the promise of a new life inspired and drove them to the western lands. While some sought refuge from the law or the brewing political, social, and economic conflicts that eventually culminated in the American Civil War, others were driven by a simple, yet unyielding curiosity and yearning for adventure. Energized by their individual motives, these early travelers created a westward frontier movement that symbolized freedom, strength, and prosperity for the entire nation.

Colorado represented an important chapter in this westward migration. Beginning in 1858, tantalizing and exaggerated echoes of "Gold!" prompted thousands from the East as well as overseas to travel the desolate, barren plains to reach the rich Colorado mountain ores. As this gold rush initiated white settlement in Colorado, the land's original occupants, Native American tribes, watched the newcomers' approach with understandable ambivalence. Colorado tribes such as the Arapaho, Cheyenne, and Ute had ties to the land that went back thousands of years, but they eventually paid the price for the white settlers' frenzied avarice for gold and land. Violent clashes between new settlers and the Arapaho and Cheyenne dominated Colorado history throughout the 1860s, and eventually culminated in the removal of natives from land that had been theirs for centuries. One early resident later offered his summary of this era in Colorado history: "Here, as elsewhere, when the Whiteman made his home on the Redman's hunting ground, it was thereafter a manhunt until the Redman with all his savage cunning gave way to the civilized cunning of the Whiteman."[1]

Set amid rolling prairies to the east and Rocky Mountain foothills to the west, the Douglas County region of Colorado lacked the gold that spurred growth elsewhere in the state. Intersected by the Cherokee and the Smoky Hill Trails, Douglas County instead served as a highway for travelers en route to other, more promising areas, such as booming Denver City or the mountain mining towns. Nonetheless, when many would-be argonauts recovered from their bouts with gold fever and descended the Rocky Mountain foothills to establish farms, ranches, or small businesses, the fertile land of Douglas County proved especially inviting. During the 1860s, as the wagon-rutted pioneer trails funneled families into the area, Douglas County, with its abundant land and resources such as lumber, rhyolite stone, and coal, gained new significance. Sawmills, ranches, farms, and dairy operations prospered, especially after the arrival of the Denver & Rio Grande and the Atchison, Topeka & Santa Fe railroads.

The political organization of Douglas County began in 1861. That November, the Territorial Legislature of Colorado established seventeen counties, one of which they named after Stephen A. Douglas, the Democratic senator from Illinois and chairman of the Senate Committee on Territories. Nicknamed the "Little Giant," Douglas had played a direct role in the Compromise of 1850 and the Kansas-Nebraska Act of 1854, key slavery compromises. After participating in a series of debates with Illinois Republican Abraham Lincoln in 1860 over slavery and popular sovereignty issues, Douglas ran an unsuccessful presidential campaign and died in June 1861. His notoriety lived on in the Colorado county that received his name.

Newly created Douglas County included a prodigious 5,160 square miles, bordered on the north by Arapahoe County, on the south by El Paso and Teller counties, on the west by Jefferson County and the South Platte River, and on the east by the Kansas state line. Frankstown, as the town was named until 1880, served as the county seat until 1874, when officials trimmed the county down to 843 square miles—creating Elbert County out of the eastern half—and forced an election in which Castle Rock became the new county seat. Today, Castle Rock, which features an unusual rock formation of the same name, continues to host the county's governmental, civic, and public transactions.

For many decades, Douglas County existed as a rural region dominated by farms, ranches, and several small towns. Later, these rural characteristics proved appealing to city dwellers and suburbanites, thousands of whom migrated to the county during the 1970s, '80s, and '90s. In the mid-1990s, astonished residents watched as Douglas County became the fastest-growing county in the country; by the end of 1999, the population had grown to more than 170,000—more than double that of just ten years earlier.

Today's residents, faced daily with the crowding and pressures that accompany unprecedented growth, may be surprised by the comments of some county third graders, who in 1977 told the *Douglas County News* why they enjoy living in the region:

> Chris: Because you can climb trees and have pine needle fights.
> Doug: Because you can have animals.
> Megan: Because it's quiet and there is more grass.
> Jina: Because at night there is no traffic.
> Tim M.: Because I like to hear the coyotes howl at night.
> Erik: Because the houses are farther apart and there is more room to play.
> Leif: Because there is more nature and hills to climb.
> Dana: Because you can have horses.[2]

As the country's fastest-growing area, Douglas County struggles to preserve its past. Cookie-cutter residential and commercial developments continue to be carved into old ranchlands, and many historic buildings are being bulldozed to make way for parking lots, shopping centers, and modern homes. Concern for historic preservation, once an unfamiliar concept, has resulted in the formation of several county historical societies and boards, designed to promote the history of the county and oversee the security of regional historic sites.

The Douglas County Historical Society was the oldest such organization. Organized in 1969, long before the surge of modern-day growth, the group met regularly to remember and discover the past through public programs, holiday celebrations, and historic displays at the former county library on Gilbert Street in Castle Rock. In 1981, the society published *Our Heritage: People of Douglas County*, an informative look at the early history of Douglas County through family and personal histories as well as essays by local authors. Not long after the release of this book, however, financial problems and attrition contributed to the dissolution of the society. The disbanded organization donated its collected archival material to the Douglas Public Library District.

The society's demise played a direct role in the formation of two new institutions: the Local History Collection of the Douglas Public Library District and the Douglas County Historic Preservation Board (DCHPB). Today both organizations tend to the preservation of Douglas County's history, albeit in slightly different ways.

The Local History Collection, Douglas County's first public repository for personal archival material, grew out of the items donated to the Douglas Public Library District when the historical society dissolved. Since 1992, archivist Johanna Harden has watched over the ever-expanding collection, now housed in the Philip S. Miller Library in Castle Rock. Tucked within the box-filled shelves and fireproof file cabinets of the crowded research room are extraordinary vestiges of Douglas County's history, including letters, photographs, diaries, manuscripts, aerial maps, architectural blueprints, and present-day community newsletters. Harden says the role of such materials is to provide essential information for the present and future by furnishing insight into past successes and failures. It is only through the donations of people from all backgrounds that the collection will retain such value, she says:

> One of the most frustrating parts of this job is people feel they have to have been rich and famous to be part of history. It saddens me when people say, "I have nothing to give because I didn't finish high school, my family wasn't rich, we didn't do anything special." When in fact, they've been a productive member of the community, raised children, worked. They were part of the fabric of the community. It's not only the rich and famous that make a community. But when you ask people for pieces of their past, their perception is that they somehow have to be larger than life. It will always be an educational process that all of these pieces of the past are important.

The DCHPB began as a volunteer arm of the county government in 1992 to pursue preservation, identification, and documentation of the area's historic resources. Those first volunteers sought to provide a central organization for the many local historical societies that had formed throughout the county. Faced with the daunting task of saving Douglas County's past amid the boom of modern growth, the board's eighteen members from all communities within the county hope to someday create a heritage center in the Cantril School building, with an emphasis on providing education and research facilities for residents. The center would have branch museums throughout the county to provide equal opportunity for historical expression and cultural community pride.

Describing past and present differences in residents' attitudes toward preservation of the county's historical sites, Clyde Jones, who has served as DCHPB chairman since its inception in 1992, suggests a dichotomous relationship between established land rights and modern development:

> Back when I first came to this county there was so much open space. I don't think people were as concerned about

> saving things in the early days as they are now. A lot of the newcomers are responsible for the increased awareness. . . . I think it's a philosophy people develop. Once they're in the neighborhoods they see something and learn a little bit about it and don't want to see it torn down. Some of the old timers probably wanted to keep things, but they sure didn't want their rights tampered with in any way so that they would ever lose their right to sell or do whatever they wanted with their land. You have a real strong sense of that in this county. The people that do own land don't want government to infringe upon their rights. They don't like all of these restrictions that come up every now and then. I guess if I were in their shoes I'd feel the same way. But now I think the good thing that has happened is that these newcomers are coming in and they feel very strongly about keeping what is there. They see things disappearing and all this newness that takes place. It's the "sameness." It's boring. If there's something over there that is in some way different and has been there a long time, why get rid of it and put in a house that looks the same as all the other new ones built nearby? That's the new mentality.

DCHPB member Kent Brandebery, former president of the Douglas County Historical Society, maintains that the society's demise paved the way for the stronger, more effective DCHPB. Brandebery's vision for the future of historic preservation in Douglas County comprises unity, sacrifice, and cooperation among both its leaders and citizenry:

> I would hope [historic preservation] goes the same way that open space went; that people see a real need for this and will support any efforts, by their tax monies, to create entities around the county that will help preserve these sites. I don't think we can do it without the help of open space, or all these entities in Douglas County like the Town of Larkspur, the Town of Lone Tree, the Town of Parker, the Town of Castle Rock, and probably the future Town of Highlands Ranch. It's got to be a cooperative thing. It will impact each one of these municipalities. I hope that the Douglas County government can be the leader in helping these communities with this and be kind of a coordinator to make this a countywide effort rather than having one group in one municipality trying to do it alone.

As residential and commercial growth of the 1970s, '80s, and '90s threatened to change forever the open vistas and natural scenery of the county, another enterprising group of citizens organized the Douglas County Open Lands Coalition to protect the county's rural qualities and preserve open land. In 1992, the coalition placed an open space land acquisition sales tax on the county ballot. When the sales tax failed, the coalition began a campaign to put the issue back before the voters in 1994.

Using petitions, surveys, door-to-door discussions, homeowners association presentations, newspaper articles, letters to the editor, and mailings, the campaign focused on the definition of open space and its importance to the present and future quality of life in the county. A cornerstone of the campaign was a strong statewide movement to prevent a parcel of land known as Southdowns, adjacent to Roxborough State Park, from being developed into a residential community. The publicity and educational focus of that campaign helped spur voters to approve a one-sixth of a cent sales tax to finance the purchase and upkeep of open space, as well as the development of parks and trails in Douglas County. Campaign leaders Micki Clark, Jennifer Drybread, Mark Weston, and Jon Farnlof, along with an army of spirited volunteers, devoted countless hours to the campaign. It was the determination and loyalty of the volunteers that Clark identified as the real force behind the campaign's success:

> If you have no hope of getting paid for your efforts and you don't expect to and there is no power in the position and you do it because you love it, then I believe that's the strongest force on earth. You cannot stop any group of people anywhere if they put their passion into something. All the lawyers and all the government in the world cannot stop people from caring if they're willing to commit their time to it.

In January 1995, the Douglas County Open Space Advisory Committee (COSAC) formed to oversee purchases of open space with funds generated by the sales tax. Powered by nine volunteer members, including town representatives, a professional planner, a county planning commissioner, and an at-large citizen, the committee identified five open-space priority areas within the county: the South Interstate 25 Corridor, the High Plateau, the Cherry Creek Corridor, the Northern Natural Area, and the Mountain Backdrop area from Perry Park north to Roxborough Park. In 1996, a $25 million bond referendum authorized the county to borrow on the 1994 sales tax in order to purchase properties as soon as they became available.

Clark, who became chair of COSAC and later president of the Douglas County Open Lands Coalition, reflected upon the achievements of these initial efforts to preserve open space. Encouraged by the acquisition of natural, scenic properties like Cherokee Ranch, Southdowns at Roxborough State Park, Prairie Canyon Ranch, Greenland Ranch, and the Lamb Spring Archaeological Site, Clark hopes that future acquisitions and management plans will be handled with the same charitable exuberance and respect exhibited by the foresighted citizens who pioneered the movement.

> My dream is that [COSAC] will continue to focus and get these fabulous jewels within the county and that they will further evolve into having good management plans so that people can actually enjoy this land and have it be a place where we can all go walk our dogs, ride our horses, bird-watch, or whatever people want to do on it while leaving the land in as much of a pristine condition as possible. I see that as the next big challenge. Where is that fine line that you need to draw between the public loving the land to death and making it accessible to those people who have paid for it? . . . I'd like to see [the acquisition of open space land] taken with the spirit of dignity and appreciation that it deserves. I'd like to see it, if possible, become less of a trump card in somebody's resume and more of a true commitment. I believe that now the commissioners are fully on board with the program. It has become a little more institutionalized than my roots would like to see, but I understand it. It would take a government to run it.

In 1993, I began researching this book as the subject of my master's thesis, which was completed and submitted to the University of Colorado at Denver two years later under the title, "Douglas County: History and Guide to Cultural Resources."

The manuscript would have never gone beyond the dusty bookshelves of academia had it not been for an urgent need to promote the preservation of Douglas County's history and historic sites, especially in light of the current explosive growth throughout the county. In 1997, I returned to the document with the desire to create a written tool for building better awareness of the county's rich heritage amid the whirlwind of this change and growth.

Why preserve these aged, often dilapidated, seemingly useless structures? Are they not just hindrances to progress and growth? Why spend the money to remodel and renovate an outdated building when one can construct a modern, fashionable structure with contemporary plumbing, wiring, and other conveniences? The reasons are simultaneously simple and complex. Historic buildings and sites represent a tangible means of connecting the past with the present by providing glimpses into the lives of the early settlers who built them. In doing so, these edifices help us understand how our communities began and evolved into their present state. They encourage a sense of place and identity by supplying the unique and original features that differentiate one community from another. By giving life and interpretation to our history in a way that textbooks, documentaries, and audio sources cannot, historic sites engender greater civic pride and heritage among citizens. Finally, these monuments, which bring so much variety and personality to the towns in which they are located, represent a distinctive and irreplaceable blend of architectural style, craftsmanship, and construction material.

The historic sites of Douglas County reflect the pioneer spirit of its early settlers. Numerous small, one-room churches and schools scattered throughout the county testify to the importance early citizens placed on education and religion. Because these structures also existed as the core of community social and political life, their importance to early settlers is immeasurable by today's standards. Old buildings that originally housed early businesses such as hotels, restaurants, banks, and general stores, particularly in Castle Rock, symbolize young Douglas County's commitment to the opportunistic qualities that typified the settlement of many towns in the Great American West. Freedom to succeed in the embrace of a welcoming, unregulated, virgin land drove settlers and adventurers west, hauling their own cultural baggage that was reflected in the architecture and style of early Douglas County buildings. Without the finances needed for elaborate architectural experimentation and design, builders created, or re-created, what modest decoration they could afford. A few more elaborate homes and public buildings display attempts to regain through design the memories of places and buildings left behind.

The historic sites of Douglas County are reminders of the past. Preservation of these sites provides life and richness to the county's history and contributes to the community's sense of pride and tradition. As more people make the county their home, a need arises for roots, civic esteem, and greater awareness of past events, present conditions, and future possibilities. This book should not be considered the definitive history of the county. It was written with the intent and hope of fostering a better understanding of the value and significance of the county's past, thus supplying context to its present and future.

Notes

1. *Record-Journal of Douglas County*, July 23, 1909, p. 1.
2. *Douglas County News*, October 20, 1977, p. 6.

CASTLE ROCK

A town will grow up there of no ordinary beauty.
—Rocky Mountain News, March 18, 1874

Castle Rock was designated the Douglas County seat in 1874, and quickly assumed the role of county leader. It grew faster than all other county towns, and as a result of this growth, is a place where old and new exist together, where historic, rhyolite buildings are surrounded by modern fast-food restaurants, gas stations, and strip malls. Present-day Castle Rock strives to connect its historic and modern elements into a harmonious town identity.

A look into Castle Rock's founding and early development naturally begins with the rocky butte itself. This highly visible rock outcropping has long been an orientation point for travelers. From a distance, the hill presents a clean silhouette crowned by a large, commanding, flat-topped rock formation that looks somewhat like an old, ravaged castle. The origin of the name is commonly attributed to the Stephen H. Long expedition of 1819–1820, but recent historical and geographical analysis indicates that although the party did indeed sight and name a rock formation "Castle Rock," they were probably observing the hill now called "Elephant Rock" located between Palmer Lake and Monument, Colorado.

Not surprisingly, later explorers and pioneers also claimed credit for naming the rock. Among them was David Kellogg, an argonaut who traveled along Plum Creek in 1858–1859 searching for gold:

> At the bend of Plum Creek stands a large flat-topped round rock resting on a pyramid-shaped base. It is an isolated part of the original rock formation, the softer part below being worn away. We find a crevice through which we climb to the top, fire off our guns and christen the place "Castle Rock," thinking we are the first to give it a name.[1]

An 1859 newspaper account declared that the Rock had been "climbed and named by Kellogg Party—But a Bob Willis claimed to have climbed and given the same name a week before."[2] An earlier explorer, John C. Fremont, is credited with naming the butte "Poundcake Rock" on July 9, 1843, because "our hungry people seemed to think it a very agreeable comparison."[3]

Whatever the origin of its name, the unique landmark posed an irresistible lure for early pioneers, and settlement at the location seemed natural. By the early 1870s, the Denver & Rio Grande Railroad had arrived and the National Land and Improvement Company was recruiting for potential town colonists; the land company spawned the formation of a small village named New Memphis, located about two miles northwest of the rock. Settled by several Tennessee families, the village survived for years as a "red hot lively town" where the "principal activity of the inhabitants was horse-racing, gambling and drinking forty-rod whiskey."[4]

Another settlement, Douglas, located about four miles south of New Memphis, became a trading post and distribution point for nearby post offices after the D&RG railroad installed a switch and water tank there in 1872. However, the origins of Douglas revolved around the discovery of a valuable stone that gave rise to a quarry industry that provided a precious source of revenue for the entire Castle Rock area.

Silas W. Madge, prospecting on one of the isolated buttes near his ranch two miles south of Castle Rock, discovered a hard, pinkish-gray volcanic rock. He extracted several samples and sent them to Denver to be assayed. The response reported no value to the rock except as a potential building material. By 1872, Madge, later labeled the "father of the lava stone industry" in Douglas County, was quarrying the igneous rock, called rhyolite, by hand and hauling it in a wagon to Douglas, where it was then shipped by rail to Denver. Each year he extracted more rhyolite, and by the early 1880s Madge employed a large number of workers, owned a boardinghouse in Douglas, and had convinced the D&RG to construct a 2.6-mile spur from Douglas to the top of his quarry. In 1881, the *Castle Rock Journal* reported the progress at the quarry:

> Mr. Madge has his railroad completed and the cars running into the quarry. . . . It is a pretty sight indeed to see the engine steaming about on top of the little mountain 500 feet above town.[5]

Rhyolite from the Madge quarry was used to build the Cantril School and Keystone Hotel in Castle Rock; the railroad depots in Castle Rock, Littleton, and Colorado Springs; the Union Depot and many other notable landmarks in Denver; and the Antlers Hotel in Colorado Springs. The Santa Fe, O'Brien, and Girardot rhyolite quarries soon opened on nearby hills and also prospered from the building boom along the Front Range. However, a lull in construction brought about by the Panic of 1893, and a switch in builders' preferences from stone to terra-cotta, cement, and cast stone, delivered a crushing blow to the rhyolite industry. From 1900 to 1920, work at the quarries slowed to the extraction of only small rock that was crushed and used for highway construction.

The area between the two boomtowns of New Memphis and Douglas survived for several years as a campsite for the region's occasional travelers. In 1869, Jeremiah Gould, a Civil War veteran from Rhode Island, moved to Colorado and established a claim on a 160-acre tract of land that later became the heart of the town of Castle Rock. That same year he bought an adjacent forty acres and built a humble cabin that locals referred to as Uncle Jimmy or Uncle Jerry's Claim Cabin. Years later, after his claim was recognized, the foresighted Gould decided to create a town named after the castle-like formation nearby. County surveyor J. D. McIntyre drew a town plan of blocks, streets, alleys, and lots and filed it on April 25, 1874, with the Douglas County clerk and recorder. Additional town land donations consisted of the Craig and Gould Addition in July 1874, made by Gould and landowner John H. Craig, founder of the settlement of Sedalia, and the Wilcox Addition of 1875, bestowed by Philip P. Wilcox, a distinguished cattleman, lawyer, and politician.

The year 1874 also saw an election for a new county seat. In February, officials divided Douglas County, and its eastern half became Elbert County. As a result of this change, Frankstown, the Douglas County seat at the time, was no longer centrally located in the county, and the populous called for a new seat election. Douglas County attorney D. D. Belden wrote a letter to the *Rocky Mountain News* in support of Castle Rock as the county seat. His letter reflects the community's genuine awe and respect for the geological formation that was the center of focus for the new settlement:

> If not "one of the seven wonders" of Colorado, Castle Rock is yet a real wonder. It is a tremendous rock, standing up in bold relief several hundred feet in height, rising up abruptly out of the plains, being visible from the cars of the Denver and Rio Grande railroad for many miles, as they pass, either way, up and down that beautiful valley. This, of itself, all other things being equal, ought to settle the question as to where the new county seat should be located. . . . I doubt not but that hundreds of persons of capital who have no business, would settle in a town located at Castle Rock, where one would not settle if the town were located out on the bare prairie, with nothing to mark or distinguish the spot. What could be more cozy or comfortable than the idea of a beautiful villa with its churches and schoolhouses nestling just there, "in the shadow of that great rock?" . . . Castle rock is a point. It is *somewhere*. Nature has done something just at that place. It has erected there a great land-mark. . . . If the county seat is located at Castle rock it will be a *permanent* location, and a town will grow up there of no ordinary beauty.[6]

On March 31, 1874, Douglas County voters selected Castle Rock as the new county seat, beating out Frankstown, New Memphis, Douglas, Glade, and Sedalia. The *Rocky Mountain News* cheered the voters' choice:

> Douglas County did the right thing in voting to locate her county seat at Castle Rock. It is one of the most picturesque points in the whole territory—adding to the charms of natural scenery a proper geographical location, with all the surroundings necessary to make a thriving and attractive town . . . Castle Rock cannot avoid becoming one of the most prosperous towns in Colorado. It will have the immediate advantages of a railway, postoffice and telegraph, and will become the focal point for the entire local trade of the county, whose capital town it will be. . . . Castle Rock will have no rival in its own county, and it is certain of being well patronized and sustained by the local pride and interest. It has all the elements and conditions at hand for an immediate, thriving and permanent growth.[7]

The *Daily Denver Tribune* also expressed optimism for the development of the new seat, musing, "We expect to have a nice little town, one that will be an honor to Douglas county and to Colorado."[8]

The new county seat grew swiftly. Planners laid out streets and alleys, divided land into plots, and for several months newspapers printed auction notices for Castle Rock lots:

> SALE OF LOTS IN THE TOWN OF CASTLE ROCK
>
> Notice is hereby given that the Commissioners of Douglas county, Colorado, will offer for sale, on Monday and Tuesday, the 22nd and 23rd days of June, 1874, Sale

> to commence at 10 o'clock a.m. each day, at the Court House in Castle Rock, (being the county seat of Douglas county), to the highest and best bidder for cash in hand, 200 LOTS. . . .[9]

The county sold about seventy-seven lots during the first auction, making a profit of $3,400. The money raised funded the construction of several county buildings, including a courthouse. Indeed, Castle Rock appeared to be "springing up as if by magic."[10] In 1881, the town incorporated, with Irving S. Morse as its first mayor. One year later Castle Rock's second mayor, local hotelkeeper Thomas Harris, opened his term with a headache of sorts:

> The boarders of the Castle Rock hotel were aroused from their peaceful slumbers by a strange and unusual noise in the rear yard of the hotel. At first a half dozen men who rushed to the window half denuded reported that the source of the deep tones which continued to vibrate upon the morning breezes was involved in mystery. In round and mellifluous tones came the words: "Good Morning, Lord Mayor of Castle Rock." Then following: "Good Morning, Mayor." Just as a number of anxious auditors were in the act of descending to investigate they saw the Mayor elect crawling out of a hogshead, where he had been familiarizing himself with his new title before venturing upon the street.[11]

The summer of 1882 saw the addition of a water reservoir located near the present site of the Philip S. Miller Library along Plum Creek Boulevard. By the following summer, the town's residents were celebrating the completion of a ditch that carried the vital East Plum Creek water from the reservoir to the town's center. With a good water supply, town beautification progressed smoothly, as trees, shrubs, and flower gardens were planted. By 1887, Castle Rock was on its way to becoming a well-landscaped town:

> The ditch which takes its water from East Plum creek runs high enough on the prominence so that every lot in town can be irrigated and every part of each lot. Trees have been set out on all of the principal streets and are making a fine growth. All kinds of shrubbery and small fruits are grown very successfully. It will be but a few years till we have as fine shade trees, as good gardens, and as delicious fruits, such as strawberries, raspberries, gooseberries, currants, etc., as in any Eastern town.[12]

A steady flow of entrepreneurs set up shop in the town. Castle Rock's first business district was located on Perry Street near the Denver & Rio Grande depot. Among the Perry Street trades were two of the town's popular hotels, the Owens House and the Harris Hotel. The Eclipse Saloon, a printing shop, a drug store, a dry goods shop, and a grocery/meat market also opened on the street. In 1887, the same year that the Atchison, Topeka & Santa Fe Railroad extended its tracks on the west side of town, the first creamery arrived in Castle Rock, which was turning out more than five hundred pounds of butter a week by 1889. Other new businesses included E. A. Palms Groceries and Clothing, the J. W. Farrell & Co. Harness and Saddlery, a real estate exchange, and stores specializing in dry goods or mowing machines.

By the turn of the century, however, Wilcox Street, located adjacent to the courthouse square, had surpassed nearby Perry Street as the town's most popular strip for business development.

Most of the street's business took place between Third and Fourth streets, where a continuous block of storefront trades formed:

> The block opposite the court house on Wilcox St. has become quite a busy business center. A couple of months ago the Colorado Telephone Company established an office in the Whittier building. Then Andrew Anderson started a saloon in Mr. Geradehand's stone building, the next improvement was when Charles Todd the druggest, and Charles Bills the butcher, moved their places of business into the block. Last week Albert Dakan started a barber shop in the room between these last named stores, and now W. P. Hambitzer has moved the building which he recently purchased from R. P. Conant to the vacant lot between the Post office and Dr. Alexander's office. The postoffice itself was moved to Wilcox street less than a month ago. These inumerous changes have worked quite a transformation, there now being a solid front of business houses from third street to fourth street.[13]

Other businesses included insurance and physician offices, a barbershop, a shoe store, a butcher, and an undertaker, reflecting the needs of a population that had reached three hundred (compared to a population of eighty-three in 1880).

In the mid-1880s, Castle Rock's residents and visitors witnessed an epidemic of gold fever. A May 1884 headline in the *Castle Rock Journal* boasted, "GOLD . . . Castle Rock to the Front With Rich Placer Discoveries. . ." and predicted, "A BOOM IS CERTAIN TO FOLLOW . . . "[14] After miners discovered "glittering gold fields" at nearby Elizabeth in early May, the newly established Castle Rock Mining Company eagerly reported that "free gold" was abundant in the Castle Rock area as well. Excitement quickly led to inflated hopes, but while the town enjoyed its own small "gold rush," the adjustment to a distinct type of visitor, the wealth-seeking argonaut, often proved awkward. An editor's note in the June 1884 issue of the *Castle Rock Journal* suggested that "old timers" were somewhat resentful of these new invaders: "The town was full of strangers last week, presumably prospectors who are not loud in their aspirations to obtain a claim in our gold field."[15] However, Castle Rock's frenzied gold fever lasted only a couple of months, as the placers dried up quickly. The town returned to quarrying, agriculture, and the official business of being a county seat.

In 1897, Castle Rock proudly opened its new schoolhouse, a six-room, two-story, rhyolite structure described by the *Castle Rock Journal* as "an ornament to the town." Perched atop "schoolhouse hill," the Cantril School, named after Douglas County resident William W. Cantril, was located four blocks east of the grand rhyolite courthouse erected in 1889–1890. As the largest and most architecturally elaborate buildings in town, the two structures attested to the importance local citizens placed on government and education. Kent Brandebery, member of the Douglas County Historic Preservation Board and longtime resident of Castle Rock, explained the close relationship between the buildings:

> The people at the turn of the century had taken great pride in their public buildings and institutions. The courthouse and the school were very significant buildings. . . . Castle Rock put up these two buildings to be admired by all the people along the Front Range of the Rocky Mountains.

As Castle Rock entered the new century, progress and modernization continued. In July 1900, the town acquired a telephone exchange, and eight to ten phones were installed. In 1901, the Douglas County Bank, the county's first financial institution, began operation in the old courthouse building on Wilcox and Fourth streets, and later moved one block south to a handsome rhyolite building, where it received the new name of First National Bank of Douglas County. In 1902, the town council voted to install gaslights in the town's business district. Eight street lamps were connected to a nearby acetylene gas plant and soon after, James Fetherolf's popular Keystone Hotel also tapped into the main gas lines. Curious town folk packed into the hotel to view the "brilliancy and beauty of the light":

> On Friday and Saturday the hotel was crowded with visitors who called to look at the beautiful acetylene light. It is no exaggeration to say that no building in Castle Rock was ever one-half as well lighted before. Many other customers are being connected, and in a few weeks' time probably 25 stores and residences will be using the new light. . . . The total cost of the plant, including about nine blocks of mains, has been about $2500. It is of sufficient capacity to supply a town several times larger than Castle Rock, and there is no doubt that the pipes will be rapidly extended to other parts of the town. . . . Certain it is that Castle Rock may well be proud of the great step in advance which it has just taken.[16]

Sidewalk construction dominated debates about community improvements for much of the decade. As early as 1889, the *Castle Rock Journal* had claimed, "More sidewalks and less stock on the streets are the pressing needs of our town."[17] The town council did not agree, and the battle raged for many years. Finally, in August 1909, the town council called a special meeting to address two pressing issues: stray chickens and the pros and cons of laying cement sidewalks. The council finally conceded that sidewalks were needed "for the convenience of the people."[18]

Victorious in the sidewalk battle, the promoters of progress continued efforts to modernize Castle Rock. In the 1920s, the blossoming town of 461 people supported businesses such as a restaurant, drug store, jeweler, blacksmith, creamery, two banks, two hotels, two garages, and two grocery stores. In 1921—following the sentiment of a *Record-Journal of Douglas County* reporter who exclaimed, "Let there be light!"—town officials approved the installation of a municipal light and power plant, with energy supplied by the Du Pont Company, which owned an explosives manufacturing operation in nearby Louviers. The Commonwealth Utilities Corporation took over the electrical plant in January 1929 with the intention of supplying power to several small communities in the county. Although financial problems caused by the Depression aborted these grandiose plans, the corporation continued electric service to Castle Rock and even installed "an ornamental lighting system" along the main thoroughfare and a beacon light on top of the historic rock to guide mail pilots. In 1931, several businesses added neon lights, giving Castle Rock metropolitan airs.

Indeed, thriving Castle Rock was developing some of the problems of a metropolis. Traffic congestion led to an August 1929 decision by the town council to install the town's first stop signs on Wilcox at the intersections of Third, Fourth, and Fifth streets. The *Record-Journal of Douglas County* praised the decision: "With so much through traffic on Wilcox Street, this precaution on the part of the councilmen was very timely."[19] The newspaper was equally impressed with the council's decision in 1936 to hire WPA workers to grade and surface two and a half miles of town streets and make road improvements along Wilcox and around courthouse square. "The town officials are giving full co-operation with this piece of improvement work and are entitled to a 'pat on the back' for their action in taking advantage of the opportunity in getting this work done."[20]

Although some of the council's decisions inspired rounds of applause, others seemed destined for controversy. In June 1931, the council announced plans to complete a much-needed modern sewage system. The estimated cost of the system was approximately $27,000, which would be financed by the sale of bonds bearing 5 percent interest. After parsimonious Denver bond houses offered only $20,000 for the bond issue, the town eagerly accepted a counteroffer, which was closer to the par value of the bonds, from Pueblo investor Joseph D. Grigsby. Consequently, many Denver investors raised an eyebrow at what they referred to as the "judgement bond racket." The *Denver Post*'s daily features of the so-called "Castle Rock chapter in the 'judgement bond' scandal" in early 1932 enraged the *Record-Journal of Douglas County*, which steamed, "As no one stands to lose a dollar in this transaction, and Bonfils [owner and editor of the *Denver Post*] will not be called upon to contribute a dime on account of it, we would kindly suggest that he keep his damned nose out of our town affairs until such a time, at least, as some wrong has been, or about to be, done."[21]

Despite the town council's insistence of no wrongdoing, the Douglas County commissioners filed a petition to examine the issue in 1932. Formal complaints from the Denver & Rio Grande Railroad and two town citizens who felt they should not be taxed for the sewage system because their property was outside the district limits prompted the commissioners' decision. The Colorado Supreme Court eventually heard the case in 1936 and decided in favor of the town and against the petitioners.

Although town activities in the 1930s centered on these attempts to expand and modernize, the financial impact of the Great Depression on Castle Rock was clearly felt in the failure of its local banks. In 1932, the Castle Rock State Bank closed its doors. A year later the First National Bank also closed, leaving Castle Rock without a financial institution and prompting the *Record-Journal of Douglas County* to suggest: "Depositors will now find it necessary to seek banking facilities elsewhere, or else find an old sock—without holes—in which to care for their reserve funds—if any?"[22] Finally in 1939, after years of struggling without banking facilities, the Bank of Douglas County opened in Castle Rock. "Sentiment in all parts of the county is very strong for having a Douglas County bank and it will, without doubt, receive hearty local support and patronage," cheered the *Record-Journal of Douglas County* following the announcement of the bank's opening.[23]

Financial difficulties during the Depression did not deter Castle Rock citizens from celebrating the holidays. One of Castle Rock's oldest traditions began in 1936 with the lighting of a Christmas star atop the rock. The original star consisted of heavy pipes, rods, and one hundred 25-watt light bulbs. In 1949, a stronger, 45-foot star replaced the weakened, weathered star. On November 28, 1965, the first annual star-lighting ceremony took place and featured a chorus and a brass choir.

Nineteen sixty-five was pivotal for the town for another, more detrimental reason. The afternoon of June 16, a tornado touched down at Palmer Lake, and torrential rains set off floods along East Plum Creek and West Plum Creek. Later called "the greatest calamity in Colorado history," the flood caused considerable damage downstream.[24] It washed out sections of

Interstate 25 and other roads and bridges, damaged or destroyed homes and buildings, and ruined crops. Six people and many ranch animals drowned. The flood smashed through a trailer park on Third Street and swept away several trailer homes. One local citizen wrote of the disaster:

> For awhile, Castle Rock was completely isolated. All highway bridges leading into town were washed out, the railroad bridge was undermined at one end, there was no mail service, either in or out, and no long-distance phoning. Many dozens of cars trying to come through Castle Rock or to by-pass it on the west highway, lined up, and many became swamped in mud. Helicopters buzzed overhead constantly, evacuating these motorists to shelters here and in Denver.[25]

The tragedy strengthened the community through mutual aid efforts that transformed Castle Rock Junior High School and several homes into emergency relief centers. The Red Cross took over the Wilcox School and converted the gymnasium into a medical center stacked with cots for victims, while volunteers helped the highway department, railroad, and utility companies with cleaning and repairing the damage wrought by the flood. The local office of the Farmers Home Administration took applications from farmers and ranchers for emergency loans.

Slowly the town began to rebuild. In December 1968, after a two-year campaign organized by Genevieve "Nicky" Mead and a hefty donation of $25,000 from Bank of Douglas County president and local philanthropist Philip S. Miller, Douglas County constructed its first county library at the corner of Third and Gilbert streets in Castle Rock. The library remained at the location until 1987, when overcrowding forced it to move into a more spacious facility at the south end of town along Plum Creek Boulevard.

In 1968, Castle Rock increased its population by 250 with the annexation of a subdivision known as Glover. In 1977, the town's first shopping complex, Village Center, opened on Wilcox Street complete with a dry goods store, restaurant, several retail shops, and Naylor's Supermarket. One year later, the Castle Rock Planning Commission approved construction of the Castle North complex, which included 120 apartment condominiums, 95 townhouses, and 45 hillside units.

Just as growth engulfed Castle Rock, a fire destroyed the town's most treasured building, the Douglas County Courthouse. On the night of March 11, 1978, Rose Ann Lucero, a seventeen-year-old Denver resident, set fire to some papers in the civic building in an attempt to create enough confusion to permit her friend's escape from a jail cell where he was being held for drunk driving. The fire spread quickly, overwhelming the rhyolite relic and sending the majestic stamped tin tower and old stone walls crashing into the basement. Only two years after being placed on the National Register of Historic Places, the building was deemed unsuitable for restoration and sentenced to death by wrecking ball despite the adamant protests of citizens.

Many townspeople felt the Douglas County Administration Building, built to replace the destroyed courthouse, was a poor substitute. During the design phase of the new building, many citizens felt the county commissioners falsely led them to believe they played an active role in selecting its architectural style. The commissioners held public meetings in which they actively sought the input of residents. The town newspaper printed drawings of the leading architectural choices and requested that readers vote for their favorites: "Act now and let your views be known. Don't wait assuming the design you want will automatically be selected."[26] Nonetheless, after soliciting residents' opinions, county commissioners reportedly ordered construction of an architectural design that had never been viewed by the public. In an interview with the author, longtime resident Kent Brandebery described the town's shock:

> When the building started to take shape, nobody recognized what was going up there. It had no resemblance to what people had seen in the paper, had voted on. People were so discouraged. We went to these meetings; we actually had input and had a chance to select what we wanted for our architectural scheme and when the whole thing came down . . . nothing . . . nothing.

County commissioners and the architectural design firm George Hoover, Karl Berg and Associates, engaged in finger-pointing after outraged citizens compared the building to a prison, an asylum, a plain box, a mausoleum, and a hunk of cinder blocks. Looking back on the controversy, architect Hoover defended his firm's work in an interview with the author. He insisted that the limited money appropriated by the county government restricted the firm to the construction of a "relatively ordinary building." He believed the town's immediate negative response to the building was due in part to the county commissioners' failure to communicate that the drawings printed in the newspaper were mere architectural concepts, not final drafts. Additionally, Hoover pointed to the town's intense sentiment and regret over the loss of their old courthouse as further reason for the rejection of the replacement.

> Generally when the building is the focus of emotion as the older one was . . . it's almost impossible to replace it. [The courthouse in Castle Rock] was really the symbol of stability and centeredness in the county. . . . It certainly wasn't a great work of architecture, but it was a memory of the past and it was really a rooted building. It felt like it had been there forever. People were married there, divorced there. [Courthouses] are the markers of the stations along life's course. This was one of those buildings.

Despite public condemnation, the new administration building remained at the center of courthouse square, a constant and painful reminder of the devastating loss of its stately predecessor. Finally in early 1998, town officials announced plans to begin a $3.2 million expansion and renovation of the building that included a new red brick façade and a stone bell tower. Residents and town officials celebrated completion of the building's facelift during a festive ribbon cutting ceremony in December 1999.

Between 1981 and early 1984, after numerous annexations, such as the Villages of Castle Rock and Plum Creek subdivisions, Castle Rock's town limits nearly tripled, growing from 2,300 acres to 7,260 acres. Gas stations, fast food restaurants, chain stores, and businesses that arose mostly west of Interstate 25 slowly overshadowed the town's rural atmosphere. In 1984, a year of very heavy growth, Castle Rock reportedly had more real estate offices and contractors than churches and restaurants combined. Some futurists predicted that the town would someday become the heart of an extensive "megalopolis," or strip city, connecting Denver to Colorado Springs or even Wyoming to New Mexico. Yet the sprawling growth continued, as the town council approved the annexations of more subdivisions—in 1984 alone, Castle Rock Ranch, Metzler Ranch, Heritage Farms,

Castle Highlands, Heckendorf Ranch, and Lincoln Meadows were all added to the town, resulting in the addition of nearly 7,700 acres. The annexations more than doubled the town's size and catapulted its population from 3,921 in 1980 to an estimated 6,000 by the end of 1984.

These actions did not go without reproach from Castle Rock citizens. Many complained that the unprecedented growth of the town posed a threat to the rural lifestyle that made living in Castle Rock so attractive. Others expressed concern over downtown traffic problems, overcrowding in schools, increase in crime, and demand for limited water and wastewater services. In 1984, disgruntled town citizens united to protest the proposed annexation of Castle Rock Ranch, a 2,260-acre residential-commercial development located south of town. Although the citizens hired two attorneys and managed to delay the town board's decision for some time, ultimately their efforts proved unsuccessful and Castle Rock Ranch received annexation approval.

Town officials did address some of the residents' concerns. In 1984, the town imposed mandatory lawn watering restrictions and began construction of an upgraded sewage plant. Also in 1984, a steering committee of local residents and business owners, led by consultant Charles King, began preparation of a business district master plan to address revitalization of downtown businesses as well as problems with traffic, parking, drainage, and pedestrian safety. Years of studies and projects eventually culminated in a 1994 Downtown Urban Design Plan, which presented ideas and proposals for Castle Rock's future that focused on transportation problems, public improvements, and economic issues. The plan also highlighted the importance of historic preservation and recommended a greater focus on a downtown heritage interpretation system that included historic markers and a town museum.

One of the plan's considerations for downtown street improvements led to a major construction project along Perry Street, Castle Rock's first business district. In order to decrease traffic on congested Wilcox Street, the plan suggested routing traffic onto Perry Street at the downtown core's north and south ends. Castle Rock voters supported the idea, and construction, headed by Hamon Contractors of Denver, began in May 1997 and was completed in June 1998. A late 1997 downtown revitalization effort led by Castle Café owner Brad Brown promised to reinstate Perry Street as an important town business strip. One of the leading real estate brokers during the renovation of several LoDo (Lower Downtown) properties in Denver, Brown directed the construction of Wilcox Square, a downtown district of renewed retail, office, and residential space that included the construction of three buildings and the renovation of three more buildings between Third and Fourth streets along Perry Street.

The growing pains of Castle Rock and Douglas County also affected the occupants of various public buildings in Castle Rock. Hired to serve the surging population, county and town employees pleaded for elbowroom amid cramped and inadequate offices. Relief arrived with the construction of several new county and town government centers. The first of these was a massive, $44 million county justice center located at the intersection of Interstate 25 and U.S. Highway 85. Begun in September 1996 and named after popular Douglas County Commissioner Robert A. Christensen, who died of a heart attack in August 1997, the center includes 192 jail cells, four courtrooms, and law enforcement offices. The Castle Rock Services Center, home to the town's maintenance, parks and recreation, and utility departments, was built adjacent to the justice center.

As the future justice and service centers rose along Interstate 25, the county also broke ground for a new county administration building at the southwest end of Third Street in downtown Castle Rock. Named after its chief financier, town philanthropist Philip S. Miller, the building opened in 1997 and now houses the offices of the county commissioners and manager, as well as the planning, finance, and other departments. Meanwhile, town officials also began planning for a new, larger town hall along Seller's Gulch on Wilcox Street's east side, as well as new police and fire stations on Perry Street.

Commercial construction in Castle Rock also escalated in the 1990s, particularly at the town's northern boundaries. The Castle Rock Factory Shops, an outlet mall constructed in 1992 and expanded in 1997, provided an enormous boost to the town's economy. In 1993, after its first year in business, sales tax figures for the Castle Rock Factory Shops (later renamed Prime Outlets at Castle Rock) equaled $2.5 million, and the trade publication *Value Retail News* named it the top outlet center in the nation. Castle Pines Commercial Village, a retail-entertainment village located adjacent to the outlet mall, and the Milestone Center, a 90,000-square-foot shopping center on Founder's Parkway, represented other commercial successes for the northern part of town.

Not surprisingly, Castle Rock's incessant commercial and residential development brought forth contentious times for the Castle Rock Town Council in the late 1990s. Heavily criticized for its 1995 approval of Diamond Ridge Estates, a development that included several highly visible homes along a ridgeline northeast of town, the council in July 1998 enacted a six-month suspension on review of ridgeline development proposals while an adequate study for preserving these areas was conducted. In March 1999, the council approved a set of high-elevation development regulations devised by a twenty-one-member "ridgeline protection" committee, much to the chagrin of several developers.

Meanwhile, Councilman Carl Alessi, an outspoken critic of Castle Rock's growth, spearheaded a citizen's initiative to enforce a six-month moratorium on all commercial and residential development proposals for the entire town. From the onset, the proposed moratorium sparked heated public debates and legal battles. Viewed as a major threat not only to commercial and residential activity, but also to public projects such as a planned library expansion and a new, much-needed elementary school, the moratorium was defeated at the polls in December 1998. Nearly four months later, Alessi challenged his fellow council members' sale of Castle Oaks, a 1,150-acre property northeast of Castle Rock that was acquired by the town when the original developer defaulted on bond payments. After formally censuring Alessi for allegations of corruption in the town government involving the land scam, the council members survived an October 1999 recall election organized by Alessi's supporters.[27] Thus, amid unresolved differences and suspicions, Castle Rock residents and officials ended a century of remarkable transformation and growth.

In a town where old structures exist alongside the new, many residents fear Castle Rock's historic buildings and sites may be overwhelmed by growth. Fortunately, preservation of historic properties has gained new momentum in Castle Rock. In 1994, the town adopted a landmark preservation ordinance and created a nine-member historic preservation board to oversee protection of the town's heritage. Successor to the short-lived Castle Rock Historic Preservation Committee (which formed briefly in 1984 to formulate a preservation plan for a historic property known as the Dyer House) the board's chief duties include adopting criteria for designation of properties as landmarks, examining applications for alterations, moving or demolishing landmark buildings, providing advice and assistance to property owners about preservation and rehabilitation issues, and developing public education programs.

Efforts to maintain harmony and balance between Castle Rock's past, present, and future are currently underway. As it is among the fastest-developing towns in Colorado, growth issues are still of vital interest to Castle Rock residents, business owners, and politicians. Perhaps the sentiments of an 1886 *Castle Rock Journal* reporter still apply today to the town located "in the shadow of that great rock":[28]

> An excellent way to ruin your town is to oppose improvements and mistrust its public men. Run it down to strangers. Go to some other town to trade. Lengthen your face when a stranger talks of locating in it. Do not invest a cent. Lay your money out somewhere else. If a man wants to buy anybody's property interfere and discourage him. Be particular to discredit the motives of public spirited citizens. Refuse to see any spirit in a scheme that does not benefit you. If you can't hog everything, judge everybody else by yourself, and accuse them of doing it.[29]

Castle Rock Historic Sites

B & B Café (1930s: builder unknown), 322 Wilcox Street.

The local hot spot for everything from town gossip to political debates to free financial advice is the B & B Café. The café has been in operation at its present spot across the street from the county administration building since 1930. B & B customers refer to it as the "Beans and Bullshit" Café, and as one patron told the author, "More business goes on at that place than at the administration building across the street."

The café's treasure is its onyx and marble bar, acquired from an abandoned Leadville saloon by B & B's first owners, Jack and Edythe Moore. The bar was constructed in Italy and moved to Leadville in the 1880s. The café also features a green pressed-tin ceiling with a bullet hole from a February 14, 1946, shootout that left Town Marshall Ray Lewis dead after he tried to apprehend escaped convict Manuel Perez. Three days earlier, eighteen-year-old Perez had shot and wounded two Denver police officers and then hidden in the gulches around Castle Rock. Hunger forced him into the B & B, where Lewis and some of the restaurant's patrons recognized him. When Lewis and Undersheriff Duncan Lowell attempted to capture Perez, a struggle ensued and one of several bullets fired struck Lewis in the heart. Perez's own wounds to the hand and ear did not elicit sympathy from furious Castle Rock residents, who reverted to an older form of western justice by attempting to hang the man from a tree in Courthouse Square. The mob was stopped, however, and Perez instead received a sentence of life in prison. He later died during a jailhouse brawl while serving his sentence in a Canon City prison.

Cantril Courthouse (1874: William Cantril, builder), 315 Fourth Street.

Three weeks after Castle Rock won the county seat election in April 1874, Douglas County's new commissioners assigned local rancher William W. Cantril to construct a temporary county courthouse in town, under the following terms:

> A building 20 feet by 40 feet and 20 feet high. Said building to be set-upon solid rock wall foundation laid in

> lime mortar. Said building to be built of good material and in a substantial matter to contain 8 windows in lower story. Said lower story to be 10 feet in height, the upper story to be 9 feet in height in the clear to contain 8 windows in the upper story. Three doors in lower story one in front and two on North side, lower story of said building to be wainscoated four feet and two coats of plaster and to be divided into three rooms the front and center rooms to be 13 by 19 and 14 x 19 and back room 10 x 19. The upper story to be in one room wainscoated and to be plastered with two coats worth.[30]

Cantril immediately began work on the building, and by May 21, 1874, the *Castle Rock Journal* reported, "The temporary court house at Castle Rock is now receiving its roofing and will be ready for occupancy about the 15th of June or before."[31] Upon completion, Cantril was paid $1,350 for his work, and the new courthouse was furnished with "one and one half dozen chairs for courtroom and Parlor chair for use of Judge of District Court—also Baize for covering Judge's and clerks desk in courtroom also matting for floor within railing and curtain for windows."[32] The courthouse also housed the county safe and documents that were transported from the former county seat of Frankstown.

In addition to serving the civic and political needs of the county, the courthouse was the scene of social and community events, including holiday celebrations, dances, lectures, dinners, and drama performances. Despite its importance to the county, in the mid-1880s many residents began to recognize the inadequacy of the small facility for a growing population. In December 1884, the *Castle Rock Journal* used the crowded conditions at a courthouse party to advocate for larger community facilities for the town.

> Could there be presented a more appropriate occasion in which to discuss the problem connected with the erection of a more commodious and neat City Hall than the one which afforded such unalloyed merriment to over one hundred people in the crowded court house last Thursday night? The house was uncomfortably crowded we are obliged to admit. . . . This was more amusingly apparent in watching the whirl of the waltzing multitude as they came up with a dull thud against the shoulders of their friends as they mingled together, each trying in vain to avoid the social collision which was inevitable. The best of feeling was exhibited on the part of the entire crowd, but is there not some way to avoid the cause which produces the effect?[33]

After a Fourth of July celebration at the courthouse, the *Journal* again cited the need for a "safer court house":

> Some thoughtless person laid a cigar on the roof of the "lean-to" at the head of the stairs. When it was discovered a hole had already been burnt in the roof. Fortunately there was but little wind at the time, otherwise the result might have been far different. Had the fire got any headway at that point, with the hall filled with dancers, loss of life might have occurred.[34]

Shortly thereafter, the construction of a larger rhyolite courthouse in 1889–1890 ended the Cantril Courthouse's era as the hub of county government and social activity. Since then, the building has been used for a variety of functions, such as the First National Bank office, the *Castle Rock Journal* office, a general store, a locksmith shop, a restaurant, a sign shop, and apartments.

Cantril School (1897: builder unknown), 320 Cantril Street.

Poised atop "schoolhouse hill," the Cantril School creates an impressive image on the landscape of the small community of Castle Rock. This two-story lava rock building features a bell tower and hipped roof supported by ornate scroll-designed cornice brackets. The main entryway to the school is set at the base of the bell tower and consists of a round arch resting upon foliated imposts. The arch is interjected by a keystone and radiating voussoirs. The building's windows are rectangular with transoms above each, with the exception of the upper bell tower windows, which consist of round arches. Benjamin Saunders added the building's northern end in 1930–1931.

Built in 1897 to replace the Castle Rock High School, which was destroyed by fire in 1896, the Cantril School was named after William W. Cantril, one of Douglas County's early pioneers and ranchers. The *Castle Rock Journal*, upon completion of the school's eight-month construction, heralded the building as "an ornament to the town."[35] It served as the first countywide school, offering courses for grades one through twelve until 1907, when a new, larger building constructed on Wilcox Street took over the county's high school courses. Cantril School then provided space for grades one through eight until 1961. From 1961 to 1968, the school served grades one through six, and from 1968 to 1984, it offered kindergarten through third grade classes. In 1984, the same year as its acceptance into the National Register of Historic Places, the Cantril School became an office building for the Douglas County School District.

Long-range goals for the building include its possible purchase by the county and eventual conversion into a county museum and archival center. In an interview with the author, Kent Brandebery, member of the Douglas County Historic Preservation Board, claimed the Cantril School was singled out as the future site for a county museum because "it is the most historically significant public building in Douglas County."

Castle Rock Depot (1875: Benjamin Hammar, builder), 420 Elbert Street.

The Castle Rock Depot was constructed in 1875 after a heated debate between the citizens of Castle Rock and the Denver & Rio Grande Railroad. Castle Rock citizens felt their nomination in 1874 as the county seat location warranted the immediate construction of a railroad station in their town. However, General William J. Palmer, founder and president of the railroad, declined the town's request, citing the existence of two well-established depots—in New Memphis, just north of Castle Rock, and in Douglas, south of town. Nonetheless, when the town won the county seat election and potential development seemed inevitable, Palmer yielded and hired a well-known stonemason named Benjamin Hammar to construct Castle Rock's depot. A leading figure in the early development of the town, Hammar supervised construction of many of the stone structures in Castle Rock and may have worked on the original Union Station in Denver.

Constructed from locally quarried and cut rhyolite stone, the Castle Rock Depot, placed on the National Register of Historic Places in 1974, possesses many decorative features. Among its most notable traits are wooden Victorian brackets located under the gabled metal roof, decorative stone lintels, running bond laid stone blocks, and a bay window composed of three single double-hung windows framed by locally cut lava stone. Two Denver citizens, William and Joyce Murray, later bought the building and moved it from its original location on Front Street near the railroad tracks to its current location on Elbert Street.

The Murrays restored and converted the old building into a home, adding a second interior story and skylights in the metal roof. Since then, the Castle Rock Depot has had several owners and served many functions, housing a center for the arts, a senior citizens center, and a studio and retail space for a glassworks company.

In September 1995, the Castle Rock Historical Society became the new owners of the building, with the help of grants from the Colorado Historical Society and the town of Castle Rock. Following the purchase, Society members began raising funds to convert the depot into a local history museum, the first of its kind in Castle Rock. Generous donations from citizens, government agencies, and businesses allowed the renovation efforts to proceed, and the Castle Rock Museum opened its doors to the public in the fall of 1997, with local history enthusiast Lionel Oberlin as museum director. In addition to displays of railroad paraphernalia, period clothing, old photos, and artifacts from pioneer churches, schools, and businesses, the museum features the original ticket cabinet, switching levers, and ticket cage from its days as an active depot.

Cedar Hill Cemetery (1875), 880 E. Wolfensberger Road.

Established in 1875, Cedar Hill Cemetery remains among the most peaceful spots in the county. Shade trees adorn the older section of the yard where many of Castle Rock's pioneers were laid to rest. Here the visitor can call upon the graves of Benjamin Hammar, Thorwald and Victoria Christensen, Judge Elias F. Dyer, William Cantril, and George E. Alexander.

In the 1880s, visitors entered the cemetery through its south side, but a new road on the cemetery's north side resulted in a north entrance. In the late 1880s, members of the Cemetery Society announced more improvements to the graveyard.

> The Castle Rock Cemetery Society would politely request all who have friends interred in the cemetery of the place, or others who desire to aid us in digging a well, putting up a wind mill and enclosing the grounds with a neat, substantial fence, to send their contributions to the treasurer of the society.[36]

The well, completed in January 1889, cost $117.75 and spanned six feet in diameter. In 1967, the yard's caretaker, Clarence Arrington, replaced wooden crosses located in the southeastern part of the cemetery, called Potter's Field, with metal plates set in concrete. He also constructed a new sign for Cedar Hill's entrance gate.

Christ Episcopal Church (1906–1907/many additions: Charles Herb, builder), 615 Fourth Street.

A fine example of rusticated, uncoursed local rhyolite stone adorns this early church. The 1906–1907 construction of the central nave, which features several stained glass Gothic lancet windows with heavy lintels and a steep gable roof with overhanging eaves, was completed by local stonemason Charles Herb, financed by Mr. and Mrs. Charles Ellis, and consecrated by Bishop C. L. Olmsted. On August 11, 1906, the Reverend Schofield, Archdeacon of the Diocese, and the Reverend James McLaughlin, who served the congregation of the nascent church, conducted a ceremony celebrating the church's construction. As part of the ceremony, members laid a marble cornerstone and placed an August 10, 1906, issue of the *Castle Rock Journal*, as well as lists of the town officers elected that spring and several prominent local clergy who served the area, behind the stone.

In 1911, Mrs. Ellis funded the addition of an east end sanctuary in memory of her husband. In 1954, a parish hall, kitchen, narthex, restrooms, and sacristy were added. That same year the congregation became a mission of Ascension Church in Denver. Three years later the congregation gained parish status and purchased extra lots and a house to the west of the church to serve as a rectory for the new minister. A 1958 purchase of land on the north side of the building and a 1965 educational wing and bell tower addition gave the church its present appearance.

The evident disgust of the *Record-Journal of Douglas County* after an act of vandalism to the church in 1935 reveals the deep adoration town residents possessed for the holy building:

> Some half-baked "critter" in human form broke loose in Castle Rock last Saturday night or early Sunday morning and thoroughly enjoyed himself for a time. One of the things that appealed to said "critter" was the breaking of one of the stained glass windows in the Episcopal Church. Now, of course, it may be possible that he was just trying to get into the house of the Lord in order to get a bit of religion—God knows he needs some of it—but we presume he was just trying to exercise a bit of "personal liberty" which he thought was guaranteed to him. However, he may discover that the limits of this "personal liberty" stuff is not boundless. . . . Such actions could only be the work of a moron mind.[37]

Christensen House (1889: John Lofe, presumed builder), 410 Jerry Street.

Now occupied by the Castle Rock Chamber of Commerce, this two-story, front-gabled, rhyolite structure was formerly home to two of Castle Rock's most prominent citizens, Thorwald and Victoria Christensen. Thorwald came to the United States in 1893 from the Island of Fyn, Denmark. He settled in Iowa and worked as a farmhand and a shoemaker before accepting a job at an Ellendale, Minnesota, bank. In 1906, Thorwald came to Castle Rock as the cashier of the First National Bank of Douglas County and eventually worked his way up to bank president. Before his death in 1957, Thorwald was widely known as a leader of Douglas County civic affairs. He operated an insurance and real estate agency, served as secretary-treasurer of the Cherry Creek Soil Conservation District, helped organize a progressive reform party known as the Citizens Party, served as president of School District No. 3, and was a chairmember of the Castle Rock Fire Department.

On September 24, 1919, Thorwald married "a beautiful socialite and leader of women's groups" named Victoria Hannold Anderson.[38] Victoria, who had been widowed two years earlier, resided at 410 Jerry Street with her son. Her family had owned the Jerry Street house (originally constructed in 1889, probably by an early Castle Rock resident, John Lofe) since 1893, and it had passed to Victoria after her mother died of double pneumonia in 1917. The house featured a steeply pitched roof with overhanging eaves, porch with wooden balustrade, and second story double-hung window with wooden lintel. Early photographs indicate that the prominent three-paned, hipped bay window was a later addition and that in its place stood the original front door to the house.

As an active member of her community, Victoria was well-respected by Castle Rock's early society. She enjoyed membership in organizations such as the Eastern Star, a woman's group equivalent to the Masons, and the Pike's Peak Grange, where she often served as lecturer. The esteem and adoration that she enjoyed from her peers is reflected on her Cedar Hill Cemetery gravestone: "OF HER IT HAS BEEN SAID: 'To have known her was a great privilege and to have her for a friend a great honor. Her goodness will continue to live in the hearts of all of us, for she was truly one of God's noble women.' "[39]

In 1992, the Christensen house became the headquarters of the Castle Rock Chamber of Commerce. The organization renovated and expanded the building in 1995, restoring all original woodwork and removing paint from rhyolite walls and carpeting from wood floors. A 1,100-square-foot south-side addition featured a bay window similar in appearance to the original one, a rhyolite-faced parapet, and a skylight connection between the old and new sections.

City Hotel (1870s: John Harris, builder), 415, 417, and 419 Perry Street.

This modest Perry Street building, formerly Castle Rock's first hotel, played a vital role in the town's early history. In 1871, its builder, an Englishman named John Harris, moved from Memphis, Tennessee, to Douglas County with his brother, Thomas. They established a town roughly two miles northwest of Castle Rock called New Memphis. John constructed a vernacular wood, front-gabled, two-story hotel with several double-hung windows to serve visitors to the new town.

The Harris brothers' high hopes for their town ended when Castle Rock became the county seat in 1874 and attracted most of the incoming settlers. In 1877, Thomas Harris moved his family and various New Memphis buildings, including the hotel, to the larger town of Castle Rock. He changed the name of the building from the Harris Hotel to the Castle Rock House and placed it only one block from the depot, an ideal location that helped his business considerably. In November 1881, Thomas shot an eagle poised atop the Castle Rock formation. Because of its six-foot wingspan, he had it stuffed, wings spread out, and hung it in the lobby of his hotel, guaranteeing an impressive spectacle for his guests.

In addition to managing his thriving hotel, Thomas Harris also held a position as the town's second mayor. Castle Rock voters reelected him in 1884, but his second term ended abruptly when he was struck by a runaway steer in the streets of Castle Rock and died five days later.

In 1890, the hotel's new owner, Philip Crawshaw, renamed it City Hotel. Ten years later, he traded it to W. R. Kendall for property along Indian Creek between Sedalia and Nighthawk. The building changed hands several times after that, but always remained a popular business in town. Sunday chicken dinners for fifty cents a plate attracted both local residents and out-of-town visitors to the City Hotel in the 1920s. In 1997, the hotel, now an apartment building, received a historic commercial properties matching funds grant (funds used by the town to match amounts paid by property owners) from the town of Castle Rock that helped pay for the construction of a new porch and restoration of its exterior doors, windows, and clapboard siding.

Douglas County Courthouse (1889–1890: W. R. Parsons and Son, architect; J. M. Anderson, general contractor), 301 Wilcox Street.

Despite its destruction by fire in 1979, the Douglas County Courthouse remains a cherished community relic. The main part of the rhyolite building stood two and a half stories high and featured a 25-foot-high central domed tower and four gable end towers. A multitude of double-hung windows adorned each side of the building, and brick chimneys projected from the main cornice.

Construction began on the courthouse in May 1889 with W. R. Parsons and Son of Topeka, Kansas, as the building's architects and J. M. Anderson of Emporia, Kansas, as general contractor. Two of the county's most talented stonemasons,

Charles Lipps and Charles Herb, prepared and sculpted rhyolite for the building's walls.

Although the *Castle Rock Journal* reported in June 1889 that, "work on the courthouse is progressing finely," an odd disagreement between two county commissioners reported in the same issue revealed the tension caused by the growing realization of the project's magnitude:

> There was quite a ripple of excitement in town yesterday caused by a difficulty among the board of county commissioners. It seems there was some dispute about the quality of the stone being used in the new court house building, which led to the trouble. The result of the difficulty was that J. P. Adams, chairman was brought before Justice Hancock on a writ sworn out by D. R. Williams charging him with assult [sic], and fined five dollars and costs.[40]

Tension also existed among town residents who questioned the county commissioners' use of funds for the building's construction, particularly that of the contractor's salary. Again the *Castle Rock Journal*'s response to these concerns revealed increasing distrust among those involved:

> There has been considerable criticism in regard to the manner in which the commissioners have conducted the business connected with the erection of the new court house, and we have been importuned from time to time to "expose the frauds" through the columns of the *Journal*. We have taken some pains to examine into the matter and while some things to a casual observer appear "shady" we have not yet been able to locate any act either of the commissioners or contractor that will justify us in public condemnation. When we do our readers will hear from us.[41]

County citizens and officials endured these distractions and were rewarded one year later, in July 1890, with the completion of a handsome county courthouse. The *Castle Rock Journal* reported that the total cost for the building, including estimates for furniture, was $33,500, and added:

> It is a fine building, there is no denying that fact, and is an honor to the county. The cost of the building is not excessive, thanks to the watchful eyes that have been upon it, and the "kicks" that came whenever an attempt was made to ring in an excessived "extra."[42]

The Douglas County Courthouse, elected to the National Register of Historic Places in 1976, stood proudly in the center of Castle Rock for nearly eighty-eight years. Tragically, on March 11, 1978, the building was destroyed by a fire started by seventeen-year-old Rose Ann Lucero, who tried to create a diversion that would allow the release of her jailed friend.

Years after its devastation, the adored Douglas County Courthouse still inspires passion among county residents, particularly those who were fortunate enough to walk within its timeless halls. To them, the building was an old friend to be forever mourned.

Dyer House (1875: Samuel Dyer, builder), 208 Cantril Street. **Private residence.**

This Victorian-style house is one of the oldest frame structures in Castle Rock. Built in three stages, the middle section was constructed first and consisted of a modified shed roof, triangular dormer, bay window, and upstairs living space. The high gable roof and porch, with decorative bracket support beams found on the front section, was constructed next, followed by the back section, which now contains a kitchen and bathroom.

Its first occupant, Samuel Dyer, son of the famous Methodist circuit preacher Father John Dyer, built the house in 1875. After being appointed county clerk and recorder in 1874, Samuel decided that the daily journey from his remote ranch in Cherry Valley to Castle Rock was too hard, considering that he had lost his left foot at the Battle of Chancellorsville during the Civil War. Six years after settling into his white frame Castle Rock house, Samuel married Esther Mary Alexander, widow of Dr. W. J. Alexander, one of the first physicians to practice in Douglas County. The two lived in the house a short time before moving to Pueblo and then to Cripple Creek with Samuel's father, who wanted to provide some much-needed spiritual guidance to the inhabitants of Colorado's gold country.

The house survived as a residence until 1984, when its owner wished to build apartments on the property and informed the town government that the house would be torn down unless relocated. Lacking a suitable relocation site, the town board opted to buy the entire property as an attempt to prevent demolition of the historic house. Subsequently, a five-member board of concerned residents, the Castle Rock Historic Preservation Committee, formed to conceive a preservation plan that ultimately included the regeneration of the Dyer House into a town museum, the creation of a public park upon the property surrounding it, and the formation of a permanent preservation fund. However, in September 1984, Castle Rock voters rejected a 1.9 mill levy tax increase that would have been used to fund the committee's plan. After this defeat, the town board put the house up for sale, and it is currently a private residence once again.

First National Bank/Douglas Masonic Lodge (1904: builder unknown), 300 Wilcox Street. **Limited public access.**

Arguably one of the most elegant buildings in Castle Rock, this Richardsonian Romanesque structure has rhyolite stone walls, a flat roof adorned with cornice brackets and frieze decorations, and a double-arched doorway. A crowning touch is the radiating voussouirs of the second-story rectangular windows.

The building was constructed in 1904 with the First National Bank of Douglas County as its initial tenant. In 1933, during the Great Depression, the bank closed its doors. The building did not reopen until 1937, when its owner, the Douglas County Masons, bought it. This structure is still used as a gathering place for Masons and received designation to the National Register of Historic Places on April 14, 1995.

Hammar House (1887: Benjamin Hammar, builder), 203 Cantril Street. **Private residence.**

Another fine example of a late nineteenth-century Castle Rock stone house is the Benjamin Hammar house, also known to local residents as the "Doctor's House." Since its construction in 1887, this one-and-a-half-story Italianate-style building has been the home of several well-known Castle Rock residents. Stonemason Benjamin Hammar, co-owner of the Castle Rock Stone Company and later owner of the Santa Fe Quarry, built the house. He and his family lived in it for two years, at which time the house reportedly served as one of the major social gathering places of Castle Rock. The *Castle Rock Journal* chronicled an early fund-raiser hosted by the Hammars.

The house was thrown open and all the people were allowed free access to all the numerous and spacious rooms of the building. The first room to the left of the entrance was occupied as the ladies apartment, and the east room was filled with those who sought entertainment in vocal and instrumentation music. The halls were festooned with large and beautiful designs, displaying to good advantage the taste of the committee as well as the host and hostess. . . . After many songs were sung the people were invited to be seated while the eatables were passed around. . . . Mrs. Randel then occupied the stool at the organ and rendered the music to "The Sword of Bunker Hill," the words of which were sung by Miss Jennie Atchinson. . . . This and other selections of vocal music ended the amusements for the evening, and the people returned home feeling that their presence at the festival had been of mutual benefit to all concerned.[43]

In 1902, Dr. George E. Alexander, a native of Connecticut who practiced medicine in Fort Collins before moving to Castle Rock, purchased the house and set up his office within. He stored a one-horse-drawn carriage used to make house calls in the backyard barn. At the time of his death in 1947, Dr. Alexander was among the country's oldest practicing physicians, having spent sixty years in the profession.

In 1988, Lionel and Starr Oberlin, members of the Castle Rock Historical Society and the Douglas County Historic Preservation Board, purchased the home and enthusiastically pursued its nomination to the National Register of Historic Places. On February 3, 1993, the house became the first residential structure in Castle Rock to receive the designation, partly because its original construction had received little alteration. The T-shaped building retains its original four-over-four wooden double-hung windows featuring lintels with stylized stone Roman arches emphasizing raised keystones with elaborate carving between the top of the window and arch. Perhaps the most notable attraction of the house is the steep pitched side gable roof with a small front gable in the center of the facade that tops a wooden Victorian balcony. The original portion of the house is made of native rhyolite stone and rests on a stone foundation.

Keystone Hotel (1901: James and Francis Fetherolf, builders), 219 and 223 Fourth Street.

This building once housed the Tivoli Saloon, one of the wildest bars in the county, where local deputies were reportedly stationed to discourage drunken cowboys from riding their horses through the establishment. James Fetherolf, owner and barkeep of the saloon and thirteen rooms of the Keystone Hotel above it, constructed the building in 1901 with his brother, Francis. They built it from native rhyolite stone, adorning it with several double-hung windows topped by flat arches and an elaborate bracketed cornice that was later removed. A hall on the second floor featured dances once a month as well as on special occasions such as New Year's Eve and Valentine's Day.

In 1930, three years after the death of James Fetherolf, Mr. G. W. Naylor and son-in-law E. J. Miller bought the Keystone Hotel and began renovating its interior. Renaming the establishment the M and N Hotel and Café, the new owners opened their doors to the public on June 7, 1930. The *Record-Journal of Douglas County* heralded the opening:

A big dance will be the feature of the evening, with supper served in the dining room and café. The place has been closed up for the past six weeks, undergoing repairs

> and remodeling. New furnishings have been installed throughout and everything is now in first class condition. The hotel rooms have been newly papered and painted, the floors have been sand papered and varnished, new beds, and bedding and new furniture installed. A counter service as well as tables have been installed in the dining room. New electric refrigeration systems have been installed in the dining room as well as a large refrigerator in the kitchen. Other up to date kitchen equipment has been installed. . . . The services and conveniences offered by this new hotel and café, which will be known as Hotel M & N Café [sic] will undoubtedly appeal to the public, and the new firm will profit thereby. We extend hearty greetings to this new firm.[44]

The building changed hands many times since then, housing a number of businesses, including a shoe shop, cafe, hardware store, grocery store, pool hall, and barber shop. In the mid-1960s, all the first-floor windows were filled in with matching colored stone.

From the mid-1930s through the early 1970s, patrons knew the establishment by its most abiding name, Castle Café and Hotel. In the mid-1990s, new owners Brad Brown and Tom Walls announced plans to re-establish a downstairs restaurant called Castle Café, with apartments on the second story. After researching its architectural history, Brown and Walls conducted an elaborate restoration project within the building that included a replica of the original Castle Café business sign, duplication of period materials and colors throughout both levels, and extraction of the stone used to fill in the original first-story windows. The innovative owners further honored the building's history by supporting its nomination to the National Register of Historic Places. The building received the designation in August 1997.

Owens House (1870s: builder unknown), 213 and 215 Perry Street. **Private residence.**

Mary Ann Foster purchased the land upon which this building now rests from William Cantril in 1875. Foster's two-story wooden home was completed by 1879 and featured a cross-gabled roof, three gabled dormers, and open-cone terraced porch with decorative railings. The contrast between arched second-story windows and first-floor rectangular windows reveals an Italianate influence.

The fifteen-room structure remained a residence until October 1879, when David Owens purchased it and converted it into a hotel. Owens, a New Yorker who moved to Colorado in 1859, tried his hand at a number of activities, including the military, mining, and ranching, before settling down in the hotel business. He advertised his hotel as a reasonably priced, first-class establishment and claimed, "Travelers, pleasure and health seekers will find this the prettiest, cosiest and neatest hotel outside of Denver." Located "in one of the healthiest and most picturesque spots in Colorado," it is no wonder the Owens House attracted tuberculosis patients and became a "home away from home" for traveling county commissioners.[45] In 1892, one of the hotel's many successive owners, John Burke, changed its name to the Cottage Hotel.

Starting in 1937, the building underwent extensive remodeling by owner Joseph Burke (brother of John), who used it as apartments. The ceiling was lowered, windows and fireplaces filled, the terraced porch torn down, and, most significantly, a stucco finish added to the entire structure. In November 1997, the Castle Rock Town Council rewarded the building with local landmark status and a matching funds grant for exterior restoration that included new front windows and trim.

St. Francis of Assisi Catholic Church (1888: John Baptiste Ehmanon, builder), 210 Third Street.

This rhyolite structure features a high-pitched gable roof with boxed cornices and a small gabled vestibule. Triangular-arched windows with protruding sills frame stained glass, and a rosette window peaks above the vestibule.

Reportedly Castle Rock's first church, St. Francis of Assisi Church was built in 1888 by German-born stonemason John Baptiste Ehmanon, who cut the native rhyolite stone in a rough manner that adds to the building's quaint appearance. Ehmanon's own funeral was held in the church in 1909. Among the more notable priests to serve St. Francis of Assisi Church was Father Dezonia Streidle, the "Padre of Kiowa Creek," who was ordained in Illinois in 1921 and spent thirty-seven years ministering in the Douglas County area. In 1966, the St. Francis congregation built a new church east of Castle Rock and put their old house of worship up for sale.

Ironically, the once-holy building is now a restaurant and bar called The Old Stone Church Restaurant. In August 1994, J. P. Cochran, owner of the restaurant, expanded the kitchen area on the building's southeast side. The addition consisted of a steeply pitched roofline, wood wall facing, and new stained glass windows.

Schweiger House (1910–1918: George Leonard, builder), 519 Wilcox Street.

This two-story, wood frame building with clapboard siding and high cross-gabled roof features patterned triangular cut wooden siding on its eastern facade. A large east-facing picture window is located on the first floor. Above this are two double-hung second-story windows topped by a miniature pointed arch attic window. The foundation walls are of rough-cut rhyolite stone, and the entrance to the building is located on its south side.

Originally constructed sometime between 1910 and 1918 by George and Evelyn Leonard, John and Anna Schweiger purchased the building in 1918. The Schweigers owned the original Happy Canyon Ranch located north of Castle Rock. John Schweiger, an Austrian native, allegedly named his ranch after a cheerful man who stayed in a nearby cabin and was prone to whistling gaily in the mornings. Schweiger worked in the mines and smelters of Georgia and Tennessee before moving to Colorado in 1869, where he worked at Horace Tabor's Sampling Mills in Leadville. Schweiger then moved to his ranch in Douglas County with several family members and his new wife, Anna. They lived there until 1918, when ill health forced him to leave his ranch and move to Castle Rock. The Castle Rock house on Wilcox Street remained in the Schweiger family for several years after John's death in 1925.

In 1964, the building was converted into a combination tea room/gift shop called the Golden Dobbin. The *Rocky Mountain News* praised the "Victorian house of treasures" for its supply of "out-of-the-ordinary gifts" and edible "delicacies."[46] The building served hungry patrons under the names French Bakery starting in June 1993 and the Augustine Grill in 1997.

Upton Treat Smith House (1902: Upton Treat Smith, builder), 403 Cantril Street. **Private residence.**

Decorative features give a distinctive appearance to this house. Besides a steep gable roof with overhanging eaves and tall, narrow sash windows, the house has rough-hewn stone lintels and wooden trim casings that resemble white picket fence designs. A hipped porch is supported by wooden posts and patterned brackets.

Upton Treat Smith, a Civil War veteran from Maine who moved to Colorado in 1869 hoping to find his fortune in gold at Central City, built the house in 1902. Like many who came before him, Smith was not successful at mining and in 1872 he went back to Maine and married Sarah E. Grout. The two returned to Colorado and settled on a homestead in West Plum Creek, eight miles southwest of Castle Rock, where they stayed for the next twenty-five years. Smith moved his family to Castle Rock in 1902 and was elected treasurer of Douglas County in 1907, a position he held for seven years. Smith also served as vice-president of the First National Bank of Douglas County and later as president of the People's Bank of Castle Rock. Affectionately labeled by the *Record-Journal of Douglas County* as "one of our best citizens," Smith died in 1925, and ten years later Sarah died.[47] Possession of the house passed to their children and has since had several owners, but it remains a residence.

Wilcox School/Town Hall (1910–1911: builder unknown), 620 and 680 Wilcox Street.

This edifice replaced a burned 1907 school building that occupied the same site. Rough-faced, square rhyolite stonework, a hipped roof, and lower-level rectangular windows with transoms adorned the rudimentary school building.

In May 1911, the community celebrated the laying of the new building's cornerstone with a ceremony conducted by the Masonic Grand Lodge. The *Record-Journal* commended the school's functionality:

> The new Douglas County High School building will be, when completed, one of the most modern and best arranged structures of its kind in the State. . . . The entire building will be of lava stone, the main part being eighty feet long by forty feet wide; or the same dimensions of the old building. In addition, there will be a front, seventeen by forty-two feet in which will be built the stairways, lavatories, typewriter room, rest room, lunch room, and Principal's office. . . . Further equipment in the form of sanitary drinking fountains, slate blackboards, good ventilation, raised seats in the laboratory, modern tables and sinks for chemicals, a good sewer system, all go to make a High School of which every citizen of Douglas County may well be proud. . . . Now let's all boost for the High School.[48]

In the mid-1930s, school officials enlarged the building to include a gym. The Wilcox School served the town's high school students until 1961 and junior high students until 1966, when the community constructed new, separate facilities for these grades. Elementary students attended Wilcox School until the mid-1980s, when they too were moved into a new building. Shortly thereafter, the Douglas County School District renovated Wilcox School for administrative offices, and in 1989 the building's gym was resurrected into a town hall. The last remodeling, by Denver architect Ron Abo, took place in 1989 and included the installation of new windows, lighting, and landscaping. Abo's exterior design masked the original rhyolite facade with multicolored brick and inset rhyolite diamonds on the frieze.

Wilson House (1897: builder unknown), 704 Wilcox Street. **Private residence.**

A broad front porch, pyramidal roof, and hipped dormer adorn this cottage. The most notable feature of the clapboard siding wooden house, however, is its turned porch posts with decorative brackets. A brick chimney straddles the rear section of the roof, and several tall, double-hung windows can be found on the sides of the house.

In 1907, Larkspur pioneer James Dallas "J. D." Wilson sold his stock ranch and moved with his wife, Sarah, to Castle Rock, where they spent the next fourteen years in this home on the north end of busy Wilcox Street. Wilson, known locally as Uncle Jimmie, owned a strong team of horses that he used to help nearby farmers and ranchers with their hauling needs. It was this occupation that ultimately led to his death. In November 1921, while hauling a load of wood, Wilson sustained fatal head injuries after falling from his wagon. He was eulogized as "obliging and faithful . . . his departure is, to any community he graces, to his family, his friends, his neighbors, and all, an irreparable loss."[49] Sarah Wilson continued to live in the house until her death in 1939, at which point ownership passed to her children. The house has since had several owners, including World War II veteran Osmer W. Sheets.

Notes

1. Robert L. Lowenberg, *Castle Rock: A Grassroots History* (Castle Rock, Colorado: Lowenberg, 1980), p. 22.
2. *Trail*, 1859, vol. 5, no. 8, p. 6, CWA Files, Colorado Historical Society.
3. *Douglas County News Press*, June 1981, Castle Rock Centennial 1881–1981 edition, p. 6.
4. Anne Moore, "The History of Douglas County, 1820–1910," in *Our Heritage: People of Douglas County*, ed. The Book Committee (Shawnee Mission, Kansas: Inter-Collegiate Press, 1981), pp. 347–348.
5. *Castle Rock Journal*, November 9, 1881, p. 3.
6. *Rocky Mountain News*, March 18, 1874, p. 2.
7. Ibid., April 14, 1874, p. 2.
8. *Daily Denver Tribune*, April 21, 1874, p. 1.
9. *Rocky Mountain News*, April 14, 1874, p. 1; June 17, 1874, p. 1.
10. Ibid., June 25, 1874, p. 4.
11. *Rocky Mountain News*, May 18, 1881, p. 4; *Castle Rock Journal*, April 12, 1882, p. 3.
12. *Castle Rock Journal*, May 25, 1887, p. 3.
13. *West Creek Mining News and the Nighthawk Mountain Echo*, May 20, 1899, p. 1.
14. *Castle Rock Journal*, May 28, 1884, p. 2.
15. Ibid., June 4, 1884, p. 3.
16. Ibid., June 13, 1902, p. 1.
17. Ibid., December 4, 1889, p. 3.
18. *Record-Journal of Douglas County*, August 13, 1909, p. 1.
19. Ibid., August 16, 1929, p. 1.
20. Ibid., June 12, 1936, p. 1.
21. Ibid., February 12, 1932, p. 1; *Denver Post*, February 10, 1932, pp. 1, 3.
22. *Record-Journal of Douglas County*, December 22, 1933, p. 1.
23. Ibid., August 18, 1939, p. 1.
24. *Douglas County News*, June 24, 1965, pp. 1, 5, 8.
25. Ibid.
26. *Douglas County News Press*, August 15, 1979, p. 4A.
27. *Douglas County News Press*, March 24, 1999, pp. 1A, 16A; April 14, 1999, pp. 1A, 16A; April 28, 1999, p. 8A; May 26, 1999, p. 8A; June 2, 1999, pp. 1A, 14A; June 9, 1999, p. 7A; June 16, 1999, p. 1A; June 23, 1999, p. 8A; July 14, 1999, pp. 1A, 16A; July 28, 1999, pp. 7A, 8A; August 4, 1999, p. 8A; August 11, 1999, p. 8A; August 18, 1999, p. 8A; September 1, 1999, pp. 1A, 7A, 8A, 20A; September 8, 1999, p. 7A;

September 15, 1999, p. 8A; September 22, 1999, pp. 7A, 10A; October 13, 1999, pp. 1A, 22A; October 20, 1999, p. 6A; October 22, 1999, pp. 1A, 18A; October 27, 1999, p. 1A; November 3, 1999, pp. 1A, 20A; December 1, 1999, pp. 1A, 18A; December 22, 1999, p. 18A.

28. *Rocky Mountain News*, March 18, 1874, p. 2.

29. *Castle Rock Journal*, December 29, 1886, p. 3.

30. Kent Brandebery, "Douglas County's First Courthouse," Draft, Quoting 1874 Commissioner Minutes, March 28, 1995, p. 256.

31. *Castle Rock Journal*, May 21, 1874, p. 4.

32. Brandebery, Quoting 1874 Commissioners Minutes, "Special Meeting June 15th A.D. 1874," p. 264.

33. *Castle Rock Journal*, December 3, 1884, p. 2.

34. Ibid., July 18, 1888, p. 1.

35. Ibid., July 23, 1897, p. 3.

36. Ibid., November 21, 1888, p. 4.

37. *Record-Journal of Douglas County*, May 17, 1935, p. 4.

38. Lowenberg, *Castle Rock: A Grassroots History*, p. 71.

39. Gravestone of Victoria Christensen, Cedar Hill Cemetery.

40. *Castle Rock Journal*, June 12, 1889, p. 3.

41. Ibid., July 10, 1889, p. 1.

42. Ibid., August 6, 1890, p. 4.

43. *Castle Rock Journal* quoted from Josephine Lowell Marr, *Douglas County: A Historical Journey* (Gunnison, Colo.: B&B Printers, 1983), pp. 162–163; *Castle Rock Journal*, April 8, 1885, p. 3; April 20, 1887, p. 3.

44. *Record-Journal of Douglas County*, April 25, 1930, p. 1; June 6, 1930, p. 1; June 13, 1930, p. 8.

45. *Castle Rock Journal*, July 13, 1881, p. 2.

46. *Rocky Mountain News*, December 26, 1964, p. 45.

47. *Record-Journal of Douglas County*, July 10, 1925, pp. 1, 8.

48. Ibid., May 26, 1911, p. 1; June 9, 1911, p. 1.

49. Ibid., November 4, 1921, p. 1; November 18, 1921, p. 1.

DECKERS

With the splendid attractions in the way of the wonderful spring water, the scenery and the fishing, Decker's ought surely to become a very famous place.
—*The Mountain Echo,* May 14, 1898

In the sleepy, secluded valley of the upper South Platte River's south fork rest a string of small, quiet communities. Throughout the history of the region, settlements have sprouted with colorful names such as Nighthawk, Twin Cedars, and Daffodil, as well as the less-colorful Pemberton, Trumbull, and West Creek. Today, the settlements that remain are collectively known as Deckers, the site of a popular turn-of-the-century health and mineral springs resort. The success of Stephen D. Decker and his resort is one of many examples of entrepreneurial activities that have occurred within the valley throughout its history. Indeed, for many years the upper South Platte River valley has been a seedbed for flowering enterprises that attempted to capitalize directly upon the extraction of resources such as timber, gold, lithia springs water, and fish. Despite the boom and bust cycles these industries saw, the region has always retained a serenity and beauty that has attracted visitors for decades.

From the 1870s through the early 1900s, the upper South Platte River valley resonated with the whirl and whine of sawmills along the river. "We visited the Platte river last week," reported an 1889 issue of the *Castle Rock Journal*, "and found that part of the country devoted largely to the lumber interests."[1] Owners of these mills took advantage of their prime location within the Plum Creek Timber Land Reserve, a 179,000-acre forest that, with the adjacent Pikes Peak Reserve, makes up part of the Pike National Forest, established in 1892. Lumber was logged from the reserves, cut in the mills, and transported by river drives or hauled overland by oxen and horse teams to South Platte Station (also known as Symes), the nearest railroad town. There, the logs were shipped to Denver and other towns. By 1879, at least ten mills operated along the river, and ten years later 200,000 feet of lumber were reportedly carried out of the area each week. Some of the most successful mill operations belonged to the John Mouat Lumber Company, the South Platte Land and Lumber Company, and the businesses of G. Kearney, S. S. Kendall, W. W. Alpine, and Tim Gill.

John Mouat and his brother Jerry also played an important role in the history of the area as the primary builders of the Sugar Creek road, part of today's State Highway 67. Roads that connected the secluded valley to Denver and Castle Rock were rare at the time, and the construction of the Sugar Creek road was considered vital to the economic survival of the area. "The people are becoming awake to the necessity of having public roads to the mountains," reported the *Castle Rock Journal*. "They should have been laid out ten years ago."[2] The grade along Sugar

Creek was more gradual than other sites in the area and, thus, better suited for road construction. Nonetheless, the Mouat brothers no doubt had business interests in mind when they chose the road's site in 1887. Their mill was conveniently located at the intersection of Sugar Creek and the South Platte River.

In 1889, a local newspaper reported the progress of the road: "They are now at work on a road up Sugar Creek, which, when completed, will be five miles long and the best mountain road the writer ever saw."[3] Gwendolin Ammons McLaughlin, one of the area's pioneers, was not as impressed by the road and remembered it as "at best only a makeshift wagon road."[4] She thought more highly of another road that wound several miles along the South Platte River on an abandoned railroad grade, from South Platte Station to just beyond Mouat's Mill on Sugar Creek. In 1885, the Denver & Rio Grande Railroad constructed the grade as part of the company's projected route to Leadville. When that plan failed, the county leased it for use as a road. It has since been widened and remains in use today.

In 1885, the Ammons family acquired the Ox Yoke Ranch, just south of Mouat's Mill, from Theodore Metz. Metz, a West Virginian who homesteaded the land with his wife and ten children sometime prior to 1876, owned several oxen and used his teams to draw freight between Leadville and Denver during the summer. One of the wooden yokes used during the hauling was suspended from the large corral gate and gave the ranch its name.

The Metz family had constructed several buildings on the Ox Yoke land, including two houses, a storeroom, a milk house, and several barns, stables, and sheds. In 1885, during a violent summer storm, a flash flood raged through the valley and swept many of these structures away. Disheartened and discouraged by the disaster, the Metz family left by the summer's end, selling the ranch and the Ox Yoke cattle brand to the Ammons family.

Although family ranches similar to the Ox Yoke property peppered the valley during the early 1880s and 1890s, the region remained sparsely populated. This seclusion appealed to Denverites and other city dwellers who favored the area as a weekend refuge. "Never before have the mountains been fresher and more inviting to persons who enjoy nature," reported the *Castle Rock Journal* in 1895.[5] The Sugar Creek correspondent for the *Castle Rock Journal* observed in August 1889, "People from Denver are frequent visitors to our creek." Another journalist in the same issue commented that the area's "grand mountain scenery" was "appreciated by the people from the metropolis who spend much time here breathing the pure air, enjoying the scenery and partaking of the hospitalities of the company."[6] However, by 1895, something besides the scenery and fresh air lured people to the area: gold fever.

In April 1895, Captain George F. Tyler triggered the short-lived gold rush of the West Creek Mining District when he sent his son to Denver with ore samples extracted from his ranch between Trout Creek and West Creek. He hoped to persuade some professional mining men to investigate the mining prospects in the area. Two months later, G. A. Kennedy arrived with a chemical assay outfit and made several tests of the Tyler ranch rock. When he reported that these tests yielded from five to fifteen dollars a sample, hundreds of argonauts flocked to the area to stake their claims. That October, a comparison of the region to infamous Cripple Creek in the *Castle Rock Journal* was filled with inflated hopes:

> Several persons who were at Cripple Creek when that camp was being developed, say that at the surface Cripple Creek could not show as much rock that run in gold or that carried as much gold as the camp here. And

> we know of no one who has examined and has said to the contrary.[7]

By December 1895, the *Castle Rock Journal* reported that, "There is now scarcely a foot of government land not covered by a claim. . . . A person can travel either north or south for five miles and be on mining claims all the time."[8]

Encouraged by this initial success, Captain Tyler established a town site to be named Tyler, Tyler City, or Bunker Hill on his ranch. In January 1896, the *Castle Rock Journal* reported, "Tyler is growing and is the only town in the West Creek district that can yet boast of a real post office."[9]

As more miners poured into the area, about 500 square miles of public land were made available to prospectors. Within weeks other campsites such as Pemberton, West Creek, North West Creek, North Cripple Creek, Ackerman, Trumbull, and Given were established. Pemberton, the largest of these camps, located on rancher Walsh Pemberton's property, established such a demand for lots "that it seemed impossible to stake them off fast enough for buyers. Lots were surveyed, sold and buildings begun, all within a day."[10] By January 1896, Pemberton was "booming. Houses are going up as rapidly as lumber can be secured."[11] Businesses in the town included restaurants, grocery stores, saloons, feed stores, butcher shops, real estate offices, surveyors' offices, a blacksmith shop, a hardware store, and a barbershop. The population of the town reached 500 in January 1896; a month later it had doubled to 1,000. The success of the town prompted a *Rocky Mountain News* reporter to muse, "Mining promises to be the leading industry in the county at no distant day."[12]

By February 1896, the inhabitants of the many campsites throughout the region agreed to unite as one town, to be called West Creek, the name of the mining district. They filed for a petition with the county commissioners that called for an election of incorporation. On March 16, 1896, all 123 votes cast were in favor, and West Creek became Douglas County's second incorporated town. The 1896 *Colorado Business Directory* gave the new town and mining district a glowing review:

> It is beautifully situated in the center of the West Creek Mining District, and is the largest town in the territory. . . . Among the other advantages, besides the mountains of undeveloped wealth, are first class water and water power. Game and fish in abundance, pure air enriched with ozone, and the most picturesque scenery. All of which, with the iron mineral springs, makes this highly favored locality a resort for both health and wealth.[13]

The *Rocky Mountain News*, prophesized a glorious future for West Creek in a bold declaration: "Its growth has been as substantial as it has been rapid. Its development will be as permanent as it will be wonderful."[14] However, the newspaper's prediction proved premature, as the flame of the West Creek Mining District's glory days died nearly as quickly as it ignited. When surface ores diminished, the miners turned to hard rock mining, which drained just as quickly, and a soaring population of 1,200 in 1896 plummeted by the next year to a mere 100. The number of saloons fell from thirteen in 1896 to two in 1897, while restaurants dropped from eight to two and hotels from four to one. By the summer of 1898, nearly two-thirds of the habitable buildings in the town were vacant. In March 1898, a columnist for the local newspaper, *The Mountain Echo*, commented on the town's paltry population during election time: "Never in the history of the town of West Creek has it been so dead that it could not support two tickets. There are now just thirty-two legal voters in the town and eleven of them are candidates."[15]

Many of the fortune-seekers who ventured to the area during the West Creek mining boom were newcomers to the world of panning, sluice boxes, and mine shafts. Among these was Stephen D. Decker, later described in the *Denver Post* as "a pioneer railroad man [who] held positions as brakeman, conductor, superintendent of construction and general superintendent on a number of railroads in this country."[16] In the mid-1890s, Decker arrived in the upper South Platte River valley to try his hand at mining. He filed a claim at the junction of Horse Creek and the South Platte River. He did not find gold, but instead found another resource that eventually made him a wealthy man. Decker's bonanza was natural, bountiful springs of lithia water, mineral water containing lithium salts. He bottled the water and marketed it as possessing miraculous healing powers effective in curing stomach, kidney, bladder, and bowel problems. The product was highly successful and demand was steady in both the United States and Europe. A local newspaper related the enormous popularity of the product:

> S. D. Decker is pushing the sale of water from his mineral spring near Trumbull with great vigor and has now reached a point where he has difficulty in supplying the demand with his limited facilities. A number of well known Denver physicians have become convinced of the medicinal value of the water from the spring and are prescribing it for their patients in a number of different diseases.[17]

Decker promptly opened a saloon as well as a general store/post office in April 1896, and called his humble settlement Daffodil. By November 1897, as the demand for his lithia water grew, Decker announced his intention to build a health resort on the land. Only one year later, *The Mountain Echo* marveled at the resort's unexpected notoriety:

> It is amazing how popular Decker's mineral springs have become in a single season. The ten or twelve cottages which Mr. Decker put up this spring are all occupied nearly all the time and applications for rates and information come in by the dozen in every mail.[18]

Decker's Mineral Springs and Resort eventually became so well established that the entire area for miles was known collectively as Deckers. In 1909, the *Colorado Business Directory* officially replaced its Daffodil listing with Deckers, but the name was not legally changed until the early 1920s, to honor the town's founder, who died in 1917.

Interestingly, Deckers was not the first South Platte River valley resort to cater to tourists. A similar enterprise, called the "O. J. Martin Place" located near the confluence of Pine Creek and the South Platte River, also attracted fishermen and nature lovers, although on a much smaller scale than Deckers. Enock Martin, a confederate Civil War veteran, and his son Owen (O. J.) came to the river country in 1876 to work in the lumber mills and filed on a 160-acre homestead that same year. They built a small log cabin with a dirt floor on the property to fulfill the legal requirements of the 1862 Homestead Act, which called for an improvement of the granted land. Years later, further improvements included the construction of a fisherman's lodge and several adjacent cabins. When Enock died, O. J. took control of the lodge, named it after himself, and around 1912 hired a man named Charlie Ethridge to cook and serve meals to the resort's guests. Ethridge's culinary whims included banging two pots together and shouting, "Chow's on!" to alert guests that a meal was served. Dorothy Roerig, a resident of the South Platte River area since 1905, recalled the quaint swinging cable bridge O. J. Martin built across the river for the convenience of his fishermen guests. Martin chided young Dorothy and her friends for dangling from the bridge during wading excursions in the river. According to Dorothy, Martin also constructed the area's only walk-in refrigerator.[19]

After O. J. Martin died in 1939, his nephew, Don Simeth, inherited the resort, but did not move there with his wife, Jane, until 1948. "Our friends thought we were crazy to quit work and go up there," Jane Simeth commented many years later, "[but] life was very interesting up there from the beginning to the end. . . . We were pioneers, because we didn't have water or electricity or telephone or anything."[20] Nonetheless, over time, the Simeths made repairs and new additions to the resort and renamed it Twin Cedars Lodge after two cedar trees that stood just outside the back door of the main lodge. Quite popular among both tourists and residents, Twin Cedars Lodge featured a grocery store where area residents could buy novelties such as cold soft drinks and beer. Four decades later, the lodge came to a tragic end. Three men, who became nervous when the Douglas County Sheriff's Office set up a summer substation at the lodge, set fire to all the lodge's buildings in an attempt to destroy illegal drugs they had stashed in one of the cabins. The incident culminated in a dramatic SWAT-team raid of the group's cabin along the South Platte River in February 1987 and the arrest of two of the men believed to have been involved in the arson.

Early guests of Decker's resort caught the Colorado & Southern railroad from Denver to South Platte Station. From there, they would be transported by stage or private conveyance fifteen miles south to Deckers. An extremely important mode of transportation for the area, the stage began rolling through the dusty roads of the upper South Platte River valley during the West Creek mining boom of the mid-1890s. The railroad brought mail three times a week to South Platte Station, where the stage picked it up and carried it as far as Deckers.

One early South Platte River valley household made stage driving a family affair. As early as 1897, the Buzbee family name was synonymous with South Platte stage travel. George, Enoch, Doc, and George Jr. transported visitors, residents, and mail for many years. Dorothy Roerig remembered driver George Buzbee, who often allowed her to sit up front with him on the stage and hold the tail end of the horses' reins as they were traveling. "Of course, I thought I was driving!" she laughed.[21] Proprietor of the stage from 1897 to 1913, George died during a December 1913 blizzard.

> George Busbee, [sic] who ran the mail stage between South Platte and West Creek, perished in the blizzard last week. His body was found near Night Hawk, Saturday by Owen Martin and Hugh Kendall. He had left South Platte Wednesday, December 3, to take the mail to West Creek, and started for home the next day. He evidently had abandoned the stage and attempted to get home horseback, but was unable to do so. One of the horses survived the storm, and it was because of having seen this horse wandering about, that Mr. Martin started out in search of the missing man. The other horse perished with its owner.[22]

George's wife contributed to the family business by serving as one of the primary mail carriers in the valley. Longtime valley resident Ethel Culver Myers fondly recalled Mrs. Buzbee's humor:

> She was fun. She would meet our cattlemen driving a herd of wild Herefords in a narrow place on the road, she would whip her team, run like hell through the middle of them scattering them to the four winds. "You can't stop the U.S. Mail!"[23]

Sometime after the Buzbee family proprietorship ended, a man known only as "Mr. Baloo" took up the reins. Dorothy Roerig claimed the new driver "was not a kind soul" and was suspected of being an alcoholic and wife beater. Hot-tempered and reckless, Mr. Baloo became enraged one afternoon when he learned that Mrs. Walgret, the stationmistress at the South Platte Station, had aided his bruised wife's desertion by placing her on the train to Denver, never to return. The incensed man shot Mrs. Walgret, set the South Platte Hotel on fire, and stole a horse for his escape. Shortly thereafter, he was shot and killed near Canon City, either by his own hand or by one of the many officers who pursued him.

In 1912, not long after this incident, the first "automobile stages," or "touring cars," arrived on the scene. Owned and run by a couple named Mr. and Mrs. Newlin, the automobile stage carried on the same activities and responsibilities as that of its horse-drawn predecessors. However, the Newlins performed their duties behind the wheel of a seven-seater car instead of behind a team of horses. The Newlins's son Ray eventually took over the business but terminated it after the Colorado & Southern shut down its passenger service to South Platte Station in 1937.

Among the most popular stage stops during the mid-1890s was the small resort and mining settlement of Nighthawk. E. L. Rogers platted the town in 1896 as part of the Nighthawk Mining District, which was named after a local species of hawk, the Bull Bat, which flies very high then suddenly plunges downward with a shrill screech. The Nighthawk Town, Mining and Improvement Company and the Nighthawk Townsite Company laid the town's lots and rented furnished and unfurnished tents of various sizes to monthly tenants. Craggie Street, Douglas Avenue, Jefferson Avenue, and El Paso Avenue featured several businesses, including E. T. Hanna's Pioneer Cash Store, I. P. Cleary's Craggie View Hotel, Henry Hiller's Restaurant, a blacksmith shop, a livery stable, and a sawmill. In 1897, speculation abounded concerning the construction in Nighthawk of "one of the handsomest and most commodius hotels in any resort in the Rocky mountains," designed by Denver architect C. Herbert Lee.[24] The grandiose plans for the Queen Anne–style hotel included a dining hall, reading room, office, and as many as thirty guest rooms, with wide porches, fireplaces, indoor plumbing, and attractive outdoor landscaping. However, construction never proceeded past laying the foundation. Instead, the town constructed a very modest building that later burned from a spark believed to have been started by match-chewing varmints.

Nighthawk's early residents envisioned a prosperous, booming future for their town. The local newspaper, *The Mountain Echo*, printed attractive descriptions of Nighthawk designed to lure investors and tourists:

> Although scarcely an hour's ride from the busy metropolis [of Denver] it has been only lately that the residents of the Capitol city have discovered what a magnificent playground nature has here provided. With towering and craggie mountains rising like grim protectors on every hand, with tall and stately pines covering the lower hills, and the silvery river threading

> its way over and under and around huge water worn rocks, bounding and leaping onward toward the wild canon below; amid these romantic environments lies the happy little town of Nighthawk.[25]

Ads published in the *Castle Rock Journal* and *The Mountain Echo* by the Nighthawk Town, Mining and Improvement Company encouraged readers to relocate to the mountain town:

> BUY LOTS IN NIGHTHAWK, Colorado's Most Beautiful Summer Resort. The Town Company is about to make Some Extensive Improvements and as soon as these are completed Prices of Lots will Advance. Build a Cottage and come and enjoy the splendid Fishing, Pure Water, and Invigorating Mountain Air. No possible danger from floods.[26]

In August 1898, *The Mountain Echo* proudly quoted a Denver newspaper: "Nighthawk has now the largest number of strangers ever domiciled within its limits at one time. . . . The fishing is fairly good, the mountain scenery grand, the mineral springs healthful, and the atmosphere lifegiving."[27]

While many visitors were lured to the area by the enchanting scenery and relaxing atmosphere, miners trekked to the town with visions of striking it rich. Many mining companies also organized in the region, including the Caledonia Nighthawk Mining and Milling Company, which owned five claims and constructed shafts and tunnels deep into the earth hoping to discover rich mineral veins and gold deposits. Although miners found only meager amounts of gold and copper, *The Mountain Echo* repeatedly put the best face on the disappointing results:

> Many experienced mining men regard the mineral indications in the immediate vicinity of Nighthawk as especially favorable. . . . The policy of those engaged in developing the mines, however, is to guard rather closely the actual value of the mineral found, fearing lest their claims be considered exaggerated boasts. They are convinced that they have good prospects and are steadily working away, confident that their perseverance will be amply rewarded in due time. They promise to startle the state at no distant date when they reveal what they so confidently expect to discover.[28]

By the 1900s, the town's mining prospects had declined considerably and its feeble boom ended. Today only a few homes, intermixed with stone foundation ruins, scatter the hillside on the east bank of the South Platte River.

During its heyday, a prosperous future for Nighthawk appeared certain, due in part to the Colorado & Southern Railway Company's projected construction of a rail extension from Denver to the great gold camp of Cripple Creek, via the South Fork of the South Platte River. Called the "Short Cut to Cripple Creek," the proposed route followed the South Fork from South Platte Station to Lake George, where it connected with the Colorado Midland at Florissant. From there it traveled the Colorado Midland tracks east to Divide, where entry to Cripple Creek was made through an arrangement with the Midland Terminal Railway Company. The *Castle Rock Journal* predicted success for the entire county pending the completion of the line:

> The advantage gained by this county will be great, for it will open up a new district, abounding in timber and

> mineral resources, and hitherto difficult of access. Then, too, some of the prettiest and grandest scenery in the state is situated in that vicinity. . . . Altogether the new railroad will be a great benefit to Douglas County.[29]

Among the many impediments to surface against the Colorado & Southern's lofty plans was the Denver Power & Irrigation Company, which planned to build a reservoir between South Platte Station and Nighthawk capable of "generating enough electricity to operate all the manufacturing plants, street railways, and electric lights in Denver."[30] In September 1899, as the Colorado & Southern began construction of its South Fork branch line, Denver Power & Irrigation Company filed suit to stop the railroad from building across its property. The newly named *West Creek Mining News and the Nighthawk Mountain Echo*, a strong supporter of the Cripple Creek cutoff, lambasted the Denver power company and offered good wishes for the railroad's efforts:

> The frantic efforts of the Denver Power & Irregation [sic] company to head off the construction of a direct line of railroad between Denver and Cripple Creek are sure to end in failure, as has everything else that company ever attempted. . . . The company has always been hard at work constructing its system ever since the spring of 1896. Sometimes two men would constitute the working force; sometimes three; more often one. The principal duties of the construction gang seemed to be to get out with shovels and a wheel barrow in plain sight of the wagon road at the two times of day when the West Creek stage went by. . . . Denver needs more direct connection with the great gold camp, and it needs it badly. . . . Success to the Colorado & Southern's new Cripple Creek line.[31]

As the *West Creek Mining News and the Nighthawk Mountain Echo* predicted, Denver Power's legal efforts failed and the Colorado & Southern resumed its branch construction with renewed vigor. By January 1900, a surveying party reached Nighthawk, and three months later workers graded and laid a temporary narrow-gauge track to the town.

However, on May 3, 1900, before the railroad could advance much further toward completing the line to Cripple Creek, a flood immersed the area. It "descended like a tidal wave fourteen feet high, ruining roads, destroying buildings and floating away everything portable in its place."[32] The *Denver Republican* reported the devastation:

> The farmers living in the South Platte valley suffered both a severe fright and what was to them heavy loss. Their lands were inundated, some of their buildings were destroyed and it is probable that many head of stock were drowned before they could be removed to a place of safety.[33]

In its account of the flood's destruction, the *West Creek Mining News and the Nighthawk Mountain Echo* revealed a devastating blow to railroad promoters: "Between Nighthawk and South Platte hardly anything remains of the grade which had been completed by the Colorado & Southern for the use of the new Cripple Creek Short Line."[34]

Oddly, it was not the flood that put the final nail in the coffin of the Colorado & Southern's Short Cut to Cripple Creek. Years before the flood, the Denver Union Water Company, headed by

Denver businessman Walter Cheesman, had begun building a 200-foot-high dam and reservoir at the mouth of Goose Creek. The May 1900 flood damaged the uncompleted dam beyond repair, and company officials chose another site downstream from the ruins to begin anew. The new site included land previously surveyed by the Colorado & Southern for its Cripple Creek cutoff. Ultimately, Cheesman and the Denver Union Water Company retained control over this disputed area, and the railroad scrapped its mountain route to Cripple Creek and instead took over the Colorado Springs & Cripple Creek District Railway, which had previously built a standard gauge line to the booming mountain town. Nevertheless, Colorado & Southern officials continued construction of the Nighthawk branch line until 1904, laying tracks as far as Twin Cedars Lodge. Used primarily to haul Cheesman Dam construction material in and out of the area, the line was abandoned in 1916.

Cheesman Dam was completed in January 1905 and contributed greatly to providing a clean water supply for growing Denver. The thirst of the city and suburban areas was far from quenched, however, and new water demands once again centered on the South Platte River. In the 1920s, the Denver Water Board, formed in 1918, purchased the unused plans for Denver Power & Irrigation Company's proposed construction of a dam between South Platte Station and Nighthawk. This dam site would later be known as Two Forks. The board did nothing with the filings until 1966, when it was evident that the future of Denver depended on an increased supply of water. They enlisted the help of the U.S. Bureau of Reclamation to plan the gargantuan project, and by 1974 the two organizations had drafted and conducted studies into the location of three proposed dam sites, all within Douglas County. The sites were West Plum Creek Dam on West Plum Creek, Ferndale Dam on the North Fork of the South Platte River, and Two Forks Dam on the South Platte River approximately one mile downstream from the North Fork junction. In early 1974, the bureau announced that of the three, construction of Two Forks Dam appeared the most efficient and would therefore be recommended as the site for the reservoir.

The announcement infuriated South Platte River area residents, Colorado outdoorsmen, and environmentalists. The dam would completely inundate twenty-nine miles of the area including the community between the North Fork and Ferndale and the South Fork to a point above Wigwam Club. In February 1974, during a packed meeting in which a Bureau of Reclamation representative outlined plans for the dam, many residents expressed their resentment over the proposed destruction of their homes in order to promote the future growth of Denver, claiming the project "amount[ed] to an annexation of Douglas County land and resources by Denver."[35] Others protested that the diversion of the mountain waters reduced the Western Slope's own chances for expansion, while still others questioned the environmental impact of the dam. One man even suggested that Denver sink wells along Colfax Avenue for its own water just as he had being doing on his land for years.

Perhaps the most devastating effects of the proposed dam on area residents were monetary, including plummeting property values, denials of loans, and neglect by county and state agencies and utility companies who refused to put money into the condemned area. The county refused to pave the roads in the region. Phone lines were "literally tacked from tree to tree" and consisted of four-person party lines, a slight improvement over the eight-person party lines that had existed in the area for years. One newspaper account claimed the neglect of the area as a result of the proposed dam left many of the valley residents living in limbo.[36]

The ominous presence of the Denver Water Board was felt even more when it purchased Decker's Resort in December 1981 from independent oilman L. W. Brooks Jr. Brooks had bought the resort in 1979 after Denver newspaper ads shouted, "BUY YOUR OWN TOWN!", "For Man Who Has It All: 1 Colorado Resort Town," and "Want to Buy a Town? Picturesque Deckers for Sale."[37]

In 1989, Concerned Citizens, an organization of landowners and sportsmen opposed to the Two Forks Dam proposal, along with nearly forty-five environmental groups that had joined them in their fight, received some devastating news. The Army Corps of Engineers had approved the dam site, as long as certain costly conditions to offset environmental damage were fulfilled. The *Rocky Mountain News* announced the next aims of the opposition groups: "Dam opponents say the heat now has to be turned on the Environmental Protection Agency and the U.S. Forest Service which must approve the $500 million water-storage project on the South Platte River."[38] One year later, to the clamorous applause of the relieved valley residents and visitors, the Environmental Protection Agency vetoed the dam project under provisions of the Clean Water Act, which specified protection for recreational areas, wildlife, and fisheries.

The victory of those opposed to the dam did not last long, however. In 1991, eight suburban water districts objected that the EPA had acted arbitrarily and capriciously in its decision, and the issue was once again brought into the federal district court. While the lawsuit dangled in legal limbo, the Denver Water Board temporarily dropped its interest in Two Forks Dam and concentrated instead on conservation techniques by replacing water meters on 87,000 Denver homes and rewarding households that installed low-volume toilets. Finally, on June 5, 1996, a federal district judge delivered yet another blow to the Two Forks project, ruling that the EPA had acted justifiably in its 1990 ruling and that the water districts could no longer pursue the matter in court without the backing of the Denver Water Board, which owned the water rights to the land in question.

While the water districts waged their legal battle with the EPA, Pike National Forest officials looked for other ways to ensure the preservation of the river. In 1995, the agency announced that it was considering applying for a National Wild and Scenic River designation for more than twenty-three miles of the South Platte River, from Cheesman Dam to Strontia Springs Reservoir, and a comparable span along the North Fork. The *Denver Post's* "Western Outdoors" columnist agreed with Pike National Forest officials who claimed the river could receive the designation because of its "recreation, fisheries, wildlife and cultural or historical resources."

> If ever a river near a major metropolitan area qualified in terms of recreational worth, it is the main-stem of the South Platte. . . . The river is also wild and immeasurably valuable because its undammed portions are natural, beautiful and free-flowing, carving a course through forested valleys, canyons and ridges as old as the limestone and granite that make up their geologic foundation.[39]

If so designated, the federal government would control river flow in those sections. This was a discouraging possibility to Denver Water Board officials, who wanted to avoid having to apply to the government when thirsty Denver residents needed extra water flow. Consequently, the water board agreed in May 1997 to hire a consultant to assist the U.S. Forest Service in devising an alternative plan for the protection of the river while maintaining local control.

For the time being, it seems, Deckers will remain above water, but the Two Forks Dam proposal has not been completely discarded. The presence of a foreboding sign along a road just south of Nighthawk that reads, "ENTERING ENDANGERED AREA" speaks of the valley residents' struggle to save their landmarks and to maintain the land that was homesteaded by their ancestors. The secluded river valley with its multitude of natural resources has sustained several generations. Entrepreneurial exploitation of the region's resources such as timber, gold, "miraculously healing" lithia mineral water, and trout fishing has entranced settlers and visitors for decades. Nevertheless, the greatest source of the area's appeal and popularity is the peacefulness of the setting and the beauty and serenity of its natural surroundings.

Deckers Historic Sites

Ammons House (1888: Elias M. Ammons, builder), 2618 South Platte River Road. **Private residence.**

Elias M. Ammons began his days as a South Platte River valley resident at Ox Yoke Ranch. Shortly before his marriage on January 30, 1889, to Elizabeth Fleming, Elias constructed a house that was later dubbed the "White House" or "Caledonia Springs" after mineral springs were discovered on a nearby hill. Located approximately one and a half miles north of Ox Yoke Ranch on land originally homesteaded by Elias's sister, Theodosia, the house contrasted greatly with the typical log cabins of the region. The two-story, clapboard building features an upstairs, full-facade balcony, and several rooms. This house, the original Ox Yoke Ranch, and property owned by other Ammons sisters along Horse Creek together constituted what was known as the Ox Yoke property.

Although Elias eventually became one of the leading cattle ranchers of the valley, his initial attempts at the trade were not without problems. He made good use of the Ox Yoke cattle brand, singeing it to the backside of Kansas cattle he purchased with his partner, Thomas Dawson. Elias's sister, Gwendolin Ammons, later related that these cattle, unadjusted to their new high-altitude environment, "grew to like the loco weed and only the loco weed. They nearly all died, slowly and rather horribly; much like an extreme alcoholic. . . . It was very disheartening."[40] Nevertheless, the experience taught Elias a valuable lesson. He purchased only cattle acclimated to the thin air for the remainder of his career and eventually became quite successful. In 1896, he was elected president of the Horse Creek and Buffalo Creek Cattle Association, and in the early 1900s, he became temporary chairman of the Douglas County Stock Grower's Association and president of the Colorado Cattle Grower's Association. He was one of three men who founded the National Western Stock Show in Denver.

In 1888, when Elias constructed his home, the *Castle Rock Journal* reported, "E. M. Ammons is doing some farming as well as stock raising. He has the finest house in this part of the country and is evidently here to stay."[41] Elias stayed in the South Platte region until 1901, when he moved his family to Denver. He was elected governor of Colorado on November 5, 1912, "by 16,000 plurality, and the entire Democratic state ticket by a large majority."[42] Following his move to Denver, Ammons sold the house to William E. Moses. Ownership of the house changed hands several times before its current owner, the Denver Water Board, purchased it in 1984. The board currently rents it to tenants.

The house has undergone some physical changes over the years, including an exterior coating of dark green paint that ended its identification as the "White House" and the addition of indoor plumbing in the 1970s.

Cheesman Dam (1905: Charles L. Harrison, builder), Wigwam Creek Road (FR211).

In the 1890s, Denver businessman Walter Cheesman envisioned the construction of a mountain reservoir that would bring pure, clean water to Denver. Private wells and an undependable and unsanitary ditch system constructed in the 1860s provided Denver's earliest water supply. On September 6, 1894, Cheesman, one of the founders of the Denver City Water Company, met with other water company leaders and incorporated the Denver Union Water Company. As company president, Cheesman immediately commenced work on his plans for a mountain reservoir, and in 1897 construction began at the mouth of Goose Creek. Not even the May 3, 1900, flood that broke through a section of the uncompleted dam and then "whirled through the canon with the speed of an express train," could vanquish the optimism of the president:

> President Cheesman of the Water company said he felt certain that [the dam] would successfully withstand the strain. The barrier which did give way was a huge pile of rock not intended to hold water, but designed, when finished, to act as a support or backing to the dam itself . . . the pile did retain a great quantity of water for hours, but, at length, was whirled away before the resistless force of the torrent, as though made of shavings of wood.[43]

However, Cheesman underestimated the damage to the dam. The structure had suffered extensive damage and had to be abandoned. Nonetheless, Cheesman did not mourn his loss for long. Charles L. Harrison, a well-known engineer who had been employed by the Panama Canal survey, was hired to design a new, stronger Cheesman Dam, and construction began on August 29, 1900, just below the junction of Goose Creek and the South Platte River, six miles south of Deckers. When the dam was completed on January 1, 1905, it stood 221 feet high and 1,100 feet long and was deemed an engineering marvel. Constructed of locally quarried solid granite ashlar blocks laid in cement mortar and featuring the gravity-arch concept that contributes to its sturdiness, the dam contains Cheesman Lake, which at times can fill to 79,100 acre-feet of water. Today, the dam, designated as a National Historic Civil Engineering Landmark in 1973, still plays an essential role in supplying water to the Denver metropolitan area.

Deckers Lodge (1897: Stephen Decker, builder), intersection of State Highways 67 and 126.

The various buildings that make up Deckers Lodge have served the community's visitors and residents for more than a century. Quaint log cabins dot the hillsides and are commanded by a large, central L-shaped lodge with a rustic restaurant/bar, grocery store, and tackle shop. A resourceful man named Stephen D. Decker originally constructed the buildings as part of a popular turn-of-the-century health resort, Decker's Mineral Springs and Resort.

Decker's former illustrious career as "a pioneer railroad man" included employment with the Atlantic & Great Western, the Erie, the Oswego Midland, the Middleton & Crawford, the Union Pacific, and finally the Denver & Rio Grande. Despite busy days on the railroad, Decker seems to have had time for other more adventurous activities:

> During the days that he ran a train in Kansas he had many troublous days with the Wilson gang and other bad men, and was usualy [sic] the hero, as he always used strategy and prevented many killings. He took part in Indian fights, and was the leader of a mixed gang of cowboys, rustlers and citizens in a chase after the Cheyenne Indians on one of their raids through Colorado.[44]

Disabled from injuries sustained in a hurricane in the mid-1880s, Decker moved to Denver, where he was employed as an adjuster for the People's Savings Bank. During the West Creek mining boom of the mid-1880s, Decker journeyed to the upper South Platte River valley, hoping to discover his fortune. Struck with the highly contagious gold fever epidemic sweeping the area at the time, he filed a claim at the junction of Horse Creek and the South Platte River. Although he did not strike gold, Decker did discover a natural spring of lithia water that he eventually bottled and marketed as possessing miraculous healing powers. The product became very successful.

In April 1896, Decker opened a general store/post office and a saloon and named the settlement Daffodil. Local legend claims that the saloon's location often leapfrogged between Douglas County on the east side of the South Platte River and Jefferson County on the west side, depending on which authorities Decker was in trouble with at the time. Nonetheless, the saloon's customers remained faithful to the business despite the unpredictability of the location.

In November 1897, Decker opened a health resort on his property. The *Castle Rock Journal* outlined the proposed design of the resort:

> On account of the healthful influence of sleeping amid the odor of the pines, a multitude of small cabins built of logs will be provided, rather than one large hotel. There will be, however, a central dining hall and large pavilion for the use of all guests.[45]

Eventually, Decker's Mineral Springs and Resort encompassed twenty-seven buildings, including a music hall for dancing and concerts. Summer festivities included taffy pulls, "rousing camp fires," and "songs and shouts of laughter mingled with the roar and rumbling of the river far below."[46] Promotional brochures called the resort "The Tourist's Paradise" and overflowed with radiant descriptions of its attractions.

> There is an air of seclusiveness at Decker's resort that is thoroughly enjoyable, and at once commends itself to those seeking a mountain retreat where they can find refreshing rest entirely free from the bustle, activity and environments incident to the more pretentious summer resorts. Here the sojourner is breathing with delight the cool and pleasant air, prolific with the odor of mountain fir and pine. . . . Nowhere in the State of Colorado presents a better or more fascinating field for the sportsman with the fishing-rod than at Decker's resort. The South Platte is fairly alive with the 'speckled beauties.'[47]

In the 1920s, the town's name was legally changed from Daffodil to Deckers to honor its founder, who died in 1917. The property changed hands several times before being purchased by the Denver Water Board in December 1981 from oilman L. W. Brooks Jr. The water board currently leases various sections of the lodge to small business owners.

Notes

1. *Castle Rock Journal*, August 14, 1889, p. 1.
2. Ibid., July 14, 1886, p. 3.
3. *Castle Rock Journal*, quoted in Josephine Lowell Marr, *Douglas County: A Historical Journey* (Gunnison, Colo.: B&B Printers, 1983), p. 242.
4. Gwendolin Ammons McLaughlin Letter to Mr. and Mrs. Harlan Doud, Typescript, p. 1, Local History Collection, Philip S. Miller Library.
5. *Castle Rock Journal*, July 10, 1895, p. 1.
6. Ibid., August 14, 1889, p. 1.
7. Ibid., October 23, 1895, p. 1.
8. Ibid., December 4, 1895, p. 1.
9. Ibid., January 15, 1896, p. 4.
10. Ibid., December 4, 1895, p. 1.
11. Ibid., January 15, 1896, p. 4.
12. Ibid., December 4, 1895, p. 1; February 5, 1896, p. 4; February 19, 1896, p. 4; *Rocky Mountain News*, January 1, 1896, p. 22.
13. *Colorado Business Directory*, 1896, p. 683.
14. *Rocky Mountain News*, February 24, 1896, p. 6.
15. *The Mountain Echo*, March 19, 1898, p. 1.
16. *Denver Post*, June 22, 1917, p. 9.
17. *The Mountain Echo*, July 17, 1897, p. 1.
18. Ibid., August 6, 1898, p. 1.
19. Dorothy Roerig, Oral History Tape, March 17, 1992, Local History Collection, Philip S. Miller Library. Dorothy Roerig, "Historical Facts," pp. 6–7, Local History Collection, Philip S. Miller Library.
20. Simeth, Jane, Oral History Tape, March 23, 1992, Local History Collection, Philip S. Miller Library.
21. Roerig interview.
22. *Record Journal of Douglas County*, December 19, 1913, p. 1.
23. Roerig, "Historical Facts," p. 14.
24. *The Mountain Echo*, October 23, 1897, p. 4.
25. Ibid., July 10, 1897, p. 4.
26. *Castle Rock Journal*, November 10, 1889, p. 3; *The Mountain Echo*, September 4, 1897, p. 4.
27. *The Mountain Echo*, August 27, 1898, p. 1, quoting *Western Progress*.
28. Ibid., July 10, 1897, p. 4.
29. *Castle Rock Journal*, January 5, 1900, p. 1.
30. *The Mountain Echo*, November 12, 1898, p. 1; December 10, 1898, p. 1.
31. *West Creek Mining News and the Nighthawk Mountain Echo*, September 23, 1899, p. 1. *The Mountain Echo* received this new, expanded name in February 1899.
32. *George's Weekly*, July 2, 1900, p. 6.
33. *Denver Republican*, May 4, 1900, pp. 1, 5.
34. *West Creek Mining News and the Nighthawk Mountain Echo*, May 12, 1900, p. 3.
35. *Douglas County News*, February 14, 1974, pp. 1, 2.
36. *Rocky Mountain News*, September 29, 1977, pp. 2C, 3C.
37. Ibid., December 23, 1978, p. 81. *Denver Post*, December 24, 1978, p. 25.
38. *Rocky Mountain News*, January 11, 1989, pp. 7, 12.
39. *Denver Post*, October 8, 1995, p. 11C.
40. Ibid., April 4, 1909, p. 11.
41. *Castle Rock Journal*, November 26, 1897, p. 2.
42. *Denver Republican*, August 9, 1903, p. 24.
43. *Decker's Mineral Springs and Resort* (Denver, Colo.: J. M. Rhoads, The Printer) pp. 3–6.
44. Gwendolin Ammons McLaughlin Letter, p. 2.
45. *Castle Rock Journal*, quoted in Marr, *Douglas County: A Historical Journey*, pp. 243, 244.
46. *Record-Journal of Douglas County*, November 8, 1912, p. 1.
47. *Denver Republican*, May 4, 1900, p. 1.

FRANKTOWN

Heritage and legacy are in the name of the town founded by James Frank Gardner.
—Lily Budd, *Douglas County News Press,* December 19, 1990

Franktown's early history promised a bustling, dynamic future for the town. Founded along Cherry Creek, which supplied the area with water, Franktown (or Frankstown, as it was known then) benefited directly from a small gold discovery at nearby Russellville that contributed to the Pikes Peak Gold Rush of 1859. Rumors of the glittering metal lured thousands of wealth-seekers through Frankstown via the Cherokee Trail. The small settlement then gained governmental recognition in 1861, when it became the first county seat of newly formed Douglas County. Despite this promising start, today Franktown is one of the county's smallest settlements. The evolution of the community that was once the center of county transactions—but whose residents are now challenged to control and manage growth and development—is a tale of chances taken, failures met, and vehement resistance to lifestyle changes.

The story of Franktown's founding begins with its southeastern neighbor, Russellville, which was named after a pioneer prospecting party. In the spring of 1858, William Green Russell and his brothers Levi and Oliver led a party of Georgia prospectors through Douglas County, en route to the California gold fields. They stopped briefly at the site of their future namesake in June, a scene that Luke Tierney, a member of the party, related in his journal:

> After travelling three-quarters of an hour, the road led us to cross the creek. One of our men, taking a pan full of gravel from its bed, washed it and found several particles of gold.[1]

Upon finding the gold dust, the group decided to follow Cherry Creek northwest, hoping to find more. Finally, in early July, suffering from attrition and frustration, the remaining men found small cavities of the "pay dirt" in the banks of Dry Creek, at its convergence with the South Platte River (in what is today Englewood). The Russell party's initial gold discovery along Cherry Creek led to the formation of Russellville, while the second fruitful discovery helped spark the Colorado gold rush and bestowed the Russells with more notoriety than as mere town namesakes.

Russellville soon grew into a habitable settlement of several log buildings and a sawmill. Later the town spawned more sawmills as well as a barn, corral, stockade, and hotel that doubled as a stage stop. The postal service established an office there on May 22, 1862. As sporadic placer mining drew many argonauts into town, one ambitious man named Charles F. Parkhurst constructed another large hotel and stage station northwest of Russellville and called it California Ranche. At the establishment, Parkhurst allegedly served "tanglewood whiskey" to thirsty Cherokee Trail travelers.

Another newcomer who had a lasting impact upon the area was James Frank Gardner. Drawn by embellished reports of sparkling western gold fields, Gardner left his hometown of Attica, New York, in 1856 and arrived in Denver in May 1859. Discouraged by his lack of mining success and an attack of typhoid fever, Gardner abandoned his dreams of gold and accepted a position at the Thomas Bayaud sawmill a few miles from Parkhurst's California Ranche. By June 1860, he had purchased an ox team and wagon and taken up a squatter's claim approximately two miles north of California Ranche. With an eye toward the future, Gardner constructed a log cabin and called his claim "Frank's Town." Years later, in 1880, by order of the state, the *s* was dropped and the town became simply Franktown. Today historians and residents often use the *s* to distinguish between the town's modern and past history.

Gardner's tiny settlement gained political recognition in November 1861 when territorial officials named it the temporary county seat of newly created Douglas County. Senator George Chilcotte, Gardner's former business and traveling partner who no doubt realized the boost the designation would provide his friend's town, encouraged the appointment. Thereafter, county transactions took place unceremoniously at Gardner's small log cabin, where the post office had been moved from Russellville on September 8, 1862. Gardner assumed the position of county clerk and recorder and later treasurer, and Sylvester Richardson, John Boggs, and Joseph Hipley served as the first county commissioners. In 1863–1864, Gardner sold his property to Samuel Brackett and transferred all county records, the town title of Frankstown, and the county seat location to California Ranche.

On December 31, 1863, however, the blossoming community received a terrible shock when fire destroyed California Ranche and several outlying buildings. In an official report to the county commissioners, Gardner related the devastating news that "all the books and papers belonging to the county, and all the official bonds of the different offices in and for the county of Douglas, were destroyed by fire."[2] Resilient town citizens reconstructed the building by January 1864, and a grand ball celebrated the reopening. Two years later, Gardner acquired the building and the 160-acre plot on which it rested from Charles Parkhurst, who moved to Denver to operate the Tremont House, one of Denver's earliest hotels.

Besides use as a hotel, stage stop, post office, and county building, California Ranche also served the defensive needs of the Frankstown community. In September 1864, the increasing threat of Indian retaliation for white infringement upon native-held lands prompted many Frankstown citizens to enlist in the Third Colorado Volunteers, a regiment raised by Colorado Governor John Evans. Commanded by Gardner, the men began their training at Denver's Camp Wheeler (now Lincoln Park) before completing the remainder of their duty at California Ranche. There, a sturdy stockade of logs was constructed around the building and down to Cherry Creek, where water could be obtained. The soldiers endured four months at the ad hoc fort, with Gardner remaining their resolute leader. Years later James Frank Gardner Jr. related an incident in which his father exemplified true heroism:

While they were camped [at California Ranche], he went out in the timber toward the mill to look after their horses, fearing the Indians would drive them away. He saw a man running toward him, pursued by a band of Indians. Father took the fellow up on his horse, turned about and started at full gallop for the stockade. The Indians chased them to within one-half mile of the stockade, then started back. Father did not find his horses but, no doubt, saved a life.[3]

The 1870s brought more conflicts to the growing town. In February 1874, officials divided Douglas County, shaping its eastern half into a new county called Elbert. The move placed Frankstown at the extreme eastern border of Douglas County, causing many citizens to call for the designation of a more centrally located county seat. During a March 31, 1874, county seat election, Frankstown competed for this designation with five other Douglas County towns: Castle Rock, Sedalia, Glade, Douglas, and New Memphis. Ironically, as reported in the *Rocky Mountain News*, sympathies for Castle Rock as the victor existed even among Frankstown residents: "At the county-seat election at Frankstown, Douglas county, that town voted 31 for Castle Rock, to 16 for Frankstown, and 7 for Memphis."[4] Countywide votes revealed 16 votes for Frankstown, 161 votes for Sedalia, 315 votes for Castle Rock, 63 for Glade, 9 for Douglas, and 30 for New Memphis—revealing a clear consensus for Castle Rock.

Months later, while Frankstown residents were adjusting to no longer being the county seat, flames again consumed California Ranche. A *Rocky Mountain News* reporter relayed the events of the destructive January 20, 1875, fire:

The fire caught from a defective flue, and, as a terrific gale was prevailing at the time, all efforts to check it were unavailing, and the building was reduced to ashes in a few minutes. A few articles of furniture were snatched from the flames. There was no insurance on either house or contents. The building was constructed of logs, which, however, had been weather-boarded, giving the house a neat appearance.[5]

The *Las Animas Leader* described the "old ranch" as "a relic of the early days of Douglas county," and lamented the destruction of what so many travelers had come to regard as a haven along the dusty Cherokee Trail: "It had once been a place of defense against the Indians, the place of meeting old friends for miles around, and its loss will be regretted by all who were familiar with its log walls and cheery fireplace."[6] The deadly bite of the 1875 fire snatched the community's most cherished building for the last time. It was never rebuilt.

After the near simultaneous losses of the county seat title and oldest community building, Frankstown changed dramatically. In 1875, only months after losing the county seat election, the town was a bustling community. A population of approximately 250 supported a general store, hotel, wagon and blacksmith shop, shoe store, lumber mill, two attorneys, and a physician. Five years later, although the town's population remained the same, the only surviving businesses were a general store, a hotel, and a wagon and blacksmith shop. By 1890, population growth had ceased and the town consisted of a saloon, blacksmith shop, general store, and a shoemaker.

The declining number of town businesses and growing newspaper reports of farming and ranching activity in the region during this period of unsteady development indicate that Frankstown residents may have hesitated to commit to careers in the trade and mercantile business. Frankstown, the former hub of county business and stage travel, both of which ended in the 1870s, no longer attracted settlers and visitors as it once had. Farming and ranching became the main livelihood for the remaining residents.

Oddly enough, the opulent farms of the Frankstown area were plowed on land formerly dismissed by skeptics as barren and infertile. In 1867, commentators for the *Rocky Mountain News* had predicted a bleak future for Frankstown and Russellville:

> Sandy and sterile, save in spots, disrupted by dry-creeks, and demoralized by grasshoppers, horned frogs, weeds and what not, there are portions of the plains that can never be cultivated, civilized or changed, put all the new processes in play that are possible to invent.[7]

Cultivation of the sandy creek soil proved difficult and demanding, but ultimately Frankstown farms, like many along the Cherry Creek valley, blossomed into productive fields. In the early 1860s, Ozro Brackett started what became "the best hay ranch between Denver and Colorado Springs," fed by an irrigation ditch constructed in 1885.[8] Other Brackett family members continued the tradition and reportedly reaped 200 tons of hay in 1890. William E. Converse also grew hay as well as corn, tomatoes, cabbages, and potatoes. George Kelty tended to a cornfield and small orchard of fruit trees, while James F. Gardner's irrigated fields yielded alfalfa and native grass.

Ranching efforts also blossomed in the area. Many early cattle ranchers sold milk to the Castle Rock Creamery, which dispatched a milk wagon to collect it. In 1895, Franktown ranchers celebrated the installation of the Hatler and Foster dairy separator. Convenient and flexible, the separator proved an enormous aid to local dairy ranchers, and with the construction of a town creamery several years later, dairy farming in Franktown contributed significantly to the great success of the industry throughout Douglas County.

As more farmers and ranchers moved into the Franktown area, a centralized irrigation system became a primary concern for the community. In 1889, agriculturists advocated the construction of a dam on Cherry Creek to aid irrigation efforts and provide badly needed flood control for the Cherry Creek valley and Denver. In response, the Denver Water Storage Company began construction of the Castlewood Dam, located about three miles south of Franktown, in December 1889. Shortly after its completion in November 1890, the project was inundated with controversy. Many Denver citizens objected to the precarious construction and dangerous state of the dam, as evidenced by the fact that it already leaked. In an issue of the *Denver Times*, W. F. Alexander, representative of the Denver Water Storage Company, assured Denverites that the dam was safe, adding, "the idea of a flood in Denver as a result of a breaking of the dam is ridiculous."[9]

Despite this reassurance, a 100-foot section of the Castlewood Dam washed out in 1897 and threatened to do the same after heavy rains filled it to capacity in 1900. This time, the insulted and defensive engineer of the dam, A. M. Welles, boldly prophesized in a letter to the *Denver Times*, "The Castlewood dam will never, in the life of any person now living, or in any generations to come, break to an extent that will do any great damage either to itself or others from the volume of water impounded, and never in all time to the city of Denver."[10]

Years later, Welles's bold prediction proved inaccurate. On August 3, 1933, summer storms again filled the reservoir to capacity and at 1:20 a.m. the walls of the dam crumbled. A fifteen-foot wall of water raged down Cherry Creek canyon. The destruction it wrought was reported in the *Record-Journal*:

> Something of the terrific force with which the water rushed down the canon was evidenced by the huge trees, torn up by the roots, and stretched along the canons and flats, down the thirty miles to Denver. Huge bowlders [sic] were carried along as though they were but pebbles and deposited as far as a quarter of a mile from the stream's normal bed. The mighty wall of water rushing down the canon swept the floor of the canon clean, down to bed rock, and demolished many beautiful and attractive places which were favorite picnic spots for thousands of people.[11]

The flood cut a path of considerable property damage not only through Cherry Creek farms and ranches, but also through Denver streets, bridges, businesses, and homes. The larger, sturdier Cherry Creek Dam was built to replace Castlewood Dam and was completed in January 1950.

Although Franktown suffered great damage from the flood, the resilient settlement survived as one of Douglas County's leading centers of both agriculture and dairy industries. Nonetheless, Franktown's agriculturists had more than floods to contend with during the 1930s. The Great Depression, which paralyzed the national economy and left millions of people unemployed, proved devastating to local farms and ranches. Years later, Wayne Wentzel, a North Dakota native who moved to Cherry Valley in 1948 and Franktown in 1963, described depression-era hardships typical among farmers all over the country:

> During the Depression time, cattle were worth nothing and hogs were worth less. Grain and corn were a nickel a bushel, oats were seven cents a bushel, wheat was twenty-eight cents a bushel, and it was just a mighty hard thing to make a living at that time. . . . If you had one pair of pants that didn't have a dozen patches on them you were pretty lucky. . . . I remember in our area where we grew up, we had a drought along with it. It wasn't only the low prices on everything but we couldn't raise anything to eat, you see? I remember we had around twenty some head of horses and we just had to turn them loose. Most of them died. . . . We bought a carload of straw and had it shipped in. Paid $36 a ton and it was half rotten. These are the things that happened to the people here. A lot of them had to be pretty tough to go through all of that.[12]

Local resident Doris Johnston recalled that the desperation and hopelessness of the Great Depression also forged unity and cooperation among neighbors:

> The neighbors helped each other. I remember when we threshed, the neighbors on all sides of us would come and help. They'd send their hired men and wagons, and team. . . . People helped each other and relied on each other and enjoyed each other.[13]

Determination and strength saw these farmers and ranchers through the worst of the national crisis and contributed to a growing sense of community pride. On May 12, 1946,

Franktown's residents set aside their shovels and plows and, along with state and county officials, dedicated a historical marker commemorating the town's first building, the California Ranche. Erected by the Colorado Historical Society and the American Pioneer Trails Association just south of the junction of State Highways 83 and 86, the ten-foot marker was constructed from petrified wood gathered by local schoolchildren and residents. The ceremony, which signified Franktown's deep reverence for its history and town founder, was highlighted by the presence of James Frank Gardner's son, who unveiled the monument.

While honoring the small-town values of the past, Franktown developed modern attributes as well. In 1962, local citizens created the Franktown Fire Department and District and constructed a station northeast of the intersection of State Highways 83 and 86. The department remained at this site until 1991, when it purchased two acres of land that included the old Franktown School and built a new, larger station. Realizing the significance of the historic school, the department remodeled the old building for use as a community museum headed by the local historical society, Historic Frankstown.

In late 1973, many Franktown residents celebrated plans to construct a much-needed public park within a two-year-old subdivision known as Whispering Pines North. The Parks Committee, which organized to oversee fulfillment of the project, pleaded with Franktown residents to help the plans become reality. "We request that every organization, businessman, and individual in the Franktown area search his heart to see where he can be of help . . . in the development of this park."[14] Proceeds from a 1974 spaghetti supper further supported the park's construction. Nonetheless, some Whispering Pines North and neighboring Whispering Pines residents did not share the community's enthusiasm and instead expressed concern that the proposed park would attract "undesirable people" that county law enforcement could not control. The disagreement found resolution during a public hearing in which the Douglas County Board of County Commissioners sided with the park's supporters. The park's construction began, and through enormous displays of munificence and volunteerism on the part of many Franktown residents and businesses, saw completion soon thereafter.

Ten years later, when landowner-turned-developer Stanislav Kopunec proposed another recreational park, opposition among the Franktown community reached new heights. The proposed attractions of Kopunec's "Fantasy Land," later renamed "Franktown Sports and Recreation Farm," included pony rides, miniature golf, a playground, a swimming pool, a BMX bicycle track, a roller-skating path, playing fields, and a picnic and barbecue area. Franktown residents, who felt the elaborate project did not complement Franktown's rural character and would congest the town's narrow streets, opposed Kopunec's sports park proposal. The protesters also pointed out that the park's fourteen-acre proposed site, which would span both sides of Cherry Creek, was located along a floodplain that would endanger the safety of its patrons. On July 2, 1984, Douglas County commissioners sided with the opposition and denied the park's application.

Throughout the contentious 1980s, Franktown's old and new residents were challenged to control and manage growth and development. Among the decade's fiercest quarrels was the issue of town incorporation. In October 1980, the Franktown Chamber of Commerce instigated a drive for town incorporation. At a December meeting held to address incorporation issues, disgruntled citizens confronted county and town representatives. Many feared the attempt to incorporate their town would lead to higher taxation and eventual annexations of high-density subdivisions. As time went on, the debate grew even hotter. Some residents questioned the suspicious nature in which pro-incorporation sympathizers collected petition signatures without proper definition of the issue at hand. Finally, in January 1981, the Franktown Chamber of Commerce voted unanimously to end the move to incorporate. The *Douglas County News Press* reflected: "Thus ends a move to incorporate the area that was controversial from the start, termed a 'riot process,' and which filled the air with rumors and considerable animosity on both sides of the move."[15]

In the late 1980s, friction between longtime residents protective of their land-use rights and newcomers who wished to preserve their quality of life arose once again—this time over a proposed subarea master plan for Franktown. In 1987, the town hired the consulting firm Shapins-Moss to complete the plan, which was adopted by the Douglas County Planning Commission two years later. The plan focused on Franktown's Influence Area, the land where development was most likely to occur, and its Rural Town Center, the area centered around the intersection of State Highways 83 and 86. A supplement to the plan outlined design guidelines for the town, including entry gateways, landscaped roadways, placement of pedestrian-scale lights adjacent to streets, and the adoption of a sign code for businesses. In addition to proposals for road improvement and construction, preservation of open lands, and creation of more parks and trails, the plan addressed land-use issues and announced, "Expansion of heavy industrial and industrial in nature land uses shall be strongly discouraged in the Franktown Influence Area." While proponents of the plan viewed it as a "land-use guide that does not take away existing rights, but protects landowners from being deluged by heavy industry," opponents argued the plan "threatens their rights, will hurt business, and is a veiled attempt to rid the area of gravel mining."[16] Although denying that their intent was to prevent gravel mining in Franktown, many proponents of the plan expressed their fear that "a string of gravel pits will one day line the scenic Cherry Creek basin and affect the quality of life, property values and wildlife that lured them to the area."[17]

Gravel mining remained a disruptive issue. An October 1993 application by Centennial Materials (owner of the McLain Gravel Pit located on Castlewood Canyon Road south of State Highway 86) for a permit to expand its establishment from 10 acres to 107 acres, promptly "raised the dust" in Franktown. Unhappy citizens formed the Franktown Citizens Coalition (FCC) to fight the proposed expansion. The group expressed concern over the visual impact of the expansion, potential highway congestion, and the proximity to residential and business areas. Other residents favored the expansion, claiming it would aid the local economy. In 1994, the county commissioners, heeding the concerns of the FCC, denied Centennial's request. By virtue of the fact that mining took place at the site before permits were required, the mining company filed a lawsuit against the county challenging the denial. The FCC, in turn, called for new taxes to raise revenue that could be used to buy the pit and, therefore, ensure local control.

Faced with the possibility of a lengthy and costly court battle, Douglas County commissioners struggled over whether to accept a settlement proposed by Centennial Materials. Instead of the twenty years originally asked for, the company proposed limiting mining at the sight to eight, with an option to apply for a continuation at the end of the term. After learning that the county had hired a mediator and was drafting a settlement, members of the FCC and the Country Lifestyle Coalition, an organization of more than 4,000 members, accused county officials of conducting secret negotiations. The matter was made worse when arbitrator Joseph Quinn, a retired Colorado Supreme Court justice, recommended the county adopt the draft settlement. Quinn reasoned that the settlement—which limited Centennial's operations to 65.5 acres for eight years without an option to renew and limited truck traffic to sixteen vehicles per hour—was "a fair and reasonable accommodation of the competing interests . . . and a feasible alternative to the uncertainty of protracted and expensive litigation."[18]

FCC members and supporters felt they had lost a battle that would forever affect the quality of life and property values of Franktown. Claiming that their "faith as citizens in the open democratic process has been completely subverted by the conduct of the current litigants," the FCC filed a motion for intervention in the McLain pit lawsuit on September 12, 1996.[19] While the motion awaited a hearing, Douglas County commissioners announced in January 1997 they had unanimously approved an out-of-court settlement with Centennial Materials. A court decision was postponed until the FCC's motion to intervene was heard, but the presiding judge ruled that the group's motion was filed too late. In February 1997, the settlement between the county and Centennial Materials received court approval, ending an issue that had consumed Franktown residents for nearly three years.

Throughout the years of tumultuous debate over the McLain Gravel Pit, Franktown continued to grow and face other challenges. In December 1990, a campaign to change the town's name posed what some felt was a significant threat to the integrity of Franktown's history. Claiming the town's name was comparable to "Hicksville," and that its usage "inhibits growth, deflates property values and sinks community pride," proponents of the name change sought to replace it with a name less rural in tone, such as Ponderosa or Castlewood.[20] Many irate Franktown residents expressed their reservations to a name change on the editorial page of the *Douglas County News Press*. Lily Budd, a member of the Franktown Women's Club, eloquently expressed the sentiment of many when she wrote of the heritage of the name and the value of its legacy:

> Anyone (oldtimer or newcomer) living in Franktown, if knowledgeable of the historical significance of the name, would certainly have "pride" in such a founding father and "value" the contributions made by James Frank Gardner. Instead of disposing of an important part of Franktown's history in favor of a "new" name, a lesson in history would surely be in order. Throwing away history does not in any way contribute to "property values" or create "community pride," it simply teaches neglect of one's heritage for generations to come.[21]

More than a century after its founding, Franktown's legacy has not been forgotten. It has been a legacy of ideas that were often never fulfilled because of differences of opinion or disparate dreams for the future. Yet amid the debates staged and factions formed, many of Franktown's citizens still share a common bond: pride in their hometown. A 1994 brochure from the Franktown Chamber of Commerce claimed the town "is rich in history and quietly approaching its future." However, if past problems, debates, and opposition to development in the area continue, Franktown will approach the future any way but quietly.

Franktown Historic Sites

Castlewood Dam (November 1890: A. M. Welles, engineer), approximately three miles south of Franktown on State Highway 83.

Although demand by local farmers for an irrigation storage system was the original impetus for building Castlewood Dam, many realized that the structure could also provide flood control along Cherry Creek, a volatile stream that occasionally carved a path of destruction through the valley into Denver. The Colorado State Assembly first raised the idea of the dam in 1889 and submitted a reservoir bill for approval. In April 1889, the *Castle Rock Journal* reported that the bill had been "defeated after a hard fight. In the mean time a private company is talking of building the reservoir and reaping the benefit."[22] Organized by Carlisle N. Greig, C. H. Rosenfeld, and W. F. Alexander, the Denver Water Storage Company engaged in construction of the dam between December 1889 and November 1890. Designed by A. M. Welles, the dam was 600 feet long and 8 feet wide, and rose 70 feet above the water surface and 92 feet above its foundation. The structure consisted of rock-fill with a masonry wall on the upper, south-facing reservoir side and a large stepping stone pattern of cement mortar laid stone on the lower, north-facing side. The reservoir covered 200 acres and had an approximate storage capacity of 3,434 acre feet of water.

Constructed on hard blue clay and sandstone, a surface that did not provide the footing needed to hold the weight of the water, Castlewood Dam immediately developed leaks as the foundation settled. A committee of dam critics formed in Denver to investigate the dam's safety and gauge the probability that it would someday give way. Despite the criticism, the *Castle Rock Journal* in April 1891 stood firm in its support of the structural integrity of the dam:

> A large delegation from Denver visited the Castlewood reservoir Friday on a tour of inspection. We have often expressed the belief that there is no possible danger to the people of Denver from this reservoir and we still believe the same.[23]

Nonetheless, faith in the dam's strength proved difficult to maintain. Heavy rainfall on August 3, 1897, washed out a 100-foot section of the walls, resulting in some damage to downstream properties and increasing apprehension among residents. Workers rebuilt the dam, but it continued to leak and threatened to break again after heavy rains in the spring of 1900 filled the reservoir to near capacity. In a letter to the *Denver Times*, engineer A. M. Welles responded sourly to the dam's critics:

> As the party who designed and constructed [the Castlewood Dam], I have for the past ten years silently and with disgust listened to the prattle of sensationalism, incompetency and vindictiveness, which, in its effects in misleading the uniformed and destroying the value of the undertaking which had so long and loudly been implored on the part of capital, is simply infamous and outrageous . . . [The dam] has for ten years withstood every test and attempt to produce disaster, and in the past few days has undergone an ordeal which few dams on earth ever endured and survived. . . . The Castlewood dam will never, in the life of any person now living, or in generations to

> come, break to an extent that will do any great damage either to itself or others from the volume of water impounded, and never in all time to the city of Denver."[24]

Between 1901 and 1902, the Castlewood Dam changed hands several times. After the Denver Water Storage Company declared bankruptcy, the Knickerbocker Investment Company purchased the dam, but promptly sold it in May 1901 to Seth H. Butler, a private entrepreneur. In February 1902, the Castlewood Dam became the property of the Denver Sugar, Land and Irrigation Company, which planned to build a sugar factory and encourage local farmers to cultivate sugar beets. The company also purchased 18,000 acres of land below the dam and advertised it as a prime area for fruit orchards. Called the "Clark Colony" after Rufus "Potato" Clark, who organized it, the project was irrigated by the Arapahoe Canal, which obtained its water from Castlewood Dam. By 1904, however, the company shelved plans for the project after problems developed over construction of the sugar factory and the road that would lead to it. The Castlewood Dam was sold to the Denver Suburban Homes and Water Company, which purchased downstream land and planted cherry trees with the intent of selling the land to newcomers. After financial difficulties arose, ownership of the dam passed to company stockholders, who organized under the name Cherry Creek Mutual Irrigation Company.

A summer storm on August 3, 1933, proved to be the last straw for the Castlewood Dam. The dam walls gave way, hurling a fifteen-foot wall of water down the valley. Its destruction received prime newspaper coverage:

> Many acres of fertile farm land lying in the path of the flood were ruined, a great number of horses and cattle were drowned, and many bridges were swept away by the huge wall of water. One bridge on the road just below the dam was swept away, as was quite a portion of the road just below the bridge. The great rush of water washed this bridge up the gulch from where it was located where it was stranded on the rocks. The steel bridge on the Franktown road went down, and it is supposed that a great many others lying in the path of the flood were swept away.[25]

The flood killed two people and many stock animals and inundated hundreds of acres of farmland. Trees were uprooted and property damaged all the way into Denver. At last citizens relinquished all faith in the dam, and it was never rebuilt.

The ruins of the structure, elected to the State Register of Historic Properties in 1995, still stand in the Castlewood Canyon State Park. The park was established in 1961 and was enlarged in 1979 and 1980 to include the dam site. After 1980, the park operated with minimal facilities until its official grand opening in June 1994.

In April 1995, the park increased in size by 256 acres north and east of its existing boundaries in exchange for granting water rights under the park to a San Diego–based water company. In November 1995, the park acquired three additional land parcels totaling seventy acres through a series of conservation easements under the supervision of the Douglas County Land Conservancy. In October 1998, 397 acres of a proposed housing development along the canyon's east rim were added to the park through ardent fund-raising by the Colorado State Parks Department, Great Outdoors Colorado, Douglas County, and the Friends of Castlewood Canyon. The Castlewood East Canyon Preservation Project, which began in 1996, plans further open-space land acquisition for the canyon's east rim, including the 978-acre Prairie Canyon Ranch.

Conrad Moschel Grave (August 4, 1864), Castlewood Canyon Road. **Limited public access.**

In 1864, volatile relations between the Southern Cheyenne and Arapaho Indian tribes and white settlers led frightened Franktown citizens to barricade themselves in California Ranche, where they built a log stockade for defensive purposes. On August 4, 1864, four Franktown men, Lawrence Welty, George Engl, Caspar Courts, and Conrad Moschel, were detailed from California Ranche to round up Engl's wandering shorthorn cattle. While the men were trying to gather the herd, approximately thirty Indians attacked them, and they attempted to escape by scattering in different directions. Engl, Courts, and Welty returned safely to California Ranche. None of the men knew of Moschel's whereabouts or fate. Six days later, a search party found Moschel's body, shot in the head, arrowed in the back, and scalped. The survivors promptly buried their comrade where he had fallen, and years later a memorial was carved in the rock above the grave. Today, the grave, which is further decorated by a granite marker, presents a sad reminder of the violence resulting from cultural clashes that reverberated throughout the West in the mid- to late nineteenth century.

Engl/Winkler Ranch (1860?: George Engl, builder), 2634 S. Castlewood Canyon Road. **Private residence.**

In 1860, Austrian immigrant George Engl filed for a homestead on a valuable, naturally irrigated stretch of land located approximately four miles south of Franktown. According to Homestead Proof Papers filed in 1870, Engl constructed a house of "hewed logs, 1½ stories, 30 x 18 ft- shingle roof and board floors," a log stable, shed, four corrals, a corn crib, milk house, and extensive "post and board fence" upon the property. Engl's highly prized shorthorn cattle, branded with his initials "GE," earned him the respect of fellow ranchers and, by 1882, a highly successful ranch.

After the death of his first wife, Engl married a fellow Austrian named Louisa Roracher, sister to one of the Engl ranch hands. When Engl died in 1896, Louisa married another Austrian named Charles Breuss. The two sold the ranch in 1919 to Louisa's nephew, Josef Winkler, an Austrian who came to the United States in 1907. Josef, described as "a life-long conservationist and a livestock producer," expanded the ranch's cattle operation and lived there until his death in 1972, whereupon the property passed into the hands of his son, former Colorado Senator Joseph Winkler, who remains its owner today. The Winkler property endures as an operating shorthorn cattle ranch and continues to use the "GE" brand, one of the oldest brands in use today. The present ranch consists of several buildings and features a two-story, rhyolite, gabled ranch house, as well as a barn, corrals, and the original homestead cabin.

Franktown Cemetery (June 21, 1870), northeast of State Highway 83 and State Highway 86 intersection.

Upon her death on June 21, 1870, early Franktown resident Clara Kelley was buried under her favorite tree. A few years after the burial, Clara's husband, James Kelley, donated the land around Clara's grave for use as a cemetery. Later land donations by Andrew Kelty and George Nez increased the size to nearly seven acres.

The cemetery is maintained through local donations and volunteers. In 1984 residents added a chain-link fence around the plot, and in 1987 they installed a black steel, arched entrance gate that read "Franktown Cemetery." The exact number of graves in the cemetery is unknown due to several unmarked, sunken holes. While the graves of several prominent Franktown pioneers can be found there, it is the grave of James Frank Gardner, the "Father of Douglas County," that attracts most visitors to the cemetery.

Franktown School (1924: builder unknown), southwest corner of State Highway 83 and State Highway 86 intersection.

Constructed in 1924 on land donated in 1908 by early Franktown violin teacher John Herren, the Franktown School replaced an earlier school building erected on property granted by James Frank Gardner in 1881. The Franktown correspondent for the *Record-Journal of Douglas County* informed readers of the new school's opening:

> The Franktown school will begin Monday, September 8th. Mr. Harvey has finished painting the teacherage, both inside and outside as well as the school house on the inside and Mrs. Boulware has moved into the teacherage.[26]

The small, gabled schoolhouse remained in use until 1966. In 1991, the Franktown Fire Department acquired the building and two acres surrounding it, to construct a new fire station. Restored and maintained by the fire department, the schoolhouse became the headquarters of Historic Frankstown, a historical society organized in 1988. The society transformed the building into Douglas County's first local history museum.

Pike's Peak Grange No. 163 (1909: Grange members, builders), 3093 State Highway 83. **Limited public access.**

The Pike's Peak Grange is possibly Colorado's last standing example of the front-gabled, vernacular wood-frame grange buildings constructed throughout the state starting in the 1860s. The white, clapboard, single-story, rectangular grange hall rests on a rhyolite and concrete foundation. On its east side, two nine-foot transomed doors open into a large meeting hall. Double-hung sash windows are found on the west, north, and south faces. In 1916, an addition provided a dining area and enlarged kitchen.

The Pike's Peak Grange is part of the Grange movement, an organization formed to advocate farmers' rights in 1867. By 1874, the movement had reached Denver. Before construction of their present grange hall, Pike's Peak Grange members met at the Fonder School and participated in the fight against powerful railroads that charged farmers high freight rates to transport goods. The large hall also served as a social hub for the area. Special events at the hall include dances, musical contests, picnics, and guest speakers. The Grange was listed on the National Register of Historic Places on October 1, 1990.

Russellville Archaeological Site (late 1850s through 1860s), along Tomichi Road and Gold Camp Way in Russellville. **Limited public access.**

Once an energetic, growing community of hopeful argonauts, foresighted merchants, and industrious lumbermen, the former site of Russellville today is a secluded residential development of five-acre home sites. The early community sprouted as a result of a small gold discovery made by the William Green Russell party in 1859, and at one time supported a post office, hotel, stage stop, barn, ice house, corral, spring house, stockade, and a few sawmills. Today only the stone spring house and two-story, wooden ice house remain.

Archaeological investigations of the Russellville area starting in 1994, conducted primarily by the Douglas County Historic Preservation Board, have uncovered a wealth of historic and prehistoric artifacts, many from the Civil War era. Hoping to prove their theory that Russellville was the site of a mid-1860s temporary Confederate military camp, the Douglas County Historic Preservation Board applied for and received a $10,000 grant from the State Historic Fund to conduct an archaeological metal detecting survey of more than 400 acres of county and private land within Russellville. Board members, volunteers, and professional archaeologists began the meticulous survey work in July 1994, and four years later had unearthed an estimated 3,000 artifacts from various sites. Among the artifacts uncovered were Civil War–era .58 caliber unspent bullets, which helped corroborate the theory that there had been a Confederate military presence in Russellville. Workers also measured, photographed, and recorded the older buildings of Russellville Ranch, the site of the original Russellville settlement, and other homesteads.

Members of the Douglas County Historic Preservation Board completed preliminary investigative fieldwork of Russellville in 1998 and have applied for designation of the area as a National Historic District. If granted, Russellville will become the third in Douglas County to receive the designation, joining the Bear Canon Agricultural District in West Plum Creek, formed in October 1975, and Louviers Village Historic District, formed in July 1999.

Notes

1. Leroy Hafen, ed. *Pike's Peak Gold Rush Guidebooks of 1859* (Glendale: Arthur Clark, 1941), p. 105.

2. Frank Hall, *History of the State of Colorado* (Chicago: Blakely Printing, 1891), p. 334.

3. J. F. Gardner Jr., "James Frank Gardner and Franktown," *Colorado Magazine*, vol. XIV, no. 5, September 1937, p. 189.

4. *Rocky Mountain News*, April 2, 1874, p. 4.

5. Ibid., January 22, 1875, p. 4.

6. *Las Animas Leader*, February 5, 1875, Newspaper Clippings Notebook, Local History Collection, Philip S. Miller Library.

7. *Rocky Mountain News*, September 16, 1867, p. 1.

8. *Castle Rock Journal*, April 15, 1885, p. 3; September 19, 1888, p. 4; October 16, 1889, p. 4.

9. *Denver Times*, May 16, 1891, p. 6.

10. Ibid., May 2, 1900, p. 2.

11. *Record-Journal of Douglas County*, August 4, 1933, p. 1.

12. "Franktown Panel," Oral History tape, September 29, 1987. Local History Collection, Philip S. Miller Library.

13. Ibid.

14. *Douglas County News*, April 11, 1974, p. 17; "Whispering Pines North File," Douglas County Planning Department.

15. *Douglas County News Press*, January 22, 1981, pp. 5, 14.

16. Ibid., October 15–16 , 1988, pp. 1, 3.

17. *Denver Post*, October 24, 1988, p. 5B.

18. *Douglas County News Press*, May 15, 1996, p. 1B; June 12, 1996, p. 1B; July 10, 1996, p. 1A; August 7, 1996, p. 1A, August 21, 1996, p. 5A.

19. Ibid., July 24, 1996, p. 1A; September 18, 1996, p. 1A; October 2, 1996, p. 5A; February 19, 1997, p. 1A.

20. Ibid., December 12, 1990, p. 1; *Rocky Mountain News*, December 18, 1990, p. 6.

21. *Douglas County News Press*, December 19, 1990, p. 4.

22. *Castle Rock Journal*, April 3, 1889, p. 1.

23. Ibid., April 29, 1891, p. 4.

24. *Denver Times*, May 2, 1900, p. 2.

25. *Record-Journal of Douglas County*, August 4, 1933, p. 1.

26. Ibid., September 5, 1924, p. 4.

HIGHLANDS RANCH

From pastoral refuge to Boomtown, USA
—Rocky Mountain News, October 16, 1994

A glance at the burgeoning subdivision that hugs C-470 reveals row after row of seemingly endless houses and streets. Indeed, it is easy to forget that Highlands Ranch, one of Colorado's fastest-growing communities, was once a vast, open cattle range with only a few ranch houses and outbuildings. As the home of some of Colorado's most notable millionaires, the land has truly been a rich man's paradise. Today, Highlands Ranch represents an example of what a developer can accomplish with a ranchman's land. The subdivision is a case study in community building in its most aggressive form. It is a modern Colorado boomtown.

Highlands Ranch originally consisted of scattered individual farms and ranches; those holdings were then consolidated into one 22,000-acre privately owned cattle range. Among the earliest pioneers was Johanne Welte, an Austrian immigrant who came to the area in the 1870s and established a successful dairy farm known as the Big Dry Creek Cheese Ranch. Welte's cheese ranch, renowned for its brick and limburger cheeses and butter, remained in business for nearly sixty years.

In 1898, Welte acquired new neighbors: John W. Springer, a wealthy, ambitious, and strong-willed man of distinguished German ancestry; and his ailing wife, Eliza Clifton Hughes, the daughter of one of the wealthiest citizens of the West, cattleman Colonel William Hughes. The couple arrived in Denver in 1897 and quickly carved a position for themselves in local affairs. With a background in politics, banking, and law, Springer easily assumed a leadership role in the city. Among many other accomplishments, he was appointed president of the National Cattlemen's Association, was a mayoral candidate (in 1904), founded the Continental Trust, and served as the director of Capitol Bank. Around the turn of the century, through a series of land purchases, Springer became the largest landholder in the future Highlands Ranch region. Upon this property he established the John W. Springer Cross Country Horse and Cattle Ranch, which became one of the top horse ranches in Colorado and the nation, with prize-winning Oldenburg stallions and German imported mares.

In 1909, five years after the death of his wife Eliza, Springer married Isabelle Patterson, a brazen, newly divorced woman he had met during a business trip to St. Louis. Enamored with his new wife, Springer named his elegant home Castle Isabelle and tried desperately to earn his beloved "Sassy" a position within Denver's society. The task proved futile, however. Addicted to nightlife, narcotics, and adventure, Isabelle's extramarital exploits culminated in the highly publicized May 24, 1911, murder at Denver's Brown Palace Hotel of one of her alleged lovers, balloonist Sylvester Louis Von Phul. The murderer was another of Isabelle's sweethearts, businessman and close Springer family friend Frank Harold Henwood. The scandal and betrayal tormented Springer, who had worked so hard for local prominence and respect. He divorced Isabelle five days after the murder and in 1913 sold the Springer Ranch to his first father-in-law, William Hughes.

When Colonel Hughes died in 1918, the ranch property, which had been renamed Sunland Ranch, passed to his granddaughter Annie Clifton Springer Hughes, daughter of John and Eliza Springer, who, oddly enough, in 1912 had married a man named Lafayette Hughes, no relation to the aforementioned Hughes family. In *Roots and Memories*, Cora Eddelman Kuykendall, who spent three years (1918–1921) of her childhood at Sunland Ranch while her father, Arthur Eddelman, was employed as ranch foreman, offered a vivid description of the mansion:

> The ball room [this room is now referred to as the Great Room] floor was covered with Navajo rugs when not being used for dancing. The largest being about 12 x 16 Ft. The furniture were massive pieces of solid oak. There was a player organ in the room and to my way of thinking the most interesting thing in the house. It is the only one of this type I have ever seen, and I have looked for one in all the museums that I have ever visited . . . the drapes in the ball room, dining room and sitting area were made of doe skin, stained with light green and brown dye. . . . In the east side of the dining room there was a large buffet. It was made of black walnut and was about eight foot high and seven foot long, and very elaborately carved. A punch bowel [sic] sat in a stand made of deer antlers that [were] so put together that they held seventy two cups, which hung from the prongs. The bowel [sic] stood on a silver serving tray that was at least 30 x 20 inches. A shelf across the north and east side of the room and about three foot from the ceiling held a collection of beer steins that had been brought over from Germany. . . . Col. Hughes had taken some horns from Texas longhorn cattle and had a love seat and two chairs made with them. The pieces were upholstered with purple leather. The polished horns against the leather was a beautiful sight. Another love seat sat along with them around the big fireplace. The wicker seat was built so that if two people were sitting on it they would be facing each other. . . . The recreation hall and library were combined and contained a pool table, large reading table, numerous book cases containing Col. Hughes' law books. One case contained Annie's books from her child hood, which included a complete set of Louisa May Alcott works. These I really did enjoy.

In 1920, Annie and Lafayette Hughes sold Sunland Ranch to Waite Phillips, an independent oil producer in Oklahoma whose brothers, Frank and Lee Eldas Phillips, founded Phillips Petroleum Company. Phillips owned the ranch for only six years before selling it to Frank E. Kistler, president of Wolhurst Stock Farms, for $425,000. Kistler established the Diamond K Ranch on the property and devoted its operation to raising Angus cattle, purebred sheep, chickens, and hogs. A fondness for entertaining inspired Kistler and his wife, Florence, to renovate the old Springer home and hire architect J. B. Benedict to add a traditional Tudor-style western wing to the original building.

The Kistler children, with thousands of acres of rolling ranchland as their backyard, enjoyed daily horseback riding excursions and summer dips in the ranch reservoir, located south of the mansion on a hill topped by a stone windmill.

Nonetheless, the family's life was not the paradise it appeared to be. In 1929, marital problems forced a hasty divorce, and Frank's subsequent marriage to Leana Antonides, widow of Denver oilman and investment broker Ralph Antonides, shocked Denver society. First wife Florence moved out with three of the Kistler children, leaving behind daughter Julia, whose love for her father exceeded a desire to remain with her mother and siblings. Sadly, her father increasingly directed his affection toward his two stepsons and did not return Julia's devotion. She died years later, and the anguished sobs of her ghost are rumored to linger among the empty mansion halls today.

In 1929, Kistler invited the Arapahoe Hunt Club to transfer its headquarters from the Denver Country Club to the vast, open hills of Diamond K Ranch. The Arapahoe Hunt Club, the oldest of its kind in Colorado, was comprised of horseback hunters who met three times a week from October through April to hunt coyotes with the assistance of some twenty-six sniffing, bellowing bloodhounds. The head of this elite hunting club was Lawrence Phipps Jr., son of former Colorado Senator Lawrence Cowle Phipps. When Kistler encountered financial difficulties in 1937, Phipps Jr. stepped in and purchased the entire Diamond K Ranch for a reported $250,000. He renamed the property Highlands Ranch, after the sweeping hills and bluffs upon which the ranch rested. By 1943, Phipps had also purchased the Welte property on Big Dry Creek after dairy production at the cheese ranch slowed, since its founder died in 1927. Phipps consolidated this property into his other landholdings, bringing the size of Highlands Ranch to 22,000 acres.

For nearly forty years Highlands Ranch survived as a cattle ranch and headquarters for the Arapahoe Hunt Club. In *A Quarter Century of the Arapahoe Hunt Club*, William W. Grant pays homage to the contributions of Lawrence Phipps Jr. to the club's integrity:

> Without his keen insistence on having the best of everything for the Hunt, without his knowledge and love of horses and hounds, without his sporting and gentlemanly instincts, and without his staunch devotion to the highest standards and behavior and dress in the hunting field, we would today have no Arapahoe Hunt in any sense of the word.

As with other owners of the ranch, Phipps Jr. also experienced marital problems. One year after he had purchased Highlands Ranch, his marriage to wife Bertha Richmond dissolved, and she moved out of the mansion with the couple's children. In 1945, Phipps Jr. married Elaine Oakes, a talented artist whose paintings still adorn many of the mansion's lavatory walls today. In May 1976, he succumbed to illness and died in his cherished mansion.

Following his death, the Lawrence Phipps Jr. estate was sold to Marvin Davis, owner of Davis Oil Corporation, for more than $13 million. Aware of the financial rewards the vast track of land could provide, Davis organized the Highlands Venturers Corporation to market the property and in 1978 sold a purchase option for the entire 22,000-acre ranch to Mission Viejo Company, a California-based housing development corporation owned by Philip Morris Incorporated. In addition to a 10,000-acre community on historic Rancho Mission Viejo in Orange County, California, Mission Viejo's plans for a 640-acre community in Aurora, Colorado, were already underway at the time of the Highlands Ranch option purchase.

In January 1978, Philip Reilly, president of Mission Viejo, told curious reporters that the company planned to transform the rolling, yucca-covered hills of Highlands Ranch into a self-supporting satellite city of Denver. Reilly claimed the company intended to use residential, commercial, and industrial development to create "an area larger than the city of Boulder."[1] The prospect of such a massive project caused concern among residents of neighboring Littleton, Denver, Arapahoe County, and Douglas County, who feared the growth of the ranch could spiral out of control and engulf surrounding communities. The *Douglas County News* compared the ranch land to a "slumbering giant" and *a Littleton Independent* headline, concerned about the future of the Arapahoe Hunt Club, asked, "Is tally-ho to be soon-forgotten cry at Highlands ranch?"[2] Uneasy about Mission Viejo's proposed housing density of 1.4 units per acre, James Wolfson, vice chairman of the Douglas County Property Owners' Association, urged fellow residents to attend public hearings and voice their concerns to Douglas County officials.

> This decision will affect our future more than any other pending Douglas County decision I can envision. . . . We are not required to accept a developer's proposal if we believe it will adversely affect us! We have the right to ask for changes. If you feel as I do, in this case you will demand a much lower density for the Highlands Ranch so that Douglas County can retain the character and life quality we now enjoy.[3]

Despite these concerns, Mission Viejo's Highlands Ranch project received approval from both the Douglas County Planning Commission and the Douglas County Board of Commissioners in September 1979. Conditions stipulated by the planning commission included the designation of several thousand acres in the southern portion of the development as permanent open space. Accepting the terms, Mission Viejo exercised its option three months later and bought the ranch for a reported $28 million.

Estimating a population of 90,000 by the year 2005, Highlands Ranch officials immediately set about planning the new community. The company suffered a setback when the State of Colorado denied fifteen well permits for the area; but after winning a lawsuit against the state in August 1980, the company began construction. Between October 1980 and January 1981, the Douglas County Planning Commission approved Mission Viejo's first and second preliminary plans. In August 1981, one year after the roar of construction machinery became commonplace on the formerly quiet ranch land, Highlands Ranch officials invited the public to a grand opening. One month later, they proudly welcomed the area's first homebuyers, Phil and Kaye Scott, with the gift of a 650-pound steer.

As more people chose Highlands Ranch as the place to raise their families, Mission Viejo realized a school was needed. Estimating that approximately two hundred elementary-age children would live in the subdivision by September 1982, company officials offered to pay all school architectural fees without financial reimbursement from the Douglas County School Board in order to get construction of the school under way. The Denver architectural firm of Barker, Rinker, and Seacat began preliminary plans for future Northridge Elementary School, while negotiations continued between Mission Viejo and the school board. After months of discussion and debate, the two parties agreed that Mission Viejo would finance the full

$3 million up front to build the educational facility. In return, the school district would lease the building for $1 a year and collect tax revenue from Highlands Ranch residents, placing the funds in a special account to be paid to Mission Viejo at the end of fifteen years. The development company's money also paid utility bills and the salary of a full-time and part-time teacher and two custodial workers.

With a new school and thriving home sales, growth in the new subdivision advanced rapidly. Douglas County commissioners approved the third and fourth sketch plans of future development in Highlands Ranch in March and April 1982. The third plan outlined the construction of 412 single-family units on 111.6 acres, one mile south of County Line Road near the intersection of Broadway and Highlands Ranch Parkway. The fourth plan called for medium-low density development of 152 homes on 109.4 acres, between Dad Clark Drive and University Boulevard. From 1982 to 1985, Northridge Community Park and Northridge Recreational Center were completed, as well as a new entrance into the development via Broadway, where a commercial center that included a convenience store, bank, gas station, and office building was planned.

Mercy Medical Center opened its Highlands Ranch surgery center at County Line Road and Broadway in December 1984, nearly a year after suing the Colorado Board of Health for denying until 1990 the construction of new hospitals in the south metropolitan area. The debate, which focused on the need for closer hospital facilities in the growing suburbs versus the cost efficiency of constructing those facilities, was highlighted by Governor Richard Lamm's 1983 veto of a bill that would have eliminated the strict review process required for approval of south suburban hospital construction. Mercy Medical Center, later renamed Highlands Ranch Health Care Plaza, offered residents of Highlands Ranch and surrounding areas immediate access to three surgical rooms, laboratory and x-ray centers, physician and dentist offices, and a pharmacy.

Aside from the delay in its medical facilities, growth at Highlands Ranch developed in several directions toward the creation of a "mosaic city" that aesthetically combined business and residential centers. By 1985, the northern business section included the Highlands Ranch Bank building, a cement factory, Fair Lanes Bowling Alley, Centennial Office Park, Ridgeline Business Park, and a convenience retail center. Golf enthusiasts celebrated the construction of the Links at Highlands Ranch, an 18-hole, 4,400-yard golf course, which opened in the fall of 1986.

Claiming "variety is the spice of life," Mission Viejo announced in March 1986 that it would open four hundred acres of Highlands Ranch land known as Eastridge to other home builders. Up to that point, Mission Viejo had handled most of the subdivision's home construction, but after ventures with Richmond Homes and Sanford Homes proved successful, the company was optimistic that the sale of parcels to other home builders would work equally as well. Eventually, many more home building corporations would purchase land in Highlands Ranch, including US Home, Oakwood, Centex, Park-Engle, High View, Kaufman and Broad, Ryland, Village, David Weekley, Falcon, Custom, Writer, D.R. Horton, Cascade, Virden, Carmel, Joyce, Pulte, Larsen, and Storck.

Since the early days of construction in Highlands Ranch, Mission Viejo officials maintained that they were working closely with residents to create a hometown atmosphere for the subdivision. Nonetheless, many residents questioned their own role and voice in the so-called partnership. In the summer of 1986, residents fumed when Mission Viejo encouraged the relocation of Elitch's Amusement Park to a 150-acre site near C-470 and Santa Fe Drive. In response to the protest, company officials announced that its plans would be dropped if 51 percent of all community households voted to reject the Elitch's project during an upcoming poll. Many opponents of the proposal questioned the fairness of the deal. "You mean if I don't vote, you're going to consider me in favor?" asked the president of a newly created organization known as Homeowners Opposed to Moving Elitch's.[4] Elitch's officials, pressured by opponents of the relocation, backed out of the agreement before the poll was held.

Less controversial parks opened during the summers of 1987 and 1989. An early phase of the Highlands Ranch Business Park opened in July 1987, southwest of the Broadway and C-470 interchange, and was reportedly 60 percent leased nine months later. Highlands Heritage Regional Park welcomed the public in the summer of 1989 after nearly three years of construction. Located at University Boulevard and Quebec Street, the ninety-acre park included an outdoor amphitheater, ball fields, playgrounds, picnic areas, and a 685-square-foot community room. The park was the largest of its kind in Douglas County and was "designed to serve both types of park users—the organized sports types and the more casual park users."[5]

Even as residents celebrated the opening of the park, a strong resentment and concern over the rate of growth in the community began to brew. In 1990, the Highlands Ranch Citizens Council emerged to give voice to these concerns. That November, the council complained that the community's officials placed too much emphasis on the development of homes and streets and not enough on new parks and schools. Stating "we want to make sure Highlands Ranch is not just going to be a collection of subdivisions connected by busy streets," the council suggested Mission Viejo revise its design plans to include smaller parks scattered throughout neighborhoods instead of large, centralized parks.

Other complaints from council members involved what were quickly coined "backyard issues." Many residents who moved into their brand new homes were dismayed when newly planned streets and houses began to encroach on their backyards. One such case took place in 1990 among residents living west of the historic Highlands Ranch Mansion, former residence of the Springer, Phillips, Kistler, and Phipps families. When residents had purchased their homes, builders allegedly assured them that South Ranch Road would not be extended past the mansion. In November 1990, when planners proposed extending the road to provide fire service to the four hundred homes planned for the area south of the mansion, irate residents claimed the move revealed dishonesty on the part of Mission Viejo builders. This backlash and sharp criticism from both residents and county planners on other planned projects sent Mission Viejo officials back to the drawing board on all but one of its filed subdivision plats. The move pleased one member of the Highlands Ranch Citizens Council, who said, "There is no other area in this state that I know of where the developer will work with you like this."[6]

Nonetheless, in December 1990, residents again cited developer dishonesty, as another controversial issue arose—this time over plans to construct the south metropolitan area's largest post office. Located on Quebec Street and University Boulevard, adjacent to a multitude of homes, the post office raised the ire of residents, county officials, and legislators. Many residents claimed home builders falsely led them to believe the area had been zoned for residential use and considered the plans yet another act of deception by developers. Despite vehement picketing of the proposed site and Mission Viejo headquarters, plans for the 46,000-square-foot structure received approval in April 1991.

Other dissatisfied residents took their grievances with Mission Viejo to court. In February 1996, a much-publicized class action lawsuit between nearly 1,000 Highlands Ranch homeowners and Mission Viejo reached the Douglas County District Court. First filed in 1992, the lawsuit alleged that Mission Viejo constructed homes between 1984 and 1990 with slab-on-grade basement floors instead of the structural wooden floors recommended for areas with expansive soil problems such as Highlands Ranch. To the relief of residents who faced expensive repair bills for cracked floors and walls, in March 1996 the jury found Mission Viejo guilty of negligence, breach of implied warranties, and violation of the state consumer protection laws. Mission Viejo immediately appealed the case, and the issue remained unresolved until April 1997, when the parties reached a private agreement that ensured Mission Viejo's participation in repair of damage to the homes.

Disagreements over the future of the swelling Highlands Ranch community continued between Mission Viejo representatives and residents. In 1990, the overwhelming growth rate in Highlands Ranch prompted a move by the Highlands Ranch Community Association (a homeowners association formed to supervise recreational activities and enforce architectural covenants) to study the plausibility of incorporation as a city. Mission Viejo representatives opposed the move, claiming it would only lead to increased taxes that would not provide any additional service. Company officials were confident that within another ten years incorporation would be more economically feasible because the community's continued residential and commercial growth would relieve it of excessive tax rates. Proponents of incorporation claimed that being a city would give Highlands Ranch residents more control over growth and "enhance community pride and keep other cities, such as Littleton, from annexing in the area."[7] Starting in 1993, the Incorporation Feasibility Committee, a fifty-member board that gathered annually to study and discuss the effects of incorporation upon Highlands Ranch, repeatedly discouraged incorporation until the community exhibited more financial stability. The conclusion in early 1997 was that incorporation was possible as long as the proposed city contracted most of its municipal services, but this failed to garner support from Mission Viejo or from the Highlands Ranch Metropolitan Districts, which questioned the necessity of adding another layer of government to the community's already confusing array of existing government agencies and organizations.

The possibility of incorporating Highlands Ranch inspired visions of a centralized civic center campus to house the future city's government offices. Located on a site west of the Broadway and Highlands Ranch Parkway intersection, the center would consist of a lush town green surrounded by public buildings such as a town hall, library, and several retail shops and restaurants lining an inviting Festival Street. Plans for a nearby Festival Plaza featured a 30-foot walkway to host community events like craft shows and farmers markets. A Civic Green area would encompass an amphitheater, stage, ice skating rink, fountains, and community lawn. In May 1999, groundbreaking for the area's 42,000-square-foot Highlands Ranch branch of the Douglas Public Library District, designed by the Denver architectural firm Humphries Poli, heralded the start of construction at the downtown area. Residential input reflected a desire for an old-fashioned, middle America–type downtown with small mom-and-pop specialty shops rather than big box retail stores. The sentiment had first been expressed by residents in 1994 following the construction of an Albertsons Shopping Center at the corner of University Boulevard and Highlands

Ranch Parkway, which was criticized for its strip mall appearance. The issue led many community leaders and residents to rally for the creation of design guidelines for what were dubbed "town centers," areas reserved for aesthetically pleasing and tasteful commercial and civic developments, designed for both automobile and pedestrian accessibility.

The greatest signal of change to modern Highlands Ranch came in early 1997, when Philip Morris announced that Mission Viejo—caretaker of Highlands Ranch for more than sixteen years—was for sale. The possibility of an ownership change incited uncertainty among residents and county and community groups regarding the future of the area. In August, Mission Viejo officials announced that a private developer, Shea Homes, had purchased the company. With experience on projects that included the Hoover Dam, Golden Gate Bridge piers, and residential development in Arizona, California, North Carolina, and Colorado, Shea Homes seemed to be a good choice as Mission Viejo's successor.

The years 1995 to 1999 saw unprecedented growth in Highlands Ranch. In addition to the completion of Thunder Ridge High School, Ranch View Junior High School, and several elementary schools, the community witnessed the opening of the new Eastridge Recreational Center, Highlands Ranch Golf Club, a 24-screen AMC "mega-theater" complex, the Columbia Health Care Plaza, Alterra Clare Bridge assisted living center, a new fire station, several churches and hotels, and countless restaurants and retail stores. Grocery store chains such as Safeway, Albertsons, King Soopers, and Cub Foods anchored several multistore retail centers. In spring 1997, construction began on Redstone Park, a fifty-three-acre community park in Westridge that included a pond, amphitheater, basketball courts, softball fields, tennis courts and more, all adjacent to Shea Stadium, a high school football stadium. Undoubtedly, the greatest commercial undertaking was the opening of the $164 million, 1.5-million-square-foot Park Meadows Town Center, situated adjacent to Highlands Ranch's northeastern boundary along C-470 and County Line Road. Designed by Chicago's Anthony Belluschi Architects, the mall attracted 180,000 visitors on its opening day, August 30, 1996, and two months later mall officials revealed that sales figures had shattered even the most optimistic projections.

While Highlands Ranch welcomed and encouraged a variety of commercial and retail enterprises, technology-based enterprises were sought for the Highlands Ranch Business Park. A 1998 decision by Lucent Technologies, a major supplier of telecommunication equipment and services, to locate a company campus in the budding business park was expected to lure similar high-tech companies.

Amid such rampant growth, Highlands Ranch faced issues that posed both beginnings and endings to the ever-changing community. In November 1995, Lone Tree subdivision, located adjacent to Highlands Ranch's eastern boundary near Park Meadows Town Center, voted to incorporate in order to reap the benefits of sales tax revenue generated from the nearby commercial developments.

While Lone Tree grappled with issues such as the election of town government officials and new zoning regulations, county commissioners approved sketch plans for the last major parcel of land in Highlands Ranch, located at the southeastern portion of the community. Designs for the 2,200-acre property included more than 6,000 residential lots as well as several schools and parks. The planned development abutted the Open Space Conservation Area known as Wildcat Mountain Reserve, an 8,200-acre wildlife refuge set aside by Mission Viejo in the

1980s. A 1999 agreement between the Highlands Ranch Community Association, developers and county officials granted Highlands Ranch 1,200 acres of the open space land for recreational activities while the remaining 7,000 acres remained a wildlife refuge with limited public access.

Highlands Ranch now ranks among the largest communities in Colorado. With a population of more than 62,000 at the end of 1999, the development is well on its way to meeting the estimated 90,000 by the year 2005. Of the subdivision's 22,000 acres, 61 percent is devoted to nonurban use (churches, parks, open space, etc.), 30 percent to residential homes, and 9 percent to business activity. Despite the majority of land zoned for nonresidential use, Highlands Ranch still resembles a sea of cloned homes flowing endlessly along the waves of formerly barren, wind-whipped prairie hills. As more attention is focused on aesthetically pleasing town centers, commercial sites, and civic and public institutions, the subdivision has countless opportunities to blossom into the self-supporting community it was designed to be. Highlands Ranch, for better or worse, is one of Colorado's best examples of a modern boomtown.

Highlands Ranch Historic Sites

Big Dry Creek Cheese Ranch (1879: Johanne Welte, builder), University Boulevard across from Grand Golf.

Big Dry Creek Cheese Ranch once consisted of a main farmhouse, large barn, sheds, corrals, privy, chicken coop, silo, cistern, ice house, workshop, and a bunkhouse. The farmhouse and barn date back to 1879 and are believed to have been the property's original structures. The two-story farmhouse consisted of white clapboard construction with four brick chimneys, full basement and attic, bay window, and gingerbread design on the eaves. Cheese manufacturing took place in the north wing of the building, while the upstairs housed living quarters. The hand-built clapboard barn featured a gable roof, two cupolas, and dormers.

Johanne Welte, a native of Austria, arrived in Denver in 1872, and by 1879 he and brother-in-law Plaziduo Gassner had purchased property in the future Highlands Ranch, where they moved their families and established a dairy ranch. Naming the ranch Big Dry Creek Cheese Ranch after a nearby gulch, Welte and Gassner produced highly renowned butter as well as brick and limburger cheeses. Gassner died in 1883, leaving the operation of the ranch to Welte. In response to the growing demand for his fine products, Welte expanded his business with the construction of a hog house, slaughterhouse, stone cistern, icehouse, granaries, and carpenter and blacksmith shops. Using dry farming techniques, he planted fields of alfalfa, corn, barley, and a variety of beet for use as livestock feed, and eventually cultivated a ten-acre orchard of fruit trees.

In January 1910, Welte deeded the entire ranch to his son-in-law Philip Renner, a German citizen who came to the United States in 1893 and later served as a board member for the Welte School, which was located just west of the cheese ranch. Welte remained a resident of the ranch and died there on January 19, 1927. Cheese production continued until 1938. The property was sold in 1943 to Glester B. Richardson, who immediately sold the ranch to Lawrence C. Phipps Jr.

The old cheese ranch buildings remained unchanged during Phipps's ownership and were part of the land sold to Mission Viejo Company in 1979. One year prior to the purchase, state archaeologists conducted a historical study of the property, at the request of Mission Viejo, with special focus given to the farmhouse and barn. In his notes, historian and professor Alan

Culpin determined that the farmhouse "is probably one of the oldest surviving homes in Douglas County, and as such is worthy of preservation as an example of the heritage of that area."[8]

Unfortunately, preservation of the cheese ranch proved too costly, so Mission Viejo destroyed all of the buildings in 1986. When county commissioners expressed outrage over this act, company representatives cited liability as the reason for the destruction: Although they had closed off and boarded up the site, efforts to prevent trespassers had proved fruitless. In 1994, the developers announced plans to turn the site into Cheese Ranch Historic Park, a fifty-acre park with biking and walking trails, picnic areas, a wildlife observation deck, interpretive signage to note the former locations of the historic buildings, and a miniature windmill. A grand opening and dedication ceremony for the historic park took place July 18, 1995.

Daniels Park (1920), Daniels Park Road, four miles south of Wildcat Reserve Parkway.

Scenic Daniels Park affords its visitors interesting history as well as spectacular views. Reportedly a popular hangout for local outlaws during the mid- to late 1800s, the park is rumored to have been the last campsite of Kit Carson just days before he died at Fort Lyons in 1868. The Territorial Daughters of Colorado erected a memorial to the western hero there in 1923.

Visitors to Daniels Park will notice several old ranch buildings located throughout the park. These are the remains of the Florence Martin Ranch, which was occupied from 1920 to 1937, and included a silo, shed, outhouse, workshop, bunkhouse, several barns, residential structures, farm animal houses, and water storage facilities. Florence Martin, an Australian who purchased the site in 1919, was a prominent Denver socialite. She and her sister, Emily, occupied the Daniels Park property during the summers and spent winters in London. In 1920, Martin donated thirty-eight acres (of approximately 2,400 acres she co-owned with Charles MacAllister Willcox) to the city of Denver to be added to the Denver Mountain Park System. The land was donated under the condition that it be named after Major William Cooke Daniels and his wife, Cicely, friends of both Martin and Willcox. The city gladly accepted the conditions, and by 1922 several campfire sites, picnic tables, and a cave-like stone shelter were constructed for visitors' enjoyment.

After fire destroyed her summer home in 1937, Martin donated another 963 acres of land, which included the ranch buildings, to the city of Denver to be incorporated into the other Daniels Park land holdings. Trails, picnic facilities, a shelter house, and a buffalo preserve were added to the newly acquired property. On June 30, 1995, Daniels Park was named to the National Register of Historic Places. It continues to reward its visitors with breathtaking views of the Front Range and eastern Colorado plains.

Highlands Ranch Mansion (1898: John Springer, builder; 1926–1937: J. B. Benedict, remodeling), South Ranch Road. **Closed to the public.**

Often referred to as The Castle, the Highlands Ranch Mansion is among the most architecturally distinct structures in Colorado. Since its original construction in 1898, numerous additions have taken place, resulting in the use of diverse building materials including wood, stone, brick, and stucco. The fenestration is varied and features many styles of windows, including casements, mullions, segmental arches, lancet arches, lintels, and radiating voussoirs. Carved wood trims frame all bargeboards, window surrounds, brackets, porch posts, and balustrades. The hipped roof has many gables and dormers. The abundance of crenellated parapets and towers projecting above the roofline give the structure a mystical, castle-like appearance. The 22,000-square-foot mansion features fourteen bedrooms, eleven bathrooms, five fireplaces, a library, a ballroom, a billiard room, a grand living room, an entry room, a butler's pantry and kitchen, a private courtyard, a game room, and a dining room and breakfast nook.

The mansion has been the home of some of Colorado's most renowned millionaires and businessmen. In 1898, John Springer, a wealthy man with a background in politics, law, and banking, began construction of an elegant mansion on his Cross Country Horse and Cattle Ranch in northern Douglas County. He added to the building for many years, completing 60 percent of its current construction.

In 1920, Waite Phillips, brother to the Phillips Petroleum Company founders, purchased the ranch and retained it until 1926, when he sold it to Wolhurst Stock Farms president Frank Kistler. Kistler changed the name of the ranch to Diamond K and hired architect J. B. Benedict in 1929 to design a classic Tudor-style addition to the mansion, featuring carved wood trims, gables, and a peaked shake-shingle roof. Nine bedrooms, hardwood floors, fireplaces, and two secret panels were included in the addition that completed the house. The mantle of the grand living room fireplace features a pictorial etching of the mansion's floor plan, a scenic view of the Front Range, and the Diamond K cattle brand. Kistler also installed a one-lane bowling alley in an elongated stone building on the mansion's east side.

Financial problems forced Kistler to sell the ranch in 1937 to Lawrence Phipps Jr., who renamed the property Highlands Ranch and lived in the mansion for nearly forty years. He died in 1976, and the ranch was sold to Marvin Davis, who organized the Highlands Venturers Corporation to market the property. In 1978, Mission Viejo, a California-based development company, entered into a purchase option agreement with Highlands Venturers and nearly two years later became the new owner of the mansion and the surrounding ranch land.

Future plans for the mansion include a 200-acre historic park for the use of Highlands Ranch residents and visitors. Designs for the park, formulated by the Highlands Ranch Historic Park Advisory Committee, include trails with interpretative signage highlighting the history of ranching in the Front Range and Colorado.

Notes

1. *Littleton Independent*, January 12, 1978, pp. 1, 2.

2. Ibid., January 31, 1978, Newspaper Clippings Notebook, Local History Collection, Philip S. Miller Library; *Douglas County News*, February 2, 1978, p. 11.

3. *Denver Post*, September 11, 1979, p. 21.

4. *Rocky Mountain News*, August 15, 1986, p. 50; October 12, 1986, p. 86.

5. *Douglas County News Press*, April 5, 1988, p. 5; February 3, 1989, p. 1.

6. *Rocky Mountain News*, November 15, 1990, p. 34; *Douglas County News Press*, December 5, 1990, p. 1.

7. *Rocky Mountain News*, August 4, 1993, p. 5A.

8. Alan Culpin, "Survey of Cheese Ranch Farmhouse at Highlands Ranch," Inventory Form, p. 2, Colorado Historical Society.

Scenes From A Fading Past

Castle Rock Depot, built 1875.
Denver Public Library, Western History Dept., #MCC-1709. Photographer: L. C. McClure

Wilcox Street, late 1920s.
DPLD, Local History Collection, #98039-235

Castle Rock

Plum Creek Flood Damage, D&RG RR South of Castle Rock, 1965.
DPLD, Local History Collection, #96013.005.029.
Photographer: John B. Norwood

Owens House, 1885. DPLD, Local History Collection, #97032-002

Cantril Courthouse, built 1874. DPLD, Local History Collection, #678.03. Photographer: Frank Reiste, 1900

Castle Rock

First National Bank/Douglas Masonic Lodge, built 1904. Courtesy: Castle Rock Historical Society

Deckers Area

Long Scraggy Peak. South Platte Stage far right.
Denver Public Library, Western History Dept., #MCC-1147. Photographer: L. C. McClure

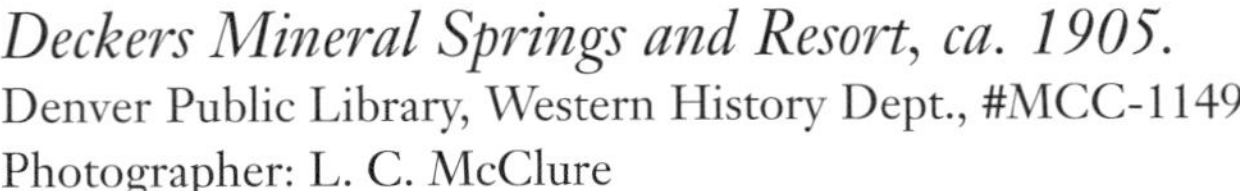

Deckers Mineral Springs and Resort, ca. 1905.
Denver Public Library, Western History Dept., #MCC-1149
Photographer: L. C. McClure

Twin Cedars Lodge, 1950s. DPLD, Local History Collection, #94051-001
Photographer: Mack Sorn

Deckers Area

Elias Ammons, 1893.
Courtesy: Colorado Historical Society, #F-1093

Mining town of West Creek, 1890s.
Denver Public Library, Western History Dept., #P-883
Photographer: H. S. Poley

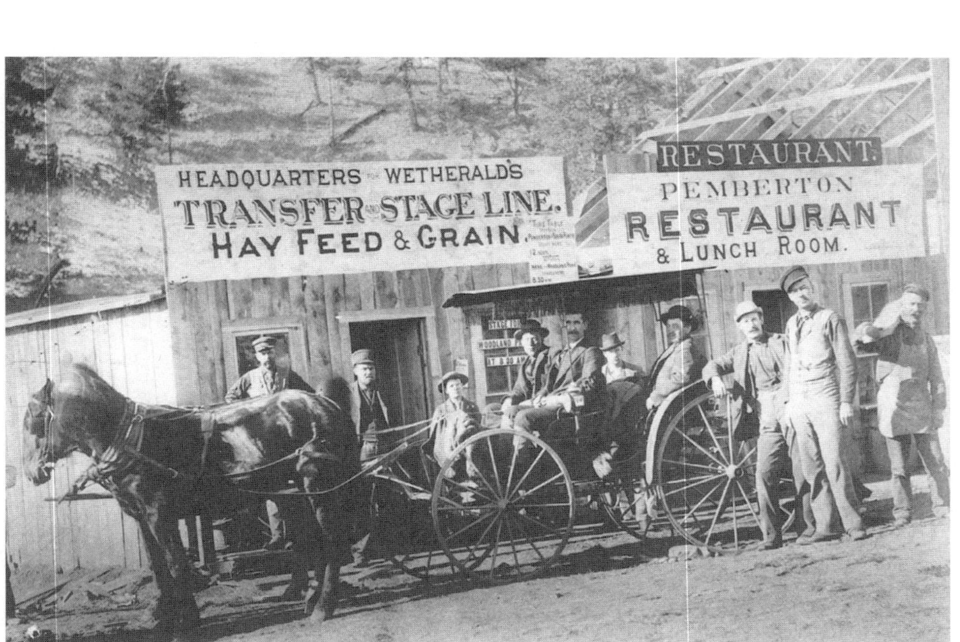

Pemberton Stage Line Passengers, 1890s.
Denver Public Library, Western History Dept., #X-13001

Deckers Area

James Frank Gardner, 1897.
"Father of Douglas County"
Courtesy: Colorado Historical Society, #10027235

The Russell Brothers, founders of Russellville.
Courtesy: Colorado Historical Society, #10027237

Leaks in the Castlewood Dam, ca. 1890.
Courtesy: Colorado Historical Society, #B1339

Franktown

Franktown School, built 1924.
DPLD, Local History Collection, #645.01

Franktown

Pike's Peak Grange #163, built 1909. Photographer: Susan Appleby

Johanne Welte.
Courtesy: Littleton Historical Museum (#513)

Big Dry Creek Cheese Ranch, built 1879.
Courtesy: Littleton Historical Museum (#505)

Florence Martin Ranch in Daniels Park.
Photographer: Susan Appleby

Highlands Ranch

Highlands Ranch

Isabelle "Sassy" Springer
Denver Public Library, Western History Dept., F-10178

Frank E. Kistler
Courtesy: Colorado Historical Society, 10027236

John W. Springer
Courtesy: Colorado Historical Society, F-1097

Highlands Ranch Mansion Great Room.
Courtesy: Shea Homes and the Highlands Ranch Historical Society

Highlands Ranch Mansion front entrance.
Courtesy: Shea Homes and the Highlands Ranch Historical Society

Highlands Ranch

Greenland Ranch, ca. 1900-1910.
DPLD, Local History Collection, #97036

Larkspur

Major Daniel C. Oakes (seated)
Charles Stobie (left), Jim Baker (right).
Courtesy: Colorado Historical Society, F-26.770

Larkspur, 1920s. D & R G Railroad in foreground. Carlson Frink Creamery, white building center. A T & S F Railroad in background. DPLD, Local History Collection, #xxx.120

Larkspur

Larkspur Town Hall
Photographer: Susan Appleby

Louviers

Louviers village, 1948.
Denver Public Library, Western History Dept., #X-12167

Louviers

Louviers, Colorado.
Denver Public Library, Western History Dept., #X-12165

Louviers Village Club, built 1917.
Courtesy: Hagley Museum and Library, Wilmington, DE

Louviers

Manager's Home, Louviers.
Denver Public Library, Western History Dept., #X-12166

Workers' Houses, pre-1920.
DPLD, Local History Collection, #94069. Photographer: Jack Colvin

Parker

Parker Post Office, 1897.
Courtesy: Colorado Historical Society, F-21.200
Photographer: Charles L. Hincke

Fonder School, built 1884.
Denver Public Library, Western History Dept., #X-12982

The Creamery, 1897.
Courtesy: Colorado Historical Society, F-21.211
Photographer: Charles L. Hincke

Colorado & Southern Railroad Station.
Courtesy: Colorado Historical Society, F-7533

Parker, March 11, 1939.
Courtesy: Colorado Historical Society, F-35.246

Ruth Memorial Chapel, built 1912-1913.
DPLD, Local History Collection, #95053-003-020
Photographer: Johanna Harden

Parker

Perry Park

Perry Park Ranch. Undated.
Denver Public Library, Western History Dept., #MCC-4216
Photographer: L. C. McClure

Nanichant House, built 1889.
DPLD, Local History Collection, #98002-002

Perry Park

Manor House on Lake Wauconda, built 1891.
DPLD, Local History Collection, #92014-319. Photographer: A. L. Schafer

Perry Park

U.S.G.S. photograph of Pleasant Park (Perry Park), ca. 1871-1872.
DPLD, Local History Collection, #2000.21.10. Photographer: Wm. H. Jackson

Hay Stacks, Perry Park.
Courtesy: Colorado Historical Society, #WHJ-2114

Perry Park Ranch.
Denver Public Library, Western History Dept., #MCC-4215
Photographer: L. C. McClure

Perry Park

Golf Course and Road Construction, ca. 1971.
DPLD, Local History Collection, #9214-066-1A. Photographer: A. L. Schafer

Roxborough Park

U.S.G.S. photograph of Roxborough Park.
DPLD, Local History Collection, #2000.21.6. Photographer: W. T. Lee

Roxborough Park
Courtesy: Colorado Historical Society, F-11.754. Photographer: Wm. H. Jackson

Roxborough Park

Sedalia

Marquis Victor in front of the Victor House.
DPLD, Local History Collection, #687-569

Cherokee Ranch, built 1924-1927.
Courtesy: Jess Stainbrook, photographer.

Sedalia

Plum Avenue, view to the southeast. Undated.
DPLD, Local History Collection, #687-525

Church of St. Philip in the Field, built 1872.
Denver Public Library, Western History Dept., #X-4070

Sedalia

Manhart Store, ca. 1900.
DPLD, Local History Collection, #687.585

Sedalia

Atchison, Topeka and Santa Fe Railroad crossover of the Denver and Rio Grande Railroad. Built 1889; eliminated during World War I.
DPLD, Local History Collection, #687.519

Divide-Spring Valley Grange #53
DPLD, Local History Collection, #94007

Spring Valley-
Cherry Valley

Bartruff-Bihlmeyer Ranch, 1890s. View to west.
DPLD, Local History Collection, #93005-006

Haywagon, Bartruff-Bihlmeyer Ranch, ca. 1905.
DPLD, Local History Collection, #95005

Spring Valley-Cherry Valley

12-foot corn grown on Gooding Ranch, 1920s.
DPLD, Local History Collection, #98041-009-002

Case Post Office at Rock Ridge Ranch, ca. 1900.
DPLD, Local History Collection, #654.13

Spring Valley-Cherry Valley

Cherry School Students, 1936-1937.
DPLD, Local History Collection, #654.12

LARKSPUR

The beautiful flowers that covered the surrounding hills but which are poisonous to livestock, suggested the town's name.
—Colorado Magazine, November 1941

For more than a century after its settlement, the small town of Larkspur, as implied by the tranquility of its name, enjoyed a peaceful existence. Located in a valley of forested buttes, with Raspberry Mountain on the west and Larkspur Mountain to the east, the town arose primarily as a shipping point for lumber and locally mined ores such as potash and clay. Larkspur remained a close-knit community well into the twentieth century, but the decision to incorporate in 1979 led to a decade of political tension and arguments that almost tore the town apart. Larkspur exemplifies the effects of big-town politics in a small-town atmosphere.

In September 1871, the tracks of the Denver & Rio Grande Railroad reached the future site of Larkspur, named after the purple wildflowers that grew prolifically in the area. Here the railroad constructed a depot, freight house, and water tank. During this time, most people viewed the railroad as a great instigator of growth and progress, and several residents from nearby Huntsville (named after Colorado Territorial Governor Alexander Cameron Hunt) relocated closer to the railroad site, where development was virtually assured.

Huntsville was one of the earliest established towns in the Colorado Territory and was home to Douglas County's first post office, authorized in February 1861 with Major Daniel C. Oakes as postmaster. A zealous Colorado booster, Oakes published a guidebook to the Colorado gold fields in 1859 that contributed enormously to the "Pike's Peak or Bust" gold rush that same year. Upon arrival in the Rocky Mountain region, many of his more naïve readers were disappointed that the glittering metal was harder to obtain than they imagined, and several burial effigies of Oakes appeared throughout the territory with epitaphs that read: "Here lies D. C. Oakes, Who was the starter of this damned hoax."[1] Nonetheless, Oakes had great faith in the future growth of the region. In 1859, he and partner William Street located a steam saw mill along Plum Creek near Sedalia. They later opened a second one in Huntsville, near a popular inn known as Mrs. Coberly's Half-Way House, which was named for its location between Denver and Colorado Springs. During the 1860s, Oakes convinced Huntsville residents to construct Fort Lincoln, a nine-room log stockade, as defense against potential Indian attacks. Locals referred to the fort as "Oakes' Folly," but were quick to withdraw the slur when souring Indian–settler relations forced thirty families to take refuge inside the stockade for six months in 1864.

On December 13, 1871, the Huntsville post office relocated

to the nearby newly constructed depot at Larkspur. By 1878, a general merchandise store, blacksmith shop, sawmill, and several dwellings had been built near the depot/post office.

Progress was steady. In 1881, the *Rocky Mountain News* reported Larkspur station's designation as a regular freight and passenger point. The lumber industry had already been established in the area for several years, and trains pulling timber-bearing cars left Larkspur frequently. In 1876, Sloan's Mill "shipped about seven million feet of lumber, one hundred thousand ties, two thousand telegraph poles, fifteen thousand cords of wood, and fifteen thousand shingles," from Larkspur, where the operation had been located since 1871.[2]

Larkspur's early merchants also enjoyed a steady patronage from town residents. J. S. McConnell operated the settlement's first general store and advertised himself as a "Dealer in Dry Goods and Groceries. Flour, Feed, and Everything Kept in a Country Store. All Ranch Produce taken in exchange for goods." W. B. Evans, McConnell's competitor, favored the vicinity's ranchers as his customers:

> "I desire to call the attention of the Ranchmen of the Divide to my stock of DRY GOODS, GENTS FURNISHING GOODS, HATS and CAPS. Groceries, Canned Goods, and Queen's ware, which I will sell at lowest Cash Prices. FLOUR and GRAIN always on hand. FARM PRODUCE TAKEN IN EXCHANGE FOR GOODS. CALL AND SEE ME. W. B. Evans."[3]

W. B. Evans's popularity extended beyond his equitable treatment of the town's consumers. His home often welcomed eager town dancers and social groups who created a celebratory atmosphere that spread throughout the house.

> On the night of March 2d, quite a number gathered at the residence of our worthy "Nasby," at Larkspur, W.B. Evans. He and his lady gracefully surrendered to the invaders, who, after disposing of the elegant supper prepared by the ladies, gave themselves over to social enjoyments, games, and a little dancing, the music being furnished by the Moorhead brothers. I say little dancing, for the reason that the room used for that purpose was too small to admit of the free movement of the dancers in quadrille, and consequently, the floor was cleared for the exclusive use of Deacon Thompson, who rendered the "double shuffle" and other steps in admirable style, as they used to be done "back in the States." It is needless to say all went home happy.[4]

Dancers had plenty of room to waltz and shuffle in the town's Victoria Casino, where imaginative masquerade balls were among the favorite events. A pavilion adjacent to the Denver & Rio Grande depot also saw many magical nights:

> There will be a dance at the Larkspur pavillion [sic] on Saturday, July 24th. The grounds will be beautifully lighted with the new glow-worm colored lights and Japanese lanterns. Special attention will be shown strangers.[5]

Many of the attendees at these popular dances traveled to Larkspur from the surrounding farms and ranches. In *Grip-Sack Guide to Colorado*, published in 1881, author George Crofutt's general curiosity as to the definition of Larkspur's name led him to turn to the obvious, most evidential source, an indication of the significance of ranching in the area: "Although this is Larkspur, you will not see the 'lark' or the 'spur,' unless the latter is a 'cowboy,' and the 'cattle on a thousand hills' are larks; but one thing is certain, when the cattle get on a *lark* it requires a great deal of spur to overtake them. Hence the name." In 1901, the Plum Creek Cattle Company purchased seven hundred acres near Larkspur to begin an extensive ranching operation. The *Denver Times* reported that the company's owners, W. S. Davis and A. G. McCann, "are having a handsome new house and barns built and will be ready for business about February 1. Both are excellent men and are a valuable addition to the community."[6]

An 1890 visitor to Larkspur and Perry Park commented, "The dairy business is the greatest industry in this country, and all the cattle look fat and sleek."[7] In 1896, Larkspur vicinity ranchers celebrated the installation of a dairy separator that gave way the next year to a creamery run by Richard Fosdick. The *Castle Rock Journal* reported that the small creamery was using about eight hundred pounds of milk a day. Starting in 1902, Clarence B. Frink joined forces with C. G. Carlson and headquartered the Carlson Frink Creamery Company in Larkspur, with branches in Castle Rock, Sedalia, Spring Valley, Kiowa, and Monument. Famous for its production of Black Canyon cheese, the creamery attracted patrons throughout the state. In the early 1920s, C. G. Carlson left the partnership and the enterprise became the Frink Creamery Company. Frink remained one of Larkspur's most important businessmen for several years and earned the respect of townsfolk and state residents alike.

> His course has been marked by steady progress since he made his initial step in the business world. Year by year he has progressed, wisely utilizing his opportunities and he is today at the head of an extensive and important creamery business that covers a wide territory and has become one of the important commercial interests of the section in which he operates.[8]

In 1921, the *Record-Journal of Douglas County* reported that from July 1920 to July 1921 Frink Creamery purchased a total of 2,484,015 pounds of milk from local farmers and produced 93,897 pounds of cheese. "Mr. Frink is deserving of considerable praise and the thanks of our entire county; and our dairymen here do show their appreciation by patronizing his creameries and supplying the large quantities of pure, rich milk that Douglas County is noted for," commented the newspaper.[9] The Frink Creamery remained an important town business until 1965, when it was washed away in the Plum Creek flood.

During its heyday, Frink Creamery had easy railroad access to outside markets not only with the established Denver & Rio Grande route, but also the Atchison Topeka & Santa Fe, which completed its tracks to Larkspur in 1887. Running parallel to its antecessor, the Santa Fe line constructed a depot just west of town and became an instant symbol of Larkspur's hopes for the future. In 1899, increased business on the line prompted Santa Fe officials to announce that eight more trains would be needed to continue the heavy workload, and "there will be both a day and night agent employed here and some improvements will be made at the station."[10]

Nonetheless, while the incoming and outgoing trains usually heralded prosperity and progress for the town, accidents were inevitable. In March 1898, a spark from a Denver & Rio Grande locomotive ignited dry pasture grass in Larkspur, "and quite an area was burned over before the flames were gotten under control."[11] A December 1900 collision on the Santa Fe line nearly resulted in a loss of life:

> Quite a serious wreck occurred here this morning on the Santa Fe. Engine 450, from Denver, while coming down to take out a work train, stopped to take water at the tank, when extra freight engine 891, from the south, came down the hill. The engineer could not hold his train and struck engine 450 at the tank, derailing the former, together with fourteen cars. Engineer Spencer and Fireman Peterson, of engine 450, reversed the engine and jumped before the collision, their engine running wild toward Denver, finally dying at Tomah, a few miles north. The depot was nearly a total wreck, and Agent Barton and family, who were in the living apartments, are considering themselves lucky not to have been badly hurt or killed. As it was, no one was hurt.[12]

Nearly thirty years later, a man involved in a 1920s collision with a train two miles south of Larkspur did not possess the same luck. In July 1929, the *Record-Journal of Douglas County* reported the findings of County Coroner S. E. Livingston:

> Mr. Livingston immediately went to the scene of the tragedy, and upon arriving there, found that the body had been moved from the center of the track, to allow the trains to pass, but there was no one around. The body was very much mutilated, having been rolled along the track for about fifty yards, but it appeared to be a mexican man about forty-five or fifty years old. As to whether the man was riding on the train or walking along the track could not be determined.[13]

Despite their dangers, the trains made Larkspur a major shipping point for resources from the region. In the early 1920s, miners extracted large deposits of high-grade potash discovered west of town and sent the ore to Denver refineries by rail. Additionally, a local mining partnership known as the Hawn Brothers reportedly extracted enough clay from a deposit on the town's north side to fill two carloads a day, which were shipped to Denver from Larkspur. Denver manufacturers used the clay for sewage pipe and pottery production.

In 1920, Larkspur's two hundred residents supported two general merchandise stores, two garages, a bakery, a post office/depot, the Larkspur Hotel, the Frink Creamery Company, and the Larkspur School, which doubled as a church. Throughout the next decade, Larkspur earned a reputation as a health and summer resort.

> Many people have benefited by spending a few months here in the summer, when the heat gets unbearable in many cities. They have come here and been refreshed and invigorated by living here and enjoying the bracing air laden with the healthful odors of the pines.[14]

From the 1920s through the 1950s, new additions and developments transpired within the Larkspur community. In 1924, the American Federation of Human Rights, made up of members of an international Co-Masonic organization, located its headquarters in a new two-story building in Larkspur Heights, just west of the Santa Fe tracks at the foot of Raspberry Mountain. Unique to the world of freemasonry in its inclusion of women as equal members, the group used the building until 1971. Operations began again in 1984, and the organization continues to provide its members "an opportunity for spiritual growth and service to humanity."[15] The building was placed on the National Register of Historic Places in 1998.

In 1930, Larkspur's population reached 250. Businesses included a grocery store, one garage, three gas stations, a post office/depot, a school, the Frink Creamery Company, a barber shop, and a restaurant. In 1950, businesses such as Virgil's Café, Jay's Café, Eagle Garage and Café, and the Larkspur Café (renamed Spur Inn and then later Spur of the Moment) catered to hungry Larkspurites.

By the 1960s, commercial developers had begun eyeing the quiet Larkspur area. A 1964 proposal to construct a "$31 million science-business-entertainment complex" one mile northwest of Larkspur, complete with convention facilities, hotels, an amusement park, and 1,900-foot space tower, was tabled after the Federal Aviation Agency ruled the tower would be a hazard to Stapleton Airport air traffic. The Frontier Boys Village, a treatment facility for emotionally disturbed boys—now called the Emily Griffith Center—opened four miles southwest of Larkspur in January 1969. The *Denver Post* described the candidates for the village:

> Boys who are delinquent, boys who are in danger of becoming delinquent, boys who are in a legal euphemism are called 'disturbed,' come to get away from the rat race of daily life, to take a breather, to learn more about their own value and establish the values by which they will live.[16]

In September 1973, Larkspur residents celebrated the opening of another educational facility for area youths. The new, expanded Larkspur Elementary School provided much-needed elbow room for its 122 pupils and their teachers, who had previously been squeezed into the community's old brick schoolhouse in the center of town. Built for an estimated cost of $355,000, the new school featured cheerful classrooms, a large gym that doubled as a cafeteria and a playground. The school's student body was drawn from Larkspur, Perry Park, Greenland, and the Divide valley.

A growing population also placed demands upon Larkspur's modest utilities. By the end of the 1970s, debate over the town's water problems resulted in a decision among residents that would cause political turmoil into the 1990s.

In 1979, tests performed by the Colorado Department of Health on Larkspur's water sources revealed that water in eleven of the twenty-two community wells was unsafe to drink. In dire need of a new water sanitation system, yet lacking the funds for such a project, Larkspur residents voted in December 1979 to incorporate in order to gain access to state and federal loans and grants.

During the first year after becoming an incorporated town, Larkspur elected a town mayor and council members, passed home rule status whereby the town gained control over local matters, and contracted for services with the county sheriff, building department, and road and bridge department. In November 1982, resident Dean Sprigg became the small town's jack-of-all-trades after accepting the concurrent positions of maintenance man, policeman, and town clerk. Also in 1982, Larkspur voters, in a move to provide a clean water system for their town, approved a 10-mill property tax to finance the construction of new water facilities. In 1983, both the state Department of Local Affairs and the Water Conservation Board offered monetary assistance in the construction of a public water system.

By the end of 1986, however, disagreements among town residents over the direction of Larkspur's growth had heated up. In December, town officials annexed 2,500 acres south of the town limits, where developers planned a $100 million resort hotel/conference center known as Spruce Mountain Ranch. The decision disappointed many Larkspur residents, who feared the project would adversely affect their rural lifestyle. Residents proved more vigilant in their efforts to put an end to a controversial "junk ordinance" adopted in April 1985 but not enforced by town officials until November 1986. The ordinance instructed residents to tidy up their property and remove unattractive objects such as old cars and deteriorating 55-gallon drums or face a $300-a-day fine. Although town officials and Mayor Ann Trueblood denounced the junk as a health hazard to the town, many enraged residents resented attempts to enforce the ordinance and responded with a movement, led by resident Myrna Been, to recall the entire town board. Years later, in an interview with the author, Been reflected upon the controversial issue that sparked her own political career:

> These people had lived out here all their lives so that they could have their junk laying around if they wanted it. Some people love their junk. An old, rusted 1942 Ford may not be important to one person, but it's not junk to others. It's their possession. One man's junk is another man's treasure. So, that junk ordinance really got the feelings going and it was what I think started the political problems in the town.

In a January 1987 article headlined, "Larkspur folks feud like the Hatfields and McCoys after incorporation," the *Denver Post* quoted one Larkspur resident as mourning the changes in her hometown: "Before we became a town, I doubt if there were ever any better friends in the country. Now we don't even talk anymore."[17] A feature in the *Rocky Mountain News*, which compared Larkspur's disagreements to the television game show "Family Feud," also had some commentary on the town's turmoil:

> The political rivalries and personality conflicts so common to small-town politics aren't so amusing anymore, and some say the struggle for power in this town of 300 is threatening to tear Larkspur apart. . . . Larkspur was a friendly community, residents say, until the town was incorporated in 1979. Then the rules changed and people started fighting over how the town should be run. They haven't stopped since.[18]

The dispute that pitted neighbor against neighbor came to a head in April 1987, when Larkspur voters opted not to recall Mayor Trueblood and the six-member council, which included her husband, Stan. Although town officials saw the results of the vote as proof of town support for their work, and for the junk ordinance in particular, opponents claimed the election "only shows that the Truebloods have a stranglehold on the town."[19] Nonetheless, in 1988 a bitterly fought town council election resulted in Stan Trueblood's failure to gain reelection. Mayor Ann Trueblood and two council members then shocked town residents and observers by announcing their resignations.

One year before relinquishing her position as mayor, Ann Trueblood aided council members in the creation of an updated version of the Comprehensive Plan for the Town of Larkspur, first written in 1984 and adopted in 1987 by the town's planning commission. The plan identified Larkspur's "planned urbanization area," the boundary of greatest expected growth, as encompassing 4,200 acres. Among the issues identified as critical were water, wastewater, transportation, and storm drainages. To address the town's water problems, the plan called for the installation of a second water tank and water treatment facilities as well as a wastewater treatment plant. Proposed transportation solutions included better access to Interstate 25, improvements to existing intersections, and construction of hiking and biking trails. The plan also recognized storm drainage problems that lingered from destruction wrought by the 1965 flood, but did not provide absolute solutions.

Not all Larkspur life during the 1980s was dominated by politics. Entertainment also found a place in the small town. After searching for several years for a permanent home, the Colorado Renaissance Festival finally settled in Larkspur in 1980. Jousting, singing, dancing, poetry reading, and eating are among the festival's events. The annual festival attracts large crowds during June and July weekends, providing an enormous boost to Larkspur's economy.

Just as the festival's knights jousted with scripted passion, Larkspur's political leadership continued to wage fervent battles well into the 1990s. After Mayor Trueblood's resignation in 1988, the top position went to Richard "Spike" Graetz, a council member of more than eight years. Six months after his reelection in April 1990, Graetz filed his resignation, leaving Larkspur's 232 residents mayorless for the second time in two and a half years. Town council member Jim Williams replaced Graetz but he, too, resigned in 1991. He was replaced by council member Florence Burch, who was elected in 1992.

The mid-1990s saw the construction of Larkspur's first community park in 1995, and in 1996 the county purchased fifteen acres of the former Greenland town site, located south of Larkspur along Interstate 25, for preservation as open space. Despite these achievements, Larkspur politics continued to be marked by controversy, polarizing the town council.

In September 1996, five months after the re-election of Mayor Burch, council members opposed to the mayor proposed an ordinance that required the town clerk position to be elected rather than appointed by the mayor, claiming it would provide the town with essential checks and balances for accounting procedures. When voters defeated the charter amendment, council member Myrna Been suggested contracting an out-of-town accountant for Larkspur's bookkeeping needs while relegating the current town clerk to clerical duties. "There has never been any money missing, but the potential is there," Been told the *Douglas County News Press*. "There is nothing personal about any of it."[20]

More controversy brewed when, in December 1996, several town residents presented the council with a signed petition requesting the termination of the town attorney. The petitioners did not cite reasons for the move, and although an initial town council vote defeated the motion to terminate the attorney, another vote taken about two months later resulted in his ouster.

In March 1997, a group of Larkspur residents banded together to put an end to what they felt was a troubled council. Coalesced as the Larkspur Petition Committee, the group demanded the resignation of council members Myrna Been, Jessa Lee Bell, and Bill Lucero. The committee said it would begin recall efforts if the three council members did not file their resignations within five days. However, the committee's actions were stalled when collected recall petitions could not be filed due to the resignation of the town clerk.

When Mayor Pro-tem Barbara Scott resigned from the council, Mayor Burch and council member Paul Manning followed suit. It was a strategic move designed to salvage what they felt was a drowning town council by forcing a special election, rather than council appointments, to determine replacements.

A summer election placed Bill Lucero, who avoided the recall attempt due to a town charter stipulation that required elected officials to stay in office for six months before being recalled, in the mayoral position. A revived recall attempt of Myrna Been and Jessa Lee Bell culminated into a November special election in which preliminary results were declared null and void due to what was called a poorly designed ballot. Finally, a new election in December recalled Jessa Lee Bell, while Myrna Been's position remained sound.

Not long after taking her post in April 1998, Larkspur's next mayor, Wandalene Hertz, was forced to face yet another division among town officials and residents. In October 1998, the town council entered negotiations with county and railroad officials concerning the proposed construction of a railroad underpass south of Perry Park Avenue. The underpass was needed to improve emergency access routes. Controversy over the issue spurred two town elections in which voters successively defeated the project, mainly due to concerns over an increase in traffic through the heart of Larkspur.

The disputes that dominated Larkspur during the 1980s and 1990s presented a sharp contrast to the serene, neighborly character that had been a trademark of the town since the early days of its settlement. Although controversial big-city politics have scarred the town, Larkspur still offers an oasis of country life between the growing cities of Denver and Colorado Springs. The town lacks sidewalks and traffic lights; one stop sign represents the sole obstacle to automobiles that travel down Larkspur's mile-long main street. Amid such modern political turmoil, many residents hope that in the future Larkspur can recover the peace of its past.

Larkspur Historic Sites

Greenland Ranch (1885: Union Real Estate, Live Stock and Investment Company), 1732 E. Noe Road. **Private residence.**

Greenland Ranch grew near the thriving town of Greenland in the 1880s. The town, laid out on a twenty-acre plot in the 1870s, received its name from poet and author Helen Hunt Jackson, who admired the green plains and hills of the area through her train window. From the 1870s to the 1920s, Greenland supported several general stores, a depot, post office, stage station, saloon, blacksmith shop, hotel, and school. The Denver & Rio Grande Railroad reached the town in the early 1870s and set up a depot in an old boxcar adjacent to the tracks before constructing a more formal building. The train line supported local industries by transporting local lumber, livestock, milk, grain, and potatoes to market.

In 1900, a deadly tale of rampant jealousy unfolded one mile west of the town of Greenland. Orville Minor, a Greenland farm hand, was shot and killed by Spencer V. Dicks, who believed the victim was trying to woo his fiancée, Miss Minnie Hutchinson. Exclaiming, "Minnie, I didn't think this of you!" Dicks also fired at his beloved, but her corset deflected the bullet and she escaped unharmed. Dicks later surrendered to authorities at Rocky Ford, east of Pueblo, Colorado.[21]

The thriving town of Greenland served as the headquarters for some of the largest ranches in the county. Among these was the 16,000-acre Greenland Breeding Farm, owned by a group of local land investors called the Union Real Estate, Live Stock and

Investment Company. An 1893 prospectus written by the ranch owners radiantly described the area:

> The location of this property, all things considered, is one unexcelled by any in the State . . . with vast stretches of undulating prairie covered with a luxuriant growth of native grasses, and dotted here and there with cultivated fields.[22]

Greenland Breeding Farm (also known as the Greenland Stock Farm) supported several hundred cattle and horses. Ranchers set aside 1,000 acres for cultivation of wheat, barley, oats, rye, potatoes, corn, and assorted vegetables. The property reportedly contained 150 miles of fencing and seven buildings with the names "Home," "Johnson," "Reddy," "McBroom," "Daniels," "Nimerick," and "Chambers." Other structures on the ranch included an icehouse, hen house, windmill, carriage house and horse barn, blacksmith shop, and silo. The largest building on the premises was a 101-foot-by-36-foot stock barn featuring "18 box stalls, capable of accomodating [sic] over 100 head of the best thoroughbreds" and a hayloft storage capacity of 110 tons.[23] Despite the fact that fire destroyed a large portion of the barn in the 1920s, it remains the largest building on the ranch today.

In 1909, John William Higby started the Greenland Land and Cattle Company on land formerly owned by the Union Real Estate, Live Stock and Investment Company. A businessman who came to Colorado in 1888, Higby assumed a partnership with the Russell-Gates Merchandise Company and operated a mercantile business in Monument and later in the town of Greenland. He operated his ranch, which became known as Greenland Ranch, until his death in 1916, whereupon it passed to his sons Louis and Carl. In 1918, the *Record-Journal of Douglas County* reported the success of the Higby brothers and other Douglas County ranchers at the Denver Stock Show:

> Messrs. Higby, of the Greenland ranch, took in a bunch of yearling Polled Shorthorns which, were awarded first prize, and also a bunch of yearling Shorthorns which captured third prize. This is a very good showing for this county when considering the class of stuff which is on exhibition at this Show.[24]

The Higby family sold parcels of Greenland Ranch throughout the years, but the headquarters of the property remained in the family until the 1980s when the Oklahoma Publishing Company, parent firm of the now-defunct *Colorado Springs Sun* newspaper, purchased it.

As the last major undeveloped parcel between Denver and Colorado Springs, Greenland Ranch was the focus of a struggle between conservationists and developers during the mid- to late 1990s. While developers envisioned housing projects and convenient Interstate 25 accessibility adjacent to shopping malls, conservationists believed the site should be set aside as an open-space reserve that would prevent the merging of Denver and Colorado Springs. Starting in 1994, the Conservation Fund, based in Boulder, conducted a biological and geographical study of a 100,000-acre area that included Greenland Ranch, using lottery money from Great Outdoors Colorado. The study no doubt aided the December 1996 purchase of fifteen acres of the former Greenland town site by Douglas County for open space preservation. The Conservation Fund negotiated the $160,000 purchase, and the county's open-space sales tax, approved by voters in 1994, provided the funds. The tax also supported the purchase of additional open-space acreage near Greenland in the latter months of 1997 and contributed, along with funds gathered from the Conservation Fund, Great Outdoors Colorado, an anonymous donor, and various foundation groups, to the final purchase of a prodigious 21,000 acres in July 2000. This purchase permanently sealed the preservation of a twelve-mile reserve between Colorado Springs and Denver.

Larkspur School (1913–1914: builder unknown), intersection of Spruce Mountain Road and Perry Park Avenue.

Located in the heart of town, this brick building served the educational needs of Larkspur children for nearly sixty years. The side-gabled structure features double-hung sash windows and a hipped roof with several hipped dormers. The interior originally consisted of two rooms, the largest of which had a stage and hosted community events and church services. Later, the school was enlarged to include a lunchroom and kitchen, and 1960 renovations included adding storage space and the transformation of the lunchroom into another classroom.

In the 1970s, after the completion of a larger, more modern facility, the Larkspur School became a private residence. In 1999, new owners announced plans to renovate it into a leased office and retail center called Schoolhouse Office Park.

Lone Tree School (1922: Leo Grout, builder), County Highway 105, 7½ miles south of Wolfensberger Road. **On private property.**

This one-room schoolhouse sits on a concrete foundation and features double-hung windows, lap siding, and a metal roof. An attached covered porch, a later addition, is located on the south side. The flooring is oak hardwood throughout.

Leo Grout constructed the school in 1922 after citizens determined that the first school, built by his father, Newton Grout, in 1872, was too small for the growing community needs. Mary Stewart Benn, granddaughter of Newton Grout, remembers attending the school that her grandfather built and the preparations of the schoolteacher before each class day began:

> The teacher had to build the fire. She had to get the water there or we wouldn't have any water to drink otherwise. And she had to see that we got our horses tied in the barn.[25]

A February 1896 issue of the *Castle Rock Journal* described a special Valentine's Day celebration at the first Lone Tree School:

> The boys and girls went in the morning dressed in their good clothes and their best manners, for they expected company in the afternoon. About two o-clock the teams began to arrive and at half past the exercises began. "America," sung by everybody, was followed by recitations and more songs by the school. Then came a valentine box in which all were much interested. Each of the children received from two to six apiece. A short recess followed so all could look at and admire their gifts from Cupid, when someone raised a shout as a big boy came in carrying a huge ice cream freezer and others followed with spoons and dishes. Then came a treat of nuts, candy, oranges, apples, fruit-cake and ice cream which they all enjoyed very much.[26]

The first school building was moved to a nearby ranch where it was used as an icehouse. The 1922 building was used as a school until approximately 1937 and was placed on the State Register of Historic Properties in 1995. No evidence remains of the barn and privy that stood near the school.

Notes

1. Marita Hayes, "D. C. Oakes, Early Colorado Booster," *Colorado Magazine*, vol. 31, no. 3, July 1954, pp. 216–224.

2. *Castle Rock Journal*, quoted in Josephine Lowell Marr, *Douglas County: A Historical Journey* (Gunnison, Colo.: B&B Printers, 1983), pp. 188–189.

3. *Castle Rock Journal*, July 5, 1882, p. 3.

4. Ibid., March 8, 1882, p. 3.

5. Ibid., July 16, 1897, p. 3.

6. *Denver Times*, January 7, 1901, p. 4.

7. *Castle Rock Journal*, June 25, 1890, p. 1.

8. Wilbur Fiske Stone, ed., *History of Colorado* (Chicago: S. J. Clark Publishing, 1913), IV, p. 406.

9. *Record-Journal of Douglas County*, December 16, 1921, p. 3.

10. *West Creek Mining News and the Nighthawk Mountain Echo*, July 29, 1899, p. 1.

11. *The Mountain Echo*, March 12, 1898, p. 1.

12. *Denver Times*, December 31, 1900, p. 1; *Castle Rock Journal*, January 4, 1901, p. 1.

13. *Record-Journal of Douglas County*, July 5, 1929, p. 1.

14. Ibid., December 16, 1921, p. 3.

15. The American Federation of Human Rights, "American Co-Masonry," n.d., Larkspur, Colorado.

16. *Denver Post*, March 14, 1969, p. 21; March 24, 1971, p. 36.

17. Ibid., January 4, 1987, p. 1.

18. *Rocky Mountain News*, February 8, 1987, p. 10.

19. Ibid., April 9, 1987, p. 33.

20. *Douglas County News Press*, November 20, 1996, p. 10A; September 11, 1996, p. 8A; April 3, 1996, p. 1A.

21. *Castle Rock Journal* August 31, 1900, p. 1.

22. The Union Real Estate, Live Stock and Investment Company, *Prospectus of the Greenland Stock Farm*, 1893, p. 7, Douglas County Historic Preservation Board files, Local History Collection, Philip S. Miller Library.

23. *Castle Rock Journal*, January 25, 1888, p. 4.

24. *Record-Journal of Douglas County*, February 1, 1918, p. 1.

25. Mary Stewart Benn and Amy Stewart Higginson, Oral History Tape, August 9, 1993, Local History Collection, Philip S. Miller Library.

26. *Castle Rock Journal*, February 19, 1896, p. 1.

LOUVIERS

With [Du Pont's] control the personnel of the village is kept the most desirable.
—Record-Journal of Douglas County, December 16, 1921

Quiet, secluded Louviers is arguably Douglas County's most unique town. Constructed, owned, and maintained by the Du Pont Company, the town originally consisted of explosives factory plant employees and their families. Although the factory's dynamite production fizzled with time, its influence over the town and its residents remains into the twenty-first century.

Louviers inherited its name from two other industrial towns. Louviers, France, the center of the woolen industry in France, was located near the hometown of Eleuthere Irenee du Pont, a French gunpowder maker. Sometime before the 1880s, Victor Marie du Pont, E. I. du Pont's brother, traveled to the United States. He established a woolen-cloth factory along Brandywine Creek in New Castle County, Delaware, and named the new community after the French town of the same name. By 1880, the du Pont family had formed E. I. du Pont de Nemours and Company and expanded its interests from textile production to the explosives industry, with the construction of a dynamite plant in Gibbstown, New Jersey.

By the turn of the century, the Du Pont Company was looking toward the Rocky Mountain region as a potential branch location for their dynamite manufacturing business. Because the nearest explosive suppliers to Colorado and most of the Western territory were located in Missouri and California, the developing mountain region desperately needed a centrally located dynamite producer to aid in railroad and highway construction, land clearings, and mineral extractions. In 1906, the Du Pont Company began construction of a branch factory on land purchased from Jacob C. Jones along Plum Creek in northern Douglas County, Colorado. Company officials selected the site for its proximity to Denver, where there was an adequate labor force, and to mountain mining operations.

The Douglas County site also offered convenient access to railroad facilities. In the 1870s, the Denver & Rio Grande Railroad had constructed a siding about four miles north of Sedalia on property owned by rancher Jonathan Kelly and later added a telephone-telegraph station called Toluca, named after a Mexican state capitol. In August 1906, as construction of the Du Pont explosives factory, named Louviers Works, progressed, workers routed spur lines from the tracks at Toluca to the factory to aid in the freighting of dynamite to outside markets. That year the *Castle Rock Journal* beamed with high expectations for the factory's future:

> It is the purpose of the powder trust to make the Colorado plant one of the largest in the United States, outside of Wilmington. The number of buildings will eventually reach 100. All will be comparatively small, in consonance with the hazardous character of the industry. The office building will be 46x50 feet and two stories in height. Besides the manufacturing plant there will be others for the generation of electricity used in the factory. Houses will also be built for the use of 400 employees of the industry. The Colorado plant will manufacture explosives, not only for the Rocky Mountain region, but also for the great west and the Orient.[1]

While the company constructed its first powder facilities, a small town called Louviers developed nearby. The town's name was only one indication of the influence the plant and the du Pont family would ultimately have on the area. In addition to guiding the growth of the plant, Du Pont's leaders supervised the town's development as well. Production of high explosives for commercial use began in 1908, and a village of workers' tents, adobe huts, and homes dug into hillsides soon sprung up adjacent to the plant. Homes belonging to top officials of the plant occupied "Management Row" atop a nearby hill. Before long, the company assumed the role of landlord by arranging construction of houses that were rented to employees for $8 to $27 a month. The company supplied electricity and coal to residents and also tended to the aesthetic development of the town by planting trees and establishing lawns.

Also in 1908, the company completed the Louviers Club, a clubhouse for the recreational use of employees. It was replaced by a larger building in 1917. During the grand opening of the new clubhouse, Du Pont officials welcomed the general public for a night of free merriment:

> The lid came off Louviers Friday night in celebration of the opening of the Louviers Club. . . . It was some party. The entertainment committee in charge of the affair got Morrison's negro Jazz band from Denver and they tore off the rag in fine style and gave everybody a good time. The Club's bowling alleys, pool and billiard table were thrown open to the public and the people who did not care to dance availed themselves of this opportunity to enjoy the Club's hospitality. It was certainly a representative bunch that gathered to celebrate this event. People from all over Douglas County as well as from Denver and other parts of the state got together to help the affair be a success, and success it was for everybody there.[2]

In 1912, Du Pont officials built a hotel to house single workers. Demolished in the early 1930s, the two-story hotel consisted of thirty-three rooms, a grocery store, dining room, pool hall, and a post office, which began service on June 25, 1907. Plant management also hired a village doctor to attend the medical needs of their employees and families and ensured educational opportunities by erecting a three-room schoolhouse in 1912.

In 1915, diverse businesses such as a general merchandise store, livery stable, and dairy producer began to take root in the town. By the mid-1920s, the population climbed to 450 and the Louviers Community Church was constructed to serve the religious needs of the inhabitants. The growth served as an indication of the Du Pont Company's commitment to the survival and steady progression of the town. The *Record-Journal of Douglas County* expressed its approval of the company's firm commitment to the community:

> Ten years ago Louviers was a veritable mushroom camp. Families lived in a triangle of tents and a row of adobe houses, with a generous intermingling of boxboard shanties. There were no streets, and the roads in and out were almost impassable. Not a modern convenience was enjoyed. Water was carried from a distance. There was no electricity, no sewerage, no fire protection. Sanitary conditions were poor, and rank growths of weeds covered the entire site. . . . This was the past: the embryo Louviers. . . . The entire village and equipment is owned and maintained by the du Pont Company. Every man with the exception of the local merchant and his assistants is in its employ. With this control the personnel of the village is kept the most desirable. The development has been roughly traced. The village of Louviers now has all the necessary municipal buildings. There are ninety good, comfortable homes, equipped with running water, bath, electric lights and furnace heat. Each home has a well-fenced yard, with lawn and trees in front and a generous garden spot in the rear. . . . The village has a modern sewage system and adequate fire protection. The streets are well kept and electrically lighted at night. There are large civic lawns, with flowers and trees, replacing the old weed patches. The most sanitary conditions are maintained. Every trace of debris is removed weekly. . . . Good roads lead in and out in all directions. . . . This is the present Louviers. Progress, achievement, and growth are measured by means of comparison.[3]

In hopes of generating similar positive media reviews of their plant, Du Pont officials invited the Central District Press Association to tour Louviers Works in June 1935. Afterward, a *Record-Journal of Douglas County* reporter expressed a newfound respect for the dynamite manufacturing business:

> To one who has never had the opportunity of taking a trip through such a plant, it is a revelation of just how little the average person knows about the operations of such a plant. . . . After visiting such a plant one comes away with his non-technical head so full of technical terms, and has traveled around over so much territory to visit different parts of the plant which are scattered around over a half section of land, that he decides that it is "SOME" job to make a stick of dynamite.[4]

As some unfortunate workers learned, however, the job of making dynamite sticks is often dangerous. In 1908, a nitroglycerin explosion claimed the life of one Du Pont employee, and three years later, residents woke to the thundering of another deadly blast.

> On Monday morning at about 7:35 o'clock, a large amount of nitroglycerine approximating 2500 pounds, exploded at the Du Pont Powder Works located at Louviers, which resulted in the instant death of three of

> the employees who were on duty in that part of the plant, demolished two of the buildings where this explosive was being manufactured, and caused such a terrific shock that it was felt for many miles in every direction from the plant. The report of the explosion was plainly heard at Castle Rock.[5]

After this tragedy, Du Pont's safety record, hailed as "one of the best in the country," remained unblemished until 1940, when an explosion of 1,600 pounds of dynamite claimed the lives of two men who were "literally blown to bits."[6] Another blast in 1947 resulted in only one employee injury and shaky nerves among nearby residents.

> A terrific blast rocked south Denver and suburban communities about 5:30 p.m. Thursday, scattered splintered wood over a five-mile area and leveled a small building at the E.I. du Pont de Nemours & Co.'s Louviers plant. . . . The explosion occurred when a ton of dynamite, believed to have been ignited by an electrical short in the company's waste house at Louviers plant, caught fire and a minute later blew up in an earth-shaking roar, spurting billows of smoke resembling that caused by an atomic fission. . . . The blast reportedly shattered all windows in the plant's buildings . . . and blew out a window in a church a half mile distant. Damage was estimated at $20,000.[7]

Residents of Louviers, acutely aware of the risks involved in living at the foot of an explosive manufacturing plant, proved unshakeable and the town continued to prosper. In 1950, Louviers supported a population of 350 and featured a general store, garage, radio and appliance dealership, and the Louviers Club, Louviers Club Library, and Louviers Community Church. Du Pont Company employees and their families helped their employer celebrate its fiftieth anniversary at an open house at the plant in June 1958. Prior to the celebration, Daniel W. Ashburn, plant manager, pointed to Du Pont's blasting role in the construction of the Pikes Peak Highway, Moffat and Blue River tunnels, Glen Canyon Dam, and major mineral mining operations as evidence of the success and value of the company's products throughout Colorado and the West.

At times, the strength of Louviers's explosives was belittled by the invincible wrath of Mother Nature. In 1954, heavy rainfall caused a flood along Plum Creek that swept away an emergency bridge. The bridge had been constructed for use in the event that both the railroad and highway bridges that provided access to the town were damaged. The *Rocky Mountain News* claimed the flood "ripped off beams from the emergency bridge and sent logs and other debris shooting down the swollen stream smashing first into the rail bridge and then the main bridge down stream."[8] With all three bridges destroyed, the town was cut off from the rest of the world for two days. Eleven years later, the powerful 1965 Plum Creek flood also swallowed the bridges, along with Louviers's sewage and water systems. The rebuilt bridges were destroyed again in 1973; this time, only the main bridge was reconstructed.

During the early 1960s, the Du Pont Company began to wean the maturing town from its attentive guardianship. A company decision in 1962 to sell land and houses to town residents, and to deed streets and parkways to the county, placed community improvements and civic affairs in the hands of its residents for the first time. Shortly after these transactions, residents formed an informal town council that had no legal basis, but would study the community's problems. Du Pont retained its control of land surrounding the core of the town upon which it vowed "there will be no subdividing," and donated the Louviers Club to the county in 1975.

The late 1960s saw the industrial nature of Louviers strengthen with the opening of two additional manufacturing plants. The first of these, Yttrium Corporation of America, a subsidiary of Molybdenum Corporation of America and Pyrites Company, produced yttrium oxide. A rare earth material, yttrium oxide, when combined with another substance, europium oxide, makes up the red phosphorus used in color television tubes, microwave devices, and mercury vapor lamps. The Ensign Bickford Company, which produced safety fuses and detonating cords, opened its Louviers plant in 1967 and two years later enlarged the facility to double its capacity.

During the early 1970s, as other industries intensified their presence in the area, the Du Pont Company continued to loosen its grip on Louviers. In 1971, citing "a continuing decline in the demand for dynamite brought about by greatly increased use of lower cost blasting agents," officials announced that the plant would cease making dynamite and reduce its employee size from 145 to 40.[9] Just before this modification took place, the plant's dynamite production concluded with a bang when an enormous blast and fire at a dynamite packing shed killed four employees. The cause of the explosion, as with most of the company's previous tragedies, was never determined.

Du Pont's cutback in employees had an unforeseen consequence for the town. Since its completion in 1908, the plant operated three shifts, which meant local men were available around the clock to respond to fire alarms. However, when the plant cut back to just one shift in 1971, the number of men available to volunteer as firefighters during daytime hours dwindled drastically. Louviers women provided the answer. After fire damaged a house during the spring of 1971 because no one was available to respond to the call, twelve Louviers "female smoke eaters" volunteered their services to the Louviers Fire Protection District. The women completed intense training in the operation of fire trucks, firefighting safety, and emergency medical assistance.

In 1980, voters approved a $125,000 bond issue to pay for the construction of a new fire station, a 500-gallon pumper truck, and a 250-gallon rescue vehicle. Shortly after this larger operation began, many fire department officials expressed resentment toward what they felt was exploitation of their services by residents who lived outside the fire district. Reportedly, nonresidents expected a response to calls but declined annexation to the district for fear of increased taxes. Finally, the department announced that starting January 1, 1981, it would no longer respond to calls outside the district boundaries unless the calls were from areas having agreements with Louviers.

Disputes continued to affect Louviers into the early 1980s. In 1982–1983, Colorado Disposal targeted a site near the town as a potential landfill location. Because nearly 94 percent of the intended trash would originate in Denver, Arapahoe, and Jefferson counties, town residents told the *Rocky Mountain News* they didn't "want other people's trash in [their] front yard and intend[ed] to do something about it."[10] Refusing to become "the dumping ground" of other counties, town residents rallied at a town meeting and vowed to stop the proposal. In addition to citing the landfill's potential to pollute local water and create an eyesore, residents argued that the proposal violated county standards that required a landfill site to be 500 feet from private property and 1,000 feet from a residential area. In a passionate letter to the *Douglas County News Press*, a fourteen-year-old Louviers girl pleaded with county residents to join her town in their landfill fight:

> People on our side of the county are fighting to stop the proposal but we need people from other parts of the county, too. They need to learn or understand that this could affect them just as much. If they travel down Santa Fe they will need to have time to spend waiting on traffic. The big truck[s] will destroy the roads and cause traffic jams.[11]

The girl's pleas helped motivate more than 150 county residents who packed the Douglas County Commissioners Hearing Room on March 8, 1983, to protest the proposal. The Planning Commission recommended denial of the plan, but before the Douglas County Board of County Commissioners could make the final decision, Colorado Disposal, bending under countywide pressure, withdrew its landfill request in April, much to the relief of the Louviers community.

As controversy united Louviers residents, the end of an era was close at hand for the small community. In October 1988, the forty remaining Du Pont employees learned that their jobs were in jeopardy as plant officials announced a possible closure of Louviers Works. "It's disappointing that all of us have devoted that much time and effort to a business that is 80 years old and built a business that has the potential of closing down," plant manager Richard Kuhn told the *Douglas County News Press*.[12] Although a sharp decrease in the demand for high explosives forced the Du Pont plant to close its doors, its influence on the town continues. Years after the plant's closing, Louviers residents still relied upon the decisions and policies of Du Pont.

In the late 1990s, with only a skeleton crew of workers at the plant, company officials examined the possibility of abandoning or selling it. The U.S. Environmental Protection Agency, however, called on Du Pont to conduct a cleanup of the site and surrounding area before any action could be taken. Residents, who had hitherto enjoyed the buffer zone of Du Pont land encircling their town, feared that the factory owners would someday sell it to developers. A resounding desire throughout the town was that Du Pont officials would eventually donate acreage for use as a greenbelt. Fran Snyder, librarian at the Louviers branch of the Douglas Public Library District and a fifteen-year resident, expressed her concern over the impact of development upon village life:

> What we would hope Du Pont would consider is kind of a greenbelt around our town because it would look real funny to have a Highlands Ranch right up bordering our old homes. The folks love living here. It's very secluded and no one knows it's here. It would be awful to have subdivisions around us.

In the late 1990s, fear of development inspired many residents to pursue nomination of the entire village as a protected historic district. After years of researching Louviers's history and consulting with historic preservation specialists concerning the benefits of such a nomination, the entire town was placed on the National Register of Historic Places as a historic district in July 1999.

In Louviers, time has seemingly stood still. The village has remained relatively untouched by modern growth. New home construction is almost nonexistent, as residents prefer the old Du Pont homes. Virtually the only way to live in Louviers is to wait for someone to sell their home. Much of the innocence and seclusion of the town can be attributed to Du Pont, its former landlord. With the creation and maintenance of a company town, Du Pont guided community growth and still holds influence through its ownership of land surrounding the village. Although the company no longer owns Louviers, the influence of the town's explosive parent will linger indefinitely.

Louviers Historic Sites

Keystone Ranch (1880s?: Jonathan Kelly, builder), Kelly Avenue, immediately west of Santa Fe Drive. **Private residence.**

Located along the west side of bustling U.S. Highway 85, just north of the Louviers town entrance, this unpretentious property was once a bustling ranch and community hub. In 1860, Ohio native Jonathan P. Kelly filed a squatter's claim upon the property before enlisting in a six-month term of service with the Colorado Home Guards the following year. Upon his return, Kelly, a well-known farmer and hunter, frequently hauled wood to Denver for income and operated a steam mill for grinding grain.

Among Douglas County's most popular establishments from the 1860s through the turn of the century, Keystone Ranch became an important stage station for travelers of the First Territorial Road between Denver and Colorado City. The postal service established an office at the site on April 7, 1863, and the Denver & Rio Grande Railroad added a siding in the 1870s and later a telephone-telegraph station called Toluca. In 1907, when the Du Pont Company completed its explosives manufacturing plant at the future site of Louviers, William C. Kelly, Jonathan Kelly's second son, envisioned a new direction for his father's ranch. With superior railroad, postal, and communication facilities, William promoted the property as "a new town, named Kelly," and assured *Castle Rock Journal* readers that it would "become the most populous in Douglas County":

> While the workmen employed at the [DuPont] powder mills will live near the scene of their work, which is two miles from Kelly, it is expected that the business which the powder industry will develop will be transacted at the new town. Both the Rio Grande and the Santa Fe companies have established stations at Kelly, and the former has erected a station building. One block in the new town has been sold for a hotel. Sites have been sold, also, for a bank, grocery store, general store, meat market, lumber yard, and a number of homes.[13]

Although the town of Kelly endured for several years as a major shipping point for Du Pont products, shoppers preferred to take the train to the thriving town of Littleton to conduct their business. Additionally, Du Pont officials provided adequate grocery, entertainment, and living accommodations for its Louviers residents. Consequently, the town of Kelly did not prosper as its founder had hoped. Today, the vestiges of this early community include two immense barns, a stone silo, and several utility shacks.

Louviers Village Club (1917: builder unknown), 7885 Louviers Boulevard.

This building features a grand block end chimney that towers over the structure and several gabled dormers. Constructed of red brick, the former clubhouse is L-shaped with a gabled roofline that spans two stories. The building currently houses a branch of the Douglas Public Library District, a gymnasium/auditorium with a stage and high vaulted ceiling, a large kitchen, and a reception room. Perhaps the greatest attraction, however, is the bowling alley, reportedly the oldest surviving alley in Colorado, with maple lanes and hand-loaded pin setters.

Set among towering evergreen trees, the Louviers Village Club recalls Louviers's early days as a company town. Du Pont officials had the building constructed in 1917 for use as a clubhouse for employees. Membership was obligatory, with fifty cents a month automatically deducted from each employee's paycheck. In their visits to the club, women confined their activities to the upstairs "women's talk room," except during monthly club dances, when they were welcome downstairs as well. The building also housed a grocery store/post office, soda shop, and billiards room. In 1918, one year after its construction, the clubhouse was converted to a temporary hospital during the worldwide flu epidemic.

In 1963, after Du Pont Company officials leased the Louviers Village Club to the town, residents formed the Village Club Board to oversee maintenance and operation of the building. In 1975, citing high taxes, the Du Pont Company donated the club to Douglas County for the use of county residents. Throughout ownership changes, the building continued to receive the attention of caring Village Club Board members, who celebrated its designation to the National Register of Historic Places on September 22, 1995.

Notes

1. *Castle Rock Journal*, August 3, 1906, p. 1; May 10, 1907, p. 1.
2. *Record-Journal of Douglas County*, November 2, 1917, p. 8.
3. Ibid., December 16, 1921, p. 3.
4. Ibid., June 21, 1935, p. 1.
5. Ibid., June 26, 1908, p. 1; July 21, 1911, p. 1.
6. *Denver Post*, February 6, 1940, p. 1; February 7, 1940, pp. 1, 5.
7. Ibid., June 27, 1947, pp. 1, 5; *Rocky Mountain News*, June 28, 1947, p. 11.
8. *Rocky Mountain News*, July 23, 1954, p. 33.
9. *Douglas County News*, January 14, 1971, p. 1; E. I. DuPont de Nemours & Company, "75th Anniversary: Louviers Works, 1908–1983," p. 6.
10. *Rocky Mountain News*, March 3, 1983, p. 70.
11. *Douglas County News Press*, March 9, 1983, p. 4A.
12. Ibid., October 11, 1988, p. 1; December 27, 1988, p. 2.
13. *Castle Rock Journal*, May 10, 1907, p. 1.

PARKER

This is where the weary traveler can get a good, square meal and the best quality of refreshments of a hot day.
—Castle Rock Journal, June 27, 1883

The present-day controversy over growth management in Parker is not new. The issue of growth has long played a role in the town's history. As in most budding western settlements, Parker's pioneers were eager to see their town develop and prosper, but as it grew, there were those who wanted to see the town retain its small-town atmosphere. The conflict between keeping Parker a friendly, peaceful small town and the push for progress and growth has divided residents, businesses, and politicians into pro-growth and anti-growth factions.

Parker's development stemmed in part from its location at the junction of two of Colorado's most-traveled pioneer trails, the Smoky Hill and the Cherokee. In 1864, George Long purchased a one-room cabin located on the George Lord Ranch, about one-and-a-half miles south of present-day downtown Parker, and had the structure moved to the convergence of the trails. Alfred Butters had built the cabin in 1863 to serve as the region's post office and called it Pine Grove after a clump of pine trees located nearby. After Long moved the cabin, it became part of the 20-Mile House, so named for its distance from Denver along Cherry Creek; the settlement that grew up around it retained the name Pine Grove. At 20-Mile House, weary travelers could rest, wash, and exchange their worn, tired horses, oxen, and mules for fresh animals, which allowed them to make a grand entrance into Denver. In an interview that appeared in a 1936 issue of *Colorado Magazine*, Mrs. Elizabeth Tallman claimed she and her sister were the first visitors to the station in 1865. She described the appearance of the building and the steps the proprietors took to ensure a good night's rest for their guests:

> There was only the kitchen, with no windows as yet, and a piece of old carpet served as a door. We were the first travelers to stop there, and Mr. and Mrs. Long had to sleep out-of-doors, as we had their bed. In the night, the coyote chorus kept the dog barking so that we could not sleep, but after a time he quieted down. The next morning I asked Mrs. Long about the dog. She said, "I got up and hung the little devil," and we thought it a most effective way to stop his barking.[1]

Six months after her stay at 20-Mile House, Elizabeth married John Tallman and moved to a ranch just two miles east of the stage stop.

During the 1860s, when clashes between local Indian tribes

and white pioneers reached a peak, frightened families refused to settle in the isolated communities outside Denver, so Elizabeth's presence in Pine Grove during this time was unusual. By the 1870s and early 1880s, the Indian threat in the region had faded and "people were becoming less afraid to get out in the open."[2] Among the newcomers to Pine Grove during the 1870s was the Parker family. A former Smoky Hill stage driver, James Sample Parker managed the Kiowa Creek Stage Station before purchasing the 20-Mile House. As traffic along the trails bustled and the town grew, Parker met the expanding demand for services by adding a blacksmith shop, a general mercantile store, an ox shoeing hoist, and the area's first official post office.

Perhaps hoping to promote further growth in Pine Grove, Parker granted a right-of-way to the Denver & New Orleans Railroad (known as the Colorado & Southern after 1898) in June 1881, and a depot was built along present-day Mainstreet. The deed instructed the railroad to construct necessary ditches and cattle guards along a one-hundred-foot-wide strip of land through the town. Starting in May 1882, "Polliwog," as the townspeople grew to refer to the train, began regularly clanging and chugging through the Pine Grove settlement. When traffic along the trails gradually decreased as a result of easier, more efficient travel by train, the prudent Mr. Parker welcomed the new travelers to his stage stop. Shortly after Parker began catering to the rail patrons, his continued success led the *Castle Rock Journal* to report, "James Parker, of the 20-mile house, is receiving a good run of trade. This is where the weary traveler can get a good, square meal and the best quality of refreshments of a hot day. Mr. Parker is a clever gentleman with whom to stop."[3]

In addition to luring travelers away from stage companies, the railroad also displaced the stages as mail carriers. Although the Pine Grove townspeople enjoyed the speedy delivery of their mail, the change posed a serious problem for the settlement. Another town along the South Platte River also claimed the name Pine Grove, and this duplication created confusion for the postal service. Parker suggested that the name of his settlement be changed to Edithville in honor of his daughter, but postal authorities objected to the length of the name. Instead, they preferred to use the name "Parker's," which was already in use for the railroad station. In the early 1880s, when the state government stipulated that the *s* be dropped from all applicable Colorado towns, the name became "Parker." The *Castle Rock Journal* reported the decision: "The name of the 20-Mile station, on the D. & N.O.R.R. has been changed to Parker, in honor of Jas. S. Parker, a worthy citizen of that place. The JOURNAL extends congratulations."[4]

Many farmers, ranchers, and miners around Parker capitalized on the opportunity afforded by the new form of transportation for the bounty they were producing. Soon the train out of Parker carried lumber, coal, livestock, and vegetables. Ranching and farming in particular flourished in the area during the 1880s and 1890s. At times, the prolific harvests of Parker's farms spawned an unusual predicament for their owners:

> The farmers on Cherry creek from Franktown to Parker have had abundant crops this season. Oats, corn and hay have all been a success. Much of the alfalfa has been cut three times. Everybody has plenty of feed and the question now is what is to be done with it. Shall we sell it in the market or buy steers to feed seems to be the question for decision just now.[5]

Reportedly, E. R. Parsons operated one of the most successful farms in the region. A master of dry farming techniques, Parsons stunned locals with his ability to transform the arid plains into lush fruit tree orchards:

> E. R. Parsons of Parker, Douglas county has been quite successful in producing a dry orchard. Trees planted in the spring of 1895 are now from ten to fifteen feet high with a spread of from seven to ten feet. One lot of forty cherries gave a yield of 400 quarts last year. He has succeeded, without any watering whatever, in growing cherries, plums, apples, pears, currants, gooseberries, caneberries, and a few peaches. He plants very close in a row and heads as low as the habits of the tree will allow. Some day this season Mr. Parsons will tell us how he has managed to do all these wonderful things in the desert land.[6]

In the 1890s, the town of Parker became one of many dairy producers in the Denver region with the opening of the Littleton Creamery. The dairy was constructed on land donated by George Parker, brother of James. In 1897, the *Castle Rock Journal* announced that Parkerites and residents of nearby Hill Top were preparing for an active dairying season. The train reportedly transported a carload of milk from the large wooden building to Denver every day.

Parker also encouraged merchant enterprises and other town businesses. By 1900, with a budding population of 253, the town boasted two hotels, three general mercantile stores, and two blacksmith shops. Nevertheless, Parker had only one saloon from 1893 through the early 1900s, despite the admonitions of the *Castle Rock Journal* editor, who grieved in 1896, "Parker is long on thirst and short on saloon."[7] Parkerites' lack of interest in the saloon business, and particularly the shady characters that usually accompanied these establishments, revealed an early desire among its residents to grow and succeed but not at the expense of peace in their town.

From the 1880s through the turn of the century, the circumstances of Parker's location encouraged more growth. In the 1880s, gold strikes began about one and a half miles southwest of the town and eventually culminated into the formation of a gold mining district known as Newlin Gulch, named after William Newlin, an early settler and rancher in the area. The usual optimistic and inflated reports of mining success at Newlin Gulch abounded in the *Castle Rock Journal*:

> Mr. S. A. Hammond, gold placer miner on Newland [sic] gulch, exhibited to a News reporter yesterday a magnificent button of the purest Cherry Creek gold. This represented the work of two men sluicing for one day, and was taken from twenty-five cubic yards of earth from the hillside or grass roots. The button was taken to Mr. E. E. Burlingame, the assayer, who found that it weighed 33 ounces and was worth $16.18. This would be an average of 65 cents per yard, the lowest this rich gulch has shown anywhere. Mr. Hammond is confident that he can double this result in the same time. . . . When these experiments develop what is universally believed of the vast wealth scattered over the Divide, the whole world shall know it.[8]

A few years later the *Castle Rock Journal* announced that the "mining boom on Newlin Gulch west of town is growing now.

The miners seem to be doing fairly well at the business if one can judge from the numbers that go in there almost daily."[9] Mining operations intensified into the 1890s with the development of several mining companies such as the American, Muldoon, Union, Maribelle, and Uncle Sam. Miners reported an estimated gold extraction value of $2 to $20 to the ton. Despite such encouraging reports, lack of water and low-quality ore eventually caused the demise of mining operations in the gulch in the early 1900s.

By the 1920s, Parker had become an important business region for the county. Three grocery stores, a hardware store, an automobile garage, a blacksmith shop, a newspaper, and several outlying ranches and farms supported a population of 414. Undoubtedly, the jewel of the town was its bank.

> The Parker State Bank attends to things financial in that corner of the county. This institution was established some eight or ten years ago and has, by courteous treatment and service, built up a good business.[10]

On November 29, 1921, the Parker State Bank became involved in a holdup straight from the pages of a gangster novel. Miss Elizabeth Schultz, assistant cashier of the bank, was forced at gunpoint by two bandits into the bank vault while her captors made off with $10,000 cash and $4,000 worth of Liberty bonds and war savings stamps. Approximately two weeks later, Denver police apprehended Ernest Krueger, alias "Big Ed Whitney," Ray "Blackie" Thomas, and Lee Norris; a fourth suspect, known as Jim "Two Gun" Brady, was caught in Casper, Wyoming. The men were charged not only with the Parker crime but also several others around Denver. Most of the stolen bank money was recovered from a suitcase hidden at Union Station in Denver.

Despite these occasional episodes of excitement, Parker remained a serenely placid, slowly growing town well into the 1930s. Businesses had grown to include one gas station, three general merchandise stores, the Cherry Creek Telephone Company, two oil companies, the Douglas County Bank, and the shops of a barber, jeweler, and blacksmith.

Although the distant whistle of the Colorado & Southern (C&S) locomotive occasionally interrupted the peace of the town, the train did not run through Parker as often as it had in the early days. An 1899 Denver–Pueblo joint-line agreement between C&S and the Santa Fe Railroad Company resulted in a re-routing of most C&S trains through Castle Rock, and downgraded the line through Parker to branch status. The change ended Parker's time as an important rail town. An increase in automobile travel and a predilection for truck freighting in the 1920s led to a further reduction of traffic along the Parker railroad branch. The final blow occurred over Memorial Day 1935, when a flash flood on Cherry Creek caused enormous damage to the C&S rail line. C&S officials finally acquiesced to their string of bad luck and asked the Interstate Commerce Commission to allow an abandonment of the line. "There's no two ways about it, the road will be missed in more ways than one, if it is allowed to be junked," mourned the *Record-Journal of Douglas County*.[11] Nonetheless, the ICC granted the request, and the track and sidings were removed by the fall of 1936.

Despite this loss, town citizens continued to take pride in their heritage. On February 1, 1946, a group of Parker pioneers and residents joined representatives of the Colorado Historical Society in dedicating a historical marker to commemorate the 20-Mile House. "Everyone who can, should make arrangements to attend this event," commanded the *Record-Journal of Douglas*

County on the day of the unveiling.[12] The marker was constructed from indigenous petrified wood gathered by Parker schoolchildren.

Located in the heart of downtown, the historical marker continues to pay homage to the town's heritage. Yet it is a heritage that some feel is being seriously ignored today. The heated growth debate that engulfs current Parker politics, business, and emotions can be traced through three decades' worth of decisions concerning the town's future.

From late 1969 to 1974, while owned by the Parker City Land Company, the town saw its most devastating defacement. In 1970, Lewis and Thomas Scifo, the company's owners, decided to reconstruct Parker into a town of "western-Victorian décor," anchored by a restaurant called Ruby Palace. Anticipating that the transformation would attract tourists, the Scifos destroyed more than a dozen pre-1920s buildings that, according to one local historian, apparently "weren't gaudy enough" to sufficiently transform the rural settlement into a "rip roaring Western town." The company declared bankruptcy in 1974, however, leaving more than 1,600 acres of land, including the main business district and several housing developments, to Bankers Trust of New York, the company's primary lender. Bankers Trust placed it on the market, where it remained for two years before being purchased by Nicholson Enterprises. Faced with an insufficient water and sanitation district and inadequate water storage facilities, owner Jim Nicholson paid $1.5 million toward the construction of a three-million-gallon water storage plant for the town. The *Denver Post* claimed the move allowed Nicholson to "more easily woo home builders" to the area.[13]

In February 1981, town citizens—in an effort to "take the future of Parker out of the hands of the Board of County Commissioners and put it into the hands of a Town Board"—voted to make Parker the third incorporated town in the county.[14] Dean Salisbury was seated as mayor, and a Quonset hut that had been used as a community center since the 1950s, served as a town hall. The incorporated area of Parker spanned approximately one square mile, totaled 285 people, and included Rowley Downs subdivision, the downtown area, and Parker Square commercial center. The passage of a sign ordinance by the Parker Planning Commission represented one of the first attempts to salvage what remained of Parker's small-town atmosphere. The ordinance called for smaller signs and encouraged shopping centers with several stores to put up only one identification sign listing the businesses.

In 1984, the *Denver Post* reported, "The philosophy of the town board and the planning commission is to approach the flowering of Parker with care and concern and conscientious, detailed planning."[15] Nevertheless, it was during this year that Parker's population soared from 500 to 1,200 with the annexation of the Villages of Parker, Town and Country Village, Stroh Ranch, and Sagewood subdivisions. The June 1984 annexation of more than two thousand acres that comprised Stroh Ranch doubled the town's size overnight and advanced town limits to within two and a half miles of Castle Rock.

Despite the construction of three shopping centers, two fast-food restaurants, and the annexations of three more subdivisions, town officials still felt they had firm control over the town's development. A 1985 *Denver Post* article referred to Parker as "a quietly booming town of ranchers and urban runaways," and claimed the town's management set a precedent for future growth-conscious development: "Home builders and economic development agencies point to Parker as an example of how a town can keep a rein on growth while rebuilding from scratch."[16]

In 1985, Parker adopted the slogan, "We'll never be a city,

but always a town," and the local newspaper pointed to the popularity of community events as evidence of the survival of a small-town atmosphere: "Parker is still a community that puts on Halloween parties, old fashioned Christmas parties and other familial-encompassing events."[17] In August 1985, when Mainstreet was paved and brick sidewalks laid along the stretch, the town celebrated with an old-fashioned carriage parade.

During the ten years following Parker's incorporation, the town's boundaries expanded from one to thirteen square miles and the population soared from nearly 300 to more than 5,400. As development continued through 1993, with the addition of more businesses, Parker's growth rate prompted many concerned citizens to form Citizens for a Better Parker. The group devised a Managed Growth Ordinance that would limit the number of building permits issued each year through use of a lottery system. The proposal quickly sparked a heated debate. Proponents of structured, controlled growth claimed restrictions were needed in order to allow Parker to keep its rural character. Opponents claimed aggressive growth was needed to fund services in the community.

Although proponents of the ordinance failed to get the 650 signatures needed to place it on the ballot, the issue of controlled growth did not die. In July 1993, the Parker Area Historical Society, founded in 1986, authored an ordinance that would create a historic preservation board and a process for selecting structures and property to be designated as landmarks. The proposal met with vehement opposition from owners of historic properties, who were concerned that the ordinance would infringe upon their property rights. Three months later, the Parker Town Council voted to postpone a decision on the ordinance, due to the presence of much opposition. The issue resurfaced in May 1997, when former historical society president Karen Kievit submitted a proposed landmark ordinance to town officials. The ordinance called for the formation of a landmark commission to oversee historic designation of sites and to aid owners in the care and preservation of these sites. This ordinance differed from the previous one in that it called for a public hearing in the event that a property owner did not agree with the historic designation. The town council approved the ordinance in June 1997 and five months later appointed the first members of the landmark commission.

In November 1994, officials completed an updated version of Parker's Master Plan, first devised in 1985. Claiming the town's vision for the future encompassed "a community with wide open spaces, country living, and hometown friendliness," the plan outlined what were seen as the major town problems and proposed ways to achieve this vision. Road improvements and enlargements, careful consideration of the benefits of future annexations, and encouragement of commercial facilities and services were among the issues addressed in the plan. The downtown area was pinpointed as the town's center, with higher residential densities encircling it and lower densities farther out. In all, the plan defined the land-use goal for Parker: "Create a community with a separate and distinct identity, which encourages and maintains a home town image, provides for quality development, preserves open space, and fosters a sense of belonging."[18]

Some Parker area residents were willing to fight to protect their quality of life. In 1994, residents of the Pinery organized to fight a rezoning proposal for higher-density lots in an area of their community. During a November 1994 public hearing before the Douglas County Planning Commission, around 600 attendees forced the delay of a decision on the proposal. In April 1995, an estimated crowd of 800 did the same, despite the fact that the developer, Great Gulf Group of Companies, offered what some felt was a 200-acre open-space bribe to county officials in exchange for the plan's approval. A deadlock among the planning commission members in early May required a final decision by the Douglas County Board of County Commissioners. In a surprise move, Great Gulf submitted changes to its plan only two hours before the scheduled June 7 hearing with the county commissioners, and the issue once again returned to the planning commission. Although opposition to the plan delayed yet another decision in September 1995, the planning commission approved the rezoning proposal that same month, against the wishes of the majority of the Pinery residents. Shortly thereafter, the Douglas County commissioners passed the rezoning request with conditions that included a decrease in density, tree preservation, and amplified architectural controls and buffer zones.

Late 1994 and early 1995 were dramatic months for the Parker Town Council. In January 1995, despite intense opposition from residents, the council approved the annexation of a proposed development on the Jacobsen property, located at Pine Drive and Homestead Hills Road. Mayor Greg Lopez immediately vetoed the council's vote, accusing several council members of ignoring the pleas of citizens to better manage the town's growth: "The fabric of Parker, the very things that makes Parker unique, a great place to live and raise a family, is being torn apart by the ill-advised decisions being made by the majority of council."[19]

Shortly after Lopez's veto, a new group called the Parker Citizens for Recall Committee, filed recall petitions against Jack Hilbert and Duane Capps for ignoring the planning board's and citizens' wishes. The recall attempt became moot when Hilbert resigned his position in June 1995 and Capps resigned in August 1995.

However, the recall attempt teemed with controversy. Many blamed Mayor Lopez for instigating "civil war" among council members by initiating a criminal investigation into what was called an "especially cozy relationship" among certain councilmen and a local development attorney. The investigation later expanded to include all council members and even the mayor himself. Although all were absolved of criminal activity, many residents continued to question the leadership of their mayor. A *Weekly News Chronicle* editorial pleaded with the mayor to take one final action for the benefit of the town:

> Mayor Lopez's performance rating with the people of Parker is at an all time low, he doesn't take responsibility, he lies, he blames others for his mistakes and he's out of control. For the sake of the entire community, Mr. Mayor, please resign.[20]

In July 1995, a majority of Parker voters voiced their political frustrations by supporting a move to change the town's form of government from mayor-council to town administrator–council, thus removing all administrative powers from the mayor and downgrading his position to part time. Soon after, Lopez announced that he would not seek reelection, and the office passed to Gary Lasater, a local businessman, in April 1996.

In February 1995, Parker voters sent a Valentine's Day message to the town council. On a February 14 ballot, they approved the Brinker amendment, which called for unanimous approval of town council members before any land could be annexed in the next decade. Proponents of the amendment claimed it would foster more deliberation over residential growth, while opponents believed it would create an autocracy in which one member of the council could block annexations.

Although some believed Parker's approval of the amendment set a precedent that the entire state should heed, others wondered how effective the decision would be. According to the *Denver Post*, "while the new rule may keep the town from expanding much beyond its present borders, it won't necessarily limit its population. There's enough land already zoned for housing within Parker to accommodate another 40,000 residents—on top of the 10,000 now living in the community."[21]

In an August 1995 article on the antigrowth movement in the West, *Time Magazine* called the Brinker amendment "one of the toughest anti-growth initiatives in the United States." The magazine also described the effects of development within Parker:

> Once a bedroom community, Parker is bursting with new streets and new residents—and is afflicted with a new sense of dislocation. From the steps of town hall, newly constructed grayish buildings can be seen spattered across a nearby hillside; at the town's outer limits, the wooden skeletons of half built houses are strewed along the landscape.[22]

As new growth surrounded Parker, residents and officials took steps to protect the small-town atmosphere of downtown Parker without sacrificing its position as the area's business center. In February 1994, Parker received a grant from the state historical society to survey, and evaluate the economic, physical, and organizational condition of downtown and the commercial districts. The grant allowed the newly created Mainstreet Advisory Committee and RNL Design, a landscape/architectural services firm, to develop a Downtown Master Plan, which was adopted by the town council in December 1995. The original plan identified a need for reducing traffic congestion and restoring a pedestrian-oriented character to Mainstreet. A July 1996 addition to the plan envisioned the fusion of Mainstreet's east and west sides with a historic park at the site of 20-Mile House on the street's west side and the development of Parker Station, a large office/retail center, on the east side.

A 1998 suggestion by several town officials to redesign O'Brien Park and raze the antiquated Quonset hut, a community center built in the 1950s, raised the ire of many nostalgic town residents. "I have so many memories involving this building," wrote one concerned citizen. "Most are about a time and tight knit community that do not exist anymore. I wonder if the great achievement of constructing this community building is really appreciated now."[23] Members of the Parker Landmarks Commission granted the building landmark status in 1999, despite its ambiguous future.

In the late 1990s, Parker became Colorado's fastest-growing town. In mid-1999, it seemed to be bursting at the seams with a projected 22,000 population base. Some residents felt certain that growth would not overcome their town. Concerned resident and historian Loyd Glasier cited water shortages, overcrowding of public facilities, and traffic problems as deterrents to future growth in Parker, but added, "We're overcrowded, overstressed, and not overjoyed."

From its early days, Parker attracted and welcomed growth, while at the same time its townspeople often distrusted and resented it. Without the cooperation and perseverance of Parker citizens, the managed growth sentiment could be subdued by successive waves of modern development. Ironically, it is the rural surroundings and small-town atmosphere that still attract settlement to Parker today, and its town planners and officials are entangled in a frantic race against time to maintain these precious traits.

Parker Historic Sites

Fonder School (1884: Hubert Fonder, builder), 5219 State Highway 83.

The Fonder School represents a fine example of the standard one-room schoolhouse so typical of nineteenth-century rural areas. This rhyolite structure features a high gable roof and bulky lintels with square keystones above the only door and each of the six windows. A transom panel sits atop the white doorway.

In the 1860s, Miriam Fonder, determined to provide quality education for local children, held school classes in the kitchen of her log cabin along Bayou Gulch between present-day Parker and Frankstown. Later these classes were moved to a log building that her husband, Hubert Fonder, helped build, located about a quarter mile north of their home. It was into this log schoolhouse that a group of local Indians wandered one day during the 1870s, much to the surprise of the teacher and students. Mocking the students, one member of the tribe picked up a book and held it upside down for a few moments, while the petrified class continued to read aloud, too frightened to do anything else, until their visitors left.

In 1884, the log schoolhouse was replaced by the stone structure that still stands today. Because many of the children traveled on horseback from distant farms and ranches, the school grounds were fenced so the horses would not wander off.

Besides serving as the area's schoolhouse until 1949, the structure was also used as a meeting place for church services, Sunday school classes, literary and lyceum clubs, and numerous socials and fraternal organizations, dances, and suppers. The Pike's Peak Grange also held its first meetings in the building.

After using the building as a storage barn for several years, Terracor, developer of the Pinery, donated it to the Denver Southeast Suburban Water and Sanitation District in 1981. The district engaged in extensive restoration of the building and built a modern addition on its south side, which is used as office space for district employees; the older schoolroom serves as a meeting room.

McMurdo/Fonder Cemetery (1871: McMurdo family), on a ridge east of State Highway 83, just south of the Pinery Country Club; five miles south of Parker.

The stark solitude of this small family cemetery is a sharp contrast to the modern subdivision that it neighbors. There are approximately twenty-five graves in the plot, five of which have unreadable markers and at least eight that are unmarked.

Readable headstones commemorate family members and friends of the McMurdo family, whose heritage in Douglas County began in the 1870s. George and Wauchope McMurdo, natives of Glasgow, Scotland, moved their family to America in 1868. They lived in Chicago and Wisconsin before purchasing a relinquished Douglas County homestead in 1872. When he was old enough, David McMurdo, their son, filed a claim to the land adjoining his parents' homestead and moved there with his new wife, Anza Monroe, in 1884. David and Anza had five children: George, Margaret, Jenny, Grace, and Mary.

The earliest readable gravestone in the cemetery bears the date July 14, 1871, and belongs to Hubert Fonder, one of Douglas County's first pioneers, who owned property a mile south of the cemetery. Fonder's gravesite was later joined by those of the McMurdo family members, a clear indication of the closeness between the two neighboring families. After Hubert Fonder, the next burial appears to have been that of Thomas, son of George and Wauchope, who died in 1877 at the age of twelve. In the 1880s, George McMurdo encircled the burial plot of his family members with a wooden fence, which was restored by the Smoky Hill Trail Chapter of the Daughters of the American Revolution in 1980 and again by the Parker Area Historical Society in 1990.

Wauchope McMurdo (died 1884) and George McMurdo (died 1896) were laid to rest in the plot, as were the cremated ashes of David McMurdo (died 1940) and Anza McMurdo (died 1955).

The cemetery is currently owned by the Parker Area Historical Society. In 1990, when the society dedicated the cemetery, 150 descendants of the McMurdo and Fonder families were present to pay homage to their ancestors.

Newlin Cemetery (1896: Newlin family), Callaway Road.

Elizabeth Newlin died in 1896 and was buried on the Newlin family property. In 1898, William G. Newlin Sr., perhaps aware of his own impending death, set aside a small plot of land next to his wife's grave for a private family cemetery. He named his son, William Newlin Jr., and daughter, Mary Newlin, trustees of the quarter-acre graveyard before being buried there himself in October 1898 at the age of seventy-four. Mary joined them after her death in 1905, and an unknown donor placed a modern gravestone over her grave sometime after 1972.

Over the years, succeeding title transfers of the Newlin Ranch excluded the quiet cemetery. It is currently owned by the Parker Area Historical Society. The cemetery, which has only the three known graves, is in fairly good condition because of the volunteer efforts of society members. A wrought iron fence encircles the graves of William Sr. and Elizabeth Newlin, and a wooden fence encloses all three graves.

Parker Cemetery (1887), located west of State Highway 83, north of the Crossroads Shopping Center.

The spacious, highly visible cemetery that occupies a steep knoll just northwest of Mainstreet and Parker Road was not the area's first. The first burials took place on a small hill east of the present-day intersection of State Highway 83 and the E-470 Tollway. However, when the little town of Pine Grove flourished around the 20-Mile House, all those interred in the old cemetery were reburied at the present cemetery site, on land donated by James Parker.

Many of Parker's first families were buried in the cemetery. When Parker himself died in 1910, a special train from Denver, where he resided, transported his remains to the town of Parker. Here he was laid to rest near his wife, Mattie, and son, Bela H., who had died at the age of six. There is no disputing the prominence of James Parker's site in Parker Cemetery. Situated in the far southwest corner, the highest spot in the yard, Parker's granite tombstone stands approximately four feet tall and is among the largest in the cemetery. However, perhaps even more visited than Parker's grave is that of young Jonathan H. Tallman. Tallman was the younger brother of the better-known John M. Tallman, first owner of the Tallman-Newlin Ranch located outside of Parker. Elizabeth Tallman, wife of John M., recounted the day her young brother-in-law was killed:

> Mr. Tallman's brother was running cattle for us east of Kiowa in 1870. Having spent the night with us, he was

> preparing to leave the next morning, when he came back into the house, picked up my baby son and hugged him close. "Elizabeth," he said, "somehow I can hardly bear to leave today." As he left the ranch, riding a mule, my husband laughingly called out, "Better get a horse, Jonathan, the Indians will catch you sure on that slow nag." The next day we found him dead, shot in the back and scalped by the Arapahoes.[24]

His epitaph is a reminder of the often violent relations between settlers and regional Native American tribes during Douglas County's early days: "Jonathan Tallman, Aged 22 years, Killed by Indians."

The well-maintained cemetery remains in use today. Aside from an incident in 1982 in which vandals overturned fifty-two tombstones, the cemetery has remained undisturbed and well cared for.

Parker School (1915: William O'Brien, builder), 19650 E. Mainstreet.

A contrast to the simple Ruth Memorial Chapel is the Parker School, a grand, two-story, boxy structure next door. Originally established as the Parker area's school, this brick building boasts a pyramidal hipped roof with eaves, two tall chimneys, and a center gable pediment supported by ornate brackets. Most notable is the large round arch that sweeps over the main double doorway and triple fanlights. Simulated lintels and keystones frame the windows.

In 1914, resident Emma Lewis sold the land on which the building was later constructed to the school district, which then consolidated schools in Pine Grove, Plainfield, Allison, and later Hilltop and Rattlesnake. In 1958, Douglas County voters decided to consolidate the entire county, and Parker high school students were bused to Castle Rock. In the mid-1960s, the old school building was abandoned in favor of new, larger schools.

When the Parker United Methodist congregation of the Ruth Memorial Chapel next door needed more room in 1970, they bought the abandoned school. The town of Parker purchased the former school and the chapel from Parker United Methodist Church in December 1995 in order to house the Mainstreet Heritage Center, a facility designated to host recreation, cultural, and civic events for area residents.

Ruth Memorial Chapel (1912–1913: William Holmes, builder), 19650 E. Mainstreet.

This Gothic Revival wooden church rests at the eastern end of downtown Parker's busy Mainstreet. Lancet-style windows adorn the north, east, and west faces of the white, two-story church, including the bell tower, while the south face contains a single rosette window. The peaked roof of the bell tower is of pyramidal construction with flared eaves. The chapel received National Register of Historic Places status in 1989 as an example of the simple one-room building typically constructed by early pioneers for holding worship services.

In the 1880s, before the chapel was built, the towns of Parker and Franktown were among the stops of pious "Circuit Riders," religious leaders who traveled to outlying districts to deliver their spiritual messages. The most significant of these riders was Father John Dyer, whose traveling religious sermons extended far across the territory. Before the construction of the Ruth Memorial Chapel, he and another rider, the Reverend McClure, preached in an old schoolhouse built by the town's namesake, James S. Parker.

Around 1910, the four-year-old son of County Superintendent of Schools Dr. Walter Heath asked his father why Parker did not have a Sunday School. Thus began Dr. Heath's dream of erecting a Methodist church in Parker. In 1912, he donated the land and $1,000 for its construction. The residents of Parker eagerly banded together to build the church under the guidance of construction supervisor William Holmes, who also drew the architectural plans. On May 25, 1913, the parishioners dedicated the church named Ruth Memorial Chapel at the request of a local family who donated a considerable amount of money toward its construction. Later renamed Parker United Methodist Church, the building served many functions for the town. It was used as a meeting place for voter caucuses, Boy Scouts, Extension Homemakers, the Art Guild, Parker Women's Study Club, and 4-H groups. The church basement also served as a classroom and library.

In 1969, the congregation moved to the Parker School building next door, but continued to use Ruth Memorial Chapel for weddings and funerals. The town of Parker purchased the chapel and former schoolhouse in December 1995, when the congregation of the Parker United Methodist Church began construction of a larger facility farther south of town. The chapel and former Parker School were united as the Mainstreet Heritage Center.

Tallman Barn (1872: John Tallman, builder), Betts Ranch Road. **Private residence.**

This 28-foot, two-story barn survives as one of the few structures in Douglas County built by an original homestead family. The rectangular barn consists of post and beam construction and is topped by a steep gabled roof. It originally featured a large door that has since been walled over. The entire structure was built with wooden pegs instead of nails.

John Tallman came to Douglas County in the 1860s and squatted on land just east of present-day Parker. The land belonged to a man named Van Buskirk, who relinquished it to Tallman in 1868. Four years later, Tallman constructed the barn immediately adjacent to his log cabin and used it to house farm animals and store hay. In 1878, citizens elected Tallman as county clerk and recorder, so he sold his 160-acre property, barn, and cabin to William and Elizabeth Newlin and moved to Castle Rock. The barn stayed in its original location until 1964, when Burr Betts moved it to his ranch about three miles west, where it remains today. Betts, originator of the Security Life Insurance Company, planned to restore the barn for use as a guesthouse. He walled over the large door, but ill health halted further remodeling efforts.

Mobile Land, the development company that owns the property upon which the barns rests, plans to retain the structure as a historical amenity within its planned development.

Tallman/Newlin Cabin (1866: John Tallman, builder; 1878: William Newlin, builder; early 1900s: Harry Newlin, renovator), Callaway Road.

In the mid-1860s John Tallman and his wife, Elizabeth, squatted on land just east of the budding town of Pine Grove. They constructed a small log cabin in 1866 and later a very large barn (now located on the former Burr Betts Ranch). The Tallmans lived at the site until 1878, when John became county clerk and recorder and the family moved to Castle Rock. William Newlin Sr. purchased the Tallman homestead and began an extensive cattle operation on the property. It is believed that the Newlins continued to use at least part of the Tallman cabin as their residence. Present-day archaeological studies indicate that various sections of the structure are still supported by logs dating to 1866. The cabin is affixed by square nails and rests on a stone foundation. In the early 1900s, Newlin's grandson Harry completely encased the log cabin in a more modern pine frame structure.

Owned by the Newlin family for several generations, the structure and property were eventually sold to various developers in the 1960s and 1970s. In early 1996, Black Creek Capital announced plans to destroy the old cabin to make way for an expansion of Canterberry Crossing, a housing development located east of the property. Fearing impending destruction of the historic house, the Parker Area Historical Society began negotiations with the developer to save the cabin. Shortly thereafter, Black Creek Capital agreed to donate the cabin to the historical society, with the stipulation that the cabin be moved several hundred feet to the east, near the Newlin family cemetery. The cabin was hoisted to its new location in May 1996 and was elected to the State Register of Historic Properties in 1997. A Colorado Historical Society grant helped complete a restoration plan for the house, and the local historical society members hope to eventually establish an historic park and educational exhibit at the site.

20-Mile House (1863: Alfred Butters, George Long, Nelson Doud, James S. Parker, builders), west of Parker Road and Mainstreet intersection.

Arguably the most significant structure in Douglas County, this early stage station served as an oasis for travelers on western pioneer trails. The original building was a one-room cabin/post office built by Alfred Butters in 1863, near the present-day Parker post office. Butters called the cabin Pine Grove in honor of a clump of trees nearby. He sold it a year later for a yoke of oxen to George Long, who moved the small cabin just west of the present-day intersection of Parker Road and Mainstreet, at the junction of the Smoky Hill Trail and the Cherokee Trail. Long believed the location along the heavily traveled trails would be a profitable place for a stage station. He later enlarged the structure and added several outbuildings on the property. Called 20-Mile House, designating its distance from Denver along Cherry Creek, the station provided weary travelers a place to rest themselves and their horses before finishing their journey into Denver.

Around 1870, Long became infatuated with a handsome mule team owned by local rancher Nelson Doud. Long offered Doud ownership of his stage station in exchange for the team. Doud accepted and settled in the house with his wife and five daughters. He built a large dining hall on the ground floor and a ballroom on the second floor. Richard B. Townshend's *A Tenderfoot in Colorado* gives a lively account of the Doud family and the barroom scuffles and excitement at their stage station. During a stop at the station, Townshend described Nelson Doud as a "cheerful Irishman of sixty or so [who] kept the bar and handed out drinks." Although Mrs. Doud tended mainly to the cooking and serving of hash, Townshend witnessed an incident in which she also revealed her defensive tactics for dealing with an unruly customer: "There came a flash of petticoats and Mrs. Dowd [sic] who had been listening from behind the door to the kitchen darted into the bar with a feminine screech and set her ten commandments in his face, dragging her nails down each cheek."[25]

During Doud's ownership of 20-Mile House, modifications gave the structure a saltbox appearance. By the mid-1870s, Doud grew tired of maintaining the stage station and sold it to James S. Parker from the nearby town of Kiowa for $2,500. Under Parker's ownership, the 20-Mile House thrived. The new owner added a blacksmith shop and mercantile store. The original Pine Grove Post Office became the first official post office for the new town growing up around the stage stop. In June 1881, Parker granted a right-of-way to the Denver & New Orleans Railroad, allowing train officials to construct necessary ditches and cattle guards along a 100-foot-wide strip of land that would run through the town. When the first trains finally chugged through town on May 11, 1882, Parker welcomed the new travelers to his stage station.

After Parker sold 20-Mile House in 1910, it changed hands several times. In 1944 Charles O'Brien purchased it and made several major changes to the property. Eventually the only remnant of the original 20-Mile House was a portion of the Pine Grove Post Office, which was being used as a garage, and some original wall and floor material from the second story. In March 1996, the Parker Area Historical Society and the property's owner, Twenty Mile Associates, negotiated the donation of a section of the property and the remnant structures to the town of Parker for the germination of Twenty-Mile House Park. The O'Brien home was demolished, except for the portion believed to be the original Pine Grove Post Office. In 1998, the historical society restored the building and celebrated its dedication with a special one-day U.S. Postal Service–authorized "Pine Grove" cancellation on outgoing letters.

Twin Houses (1885: builder/architect unknown), intersection of State Highway 83 and Stroh Road. **Private residence.**

Many of Douglas County's early citizens were ambitious and opportunistic. Several of them attempted to capitalize on the rich natural resources indigenous to the region. One man, F. H. Allison, discovered natural mineral water flowing from a spring on his property near the present-day Stroh Ranch subdivision, and immediately established a health resort for tuberculosis patients. Built in 1885, the facility was comprised of two identical two story, gable-roofed houses. It was given the ostentatious name of Ponce de Leon Chalybeate Springs, but was often referred to simply as the Twin Houses. The houses were white clapboard construction and possessed symmetrically placed upstairs and downstairs windows and a full facade porch with ornate Victorian post brackets. Within a few years Allison's resort was highly successful, and the proprietor boasted to the *Castle Rock Journal* in 1892 that he "has both his houses full of guests and has turned away several for lack of accommodations."[26]

After Allison sold the resort around 1900, the two houses changed hands several times and were used by later owners as hotels, hostelries, homes, and barns. The structures remained side by side until the 1970s, when a woman known only by her married name of Mrs. Louis Kraglund purchased one of the houses and moved it seven miles north to her Arapahoe County home, just off State Highway 83 near the 17-Mile House. This twin building was renovated and used as a clothing boutique called Glitzy Glitz Girls. Today the restored Arapahoe County house bears little resemblance to its deteriorating Douglas County twin, which is used at this writing as a barn and storage facility.

Notes

1. James R. Harvey, "Pioneer Experiences in Colorado," *Colorado Magazine*, vol. XIII, no. 4, July 1936, pp. 145–146.

2. Elizabeth Tallman, "Early History of Parker and Vicinity," *Colorado Magazine*, vol. XXIII, no. 3, May 1946, p. 186.

3. *Castle Rock Journal*, June 27, 1883, p. 3.

4. Ibid., March 8, 1882, p. 3.

5. Ibid., October 16, 1889, p. 4.

6. Ibid., March 17, 1899, p. 2; January 18, 1907, p. 1.

7. Ibid., April 15, 1896, p. 4.

8. Ibid., June 10, 1885, p. 3, quoting from the *Rocky Mountain News*.

9. Ibid., July 25, 1894, p. 4.

10. *Record-Journal of Douglas County*, December 16, 1921, p. 5.

11. Ibid., August 14, 1935, p. 1.

12. Ibid., February 1, 1946, p. 1.

13. *Denver Post*, August 11, 1985, pp. 1F, 8F.

14. Ibid., February 25, 1981, p. 17; January 14, 1981, NSE-8; February 18, 1981, NSE-6. Castle Rock and Larkspur were Douglas County's other two incorporated towns.

15. Ibid., January 22, 1984, p. 1I, 4I.

16. Ibid., August 11, 1985, pp. 1F, 8F.

17. Ibid., August 18, 1985, p. 1E.

18. "Town of Parker Master Plan," November 1994, p. 23.

19. *Weekly News Chronicle*, January 25, 1995, p. 1.

20. Ibid., April 19, 1995, p. 3.

21. *Denver Post*, February 16, 1995, pp. 1B, 5B; February 17, 1995, p. 10B.

22. Christopher John Farley, "Sorry, No Vacancies," *Time Magazine*, vol. 146, no. 6, August 7, 1995, pp. 34–35.

23. *Douglas County News Press*, December 23, 1998, p. 7A.

24. Harvey, "Pioneer Experiences in Colorado," pp. 148–149.

25. Richard B. Townshend, *A Tenderfoot in Colorado* (Norman, Okla.: University of Oklahoma Press, 1968), pp. 55–56, 63.

26. *Castle Rock Journal*, November 30, 1892, p. 4.

PERRY PARK

Nature has been lavish in the display of her handiwork, creating for the purpose a most enchanting spot . . .
—Perry Park, Colorado, 1890

The peaceful magnificence of Perry Park's enormous scarlet rock formations, countless regiments of tall, stoic pine trees, and vast open land inspires images that belie the precarious nature of the area's history. Starting in the mid-nineteenth century, Perry Park existed as the successive home and working ranch of some of Colorado's wealthiest families. The area endured two attempts by developers to create upscale communities amid its awe-inspiring natural beauty. Today's residents, abandoned by the very developers who sold them such visions of paradise, are attempting to recover from a struggle that required determination among many hurdles.

Native Americans were the first to marvel at the mysterious rock formations of the Perry Park area. For centuries, the Ute, Kiowa, Arapaho, and Cheyenne traversed and often settled in the pristine place. Early legends reflect their efforts to decipher the drama behind the unusually human-like shapes of the towering rocks. One legend, recorded in the late 1800s, told of a time when powerful and complacent "giants and giantesses" refused to heed the warning of Mokahna, a prophet who admonished them for their neglect of the god Gitche Manito, Master of Life. The legend explains:

> Suddenly the great wrath of their God came upon them, and all living things were instantly but stone images of their former selves. Tumpwichits (Toom-pa-kee-tis), the great chief and wilful leader of this rebellion was reduced from great power and majesty to a dwarf, and condemned to stand on this height ever gazing upon his brave warriors, who lie prostrate or tower in their majestic height before him. Near by sings the voice of his beloved Wahuneep in the falls of Muaga (Moo-ah-ga) canon where she becomes a fountain of tears at the sight of her silent and stony lover. In this state they must ever remain, until the veil of the Prophet Chief, the great Mokahna, is lifted. Then they will be set free, to the joy and gladness of a new life in this garden of the Rockies.[1]

The Ferdinand Hayden geological survey expedition, possibly unaware of the tragic myth associated with the area, named the valley Pleasant Park in 1869. The designation seemed appropriate for a region so rich in geological history. The eroded sandstone and shale rock formations were formed during the Upper Cretaceous Period, and mineral deposits in the area include gypsum, limestone, sand, and clay. During an 1891 convention of the Denver Society of Civil Engineers, Professor P.H. Van Diest claimed the area "has its massive portals and queer shaped rocks, but combines with solemn and awful grandeur, loveliness and attractive variety."[2]

John Dietz Perry, a distinguished St. Louis businessman, first saw this captivating scene in the early 1870s. President of the Kansas Pacific Railroad, Perry was instrumental in providing a direct line from Kansas to Denver in 1870. He became acquainted with the West Plum Creek area during earlier railroad surveys, and by 1872 he had acquired approximately 4,000 acres in Pleasant Park for use as a working ranch. Perry renamed his new property Perry Park Ranch and promptly constructed a house and ranch buildings within a colorful gorge partially formed by a 300-foot ridge called Nanichant Rock. Like the Native Americans before them, the Perry family enjoyed naming the unusual rock formations surrounding their new home. Names like Castle Ridge, Kenilworth Castle, Washington Monument (known today as Sentinel Rock), the Walls of Jericho, Cashmere Ridge, and Haystacks Ranch reflect places the family had visited during their world travels.

Although most Perry family members lived at the ranch during the summer and fall only, Charles Perry, the eldest son, happily called the area home year-round. Charles raised shorthorn cattle on the ranch and managed all of the farming operations until August 1875, when the Perrys hired Upton T. Smith, one of Douglas County's most renowned pioneers, as farmer. Charles remained foreman of the ranch until the fall of 1876, when he died after being kicked by a horse.

Visitors to Perry Park traveled by train first to nearby Larkspur, then by stage to the remote rocky hills of the ranch. A small inn existed for those sojourners who wished to prolong their stay. The ranch was also a popular picnic spot for residents of both Denver and Colorado Springs, and the Perrys were accustomed to visits from sightseers. In the fall of 1873, a different type of visitor called upon the ranch: an English woman named Isabella Bird, who traveled by horseback alone through the Rocky Mountain region during 1873. Bird had many adventures on her trip, including a successful ascent of Long's Peak. She was the second woman in Colorado history to climb it. Bird recorded her experiences in letters to her sister in England, and those letters were the basis for her book, *A Lady's Life in the Rocky Mountains*. One letter, dated October 28, 1873, is richly colored with scenic descriptions and provides precious insight into early life at Perry Park Ranch:

> Finding that there would be risk in trying to ride till nightfall, in the early afternoon I left the road and went two miles into the hills by an untrodden path, where there were gates to open, and a rapid steep-sided creek to cross; and at the entrance to a most fantastic gorge I came upon an elegant frame house belonging to Mr. Perry, a millionaire, to whom I had an introduction which I did not hesitate to present, as it was weather in which a traveler might almost ask for shelter without one.
>
> Mr. Perry was away, but his daughter, a very bright-looking, elegantly-dressed girl, invited me to dine and remain. They had stewed venison and various luxuries on the table, which was tasteful and refined, and an adroit, colored table-maid waited, one of five attached Negro servants who had been their slaves before the war. After dinner, though snow was slowly falling, a gentleman

> cousin took me for a ride to show me the beauties of Pleasant Park, which takes rank among the finest scenery of Colorado, and in good weather is very easy of access. It did look very grand as we entered it by a narrow pass guarded by two buttes, or isolated upright masses of rock, bright red, and about 300 feet in height. The pines were very large, and the narrow canyons which came down on the park gloomily magnificent. It is remarkable also from a quantity of "monumental" rocks, from 50 to 300 feet in height, bright vermilion, green, buff, orange, and sometimes all combined, their gay tinting a contrast to the disastrous-looking snow and the somber pines.

In the late 1870s, John Perry decided to gradually break his connection with the ranch. Prior business obligations with the Kansas Pacific Railroad, two Colorado branch railroads, and other business enterprises out of state, along with the death of son Charles, no doubt contributed to his decision. In August 1879, he placed half of the property up for sale. The *Rocky Mountain News* announced that the sale posed a "rare chance for a man with means who is seeking a home in Colorado," and described the ranch's attributes:

> It contains about 5,000 acres, under good fence, 4½ miles along the base of the mountains. The improvements consist in part of two good frame houses each with a rock milk house, with a running stream of water through each, large barns and other houses. These farms are well stocked with a herd of high grade cattle, horses, work mules, farming implements suited to an extensive farm, and there are two or three hundred acres of good land under ditch, most of it suitable for wheat, rye, oats, and barley.[3]

While family and business obligations took him away from his beloved Perry Park, Perry recognized the property's potential as a first-class summer resort for Colorado tourists and spent the next few years searching for a responsible party to manage this retreat. Unfortunately for Perry, who was now attempting to run his Perry Park estate from his permanent home in St. Louis, Missouri, several such business arrangements fell through. One difficulty was reported in an 1882 issue of the *Castle Rock Journal*, which loudly reprimanded the new operators of the Perry Park Hotel for serving "a mock dinner and a worse supper" to Fourth of July partiers at the ranch. The debacle seemed to threaten the reputation of the entire ranch, and the newspaper reported that several older citizens were overheard lamenting the days when "the gentlemanly Perry boys" hosted other annual receptions. The article concluded with a cryptic warning to the new proprietors: "Douglas County may contain thousands of dummies and numbskulls, but when the wind is right, they can tell a hawk from a hand-saw."[4]

Frustrated and tired after years of incompetent partnerships, Perry finally sold the remaining Perry Park land to the Red Stone Town, Land & Mining Company in May 1888, accepting a stockholder's position in the company. He hoped that his dream of turning Perry Park into a first-class resort would be realized under the company's leadership. The company's elected president, General Bela M. Hughes, Denver Pacific Railroad's first president and a staunch advocate of transportation links between Colorado and the East, wholeheartedly supported Perry's vision. Hughes and Perry had become friends during Perry's earlier efforts to connect Kansas and Colorado with rail lines.

Ironically, transportation was one of the issues that eventually set the Red Stone Town, Land & Mining Company's plans awry in Perry Park. The remoteness of the area made a convenient, reliable form of transportation vital to its survival as a resort. Weighing its options, the company chose to construct a rail line from Sedalia to Palmer Lake, in northern El Paso County. Optimistic stockholders formed a separate organization called the Perry Park Railroad Company and hired a surveyor to estimate the cost. The line would be routed through Perry Park to serve the needs of the resort's patrons as well as to provide freight services for mining operations in the area.

Meanwhile, the Red Stone company refined its designs for the resort. After a dam was constructed across Bear Creek to form Lake Wauconda (an Indian name for Almighty God), the company changed the resort's name to the Village of Lake Wauconda and specified plans for three additional lakes. A lakeside casino, chapel, library-museum, and a full relief sculpture of Castle Ridge, designed by sculptor Preston Powers, were also proposed. Other plans included two more residential developments in addition to the original one on Lake Wauconda. One of these, to be called the Town of Perry, was to be located at the resort's eastern entrance gate. It was intended to provide reduced-priced housing for those who could not afford the more extravagant dwellings closer to the lake, and was also to house the company's business offices.

Once lots were platted and priced in the Village of Lake Wauconda, the company proposed strict regulations concerning the construction of buildings and fences and strongly recommended the use of native building materials whenever possible. It was hoped that rules such as these would protect the natural surroundings and make the resort more attractive to tourists. To accomplish these goals, the company hired the architectural firm, Andrews, Jaques & Rantoul, as well as renowned landscape designer Frederick Law Olmsted to oversee construction efforts. In an 1890 analysis titled "Feasibility of Perry Park as a Resort," Olmsted prophesized success for the resort as long as its natural state was respected:

> Kept clear of such puerile and cockneyfied structures as are too generally allowed to put nature out of countenance in places of summer resorts, as well of such as would be offensive from their rudeness and shabbiness, I should think that Perry Park would soon be found very attractive, first, to tourists, led chiefly by curiosity, second, to persons seeking rest and refreshment under the influence of invigorating mountain air, of a landscape that will grow more pleasing as it becomes more familiar, and of incitements to out of door contemplative occupations, such as are to be found abundantly in the conditions that have been described.

In the summer of 1889, the company opened Nanichant House, a two-story frame building with a large veranda, immense stone fireplace, thirty guest rooms, lobby, dining room, and modern kitchen. Originally located at the foot of Nanichant Rock, the hotel was later moved a few yards west at the opening of Bear Creek Canyon. The name *Nanichant*, meaning echo, came from the Native American legend in which the cries of Wahuneep, Chief Tumpwichits' beloved, echoed throughout the canyon. Consequently, the inn was informally referred to as Hotel Echo.

Nanichant House enjoyed a steady flow of guests. Dances,

hayrides, ice-skating, and oyster suppers were among the favorite activities of younger patrons, while the older clientele sought relaxation and privacy. Locals like Charles A. Nickson, who grew up at a ranch nearby, also enjoyed the hotel's festivities.

> With the hotel going in the summer it made for lively times in the neighborhood. The large dining room afforded a good place in which to dance and there were parties and hayrides and it was always a thrill to be in the large lobby with rustic finish and large fireplace.[5]

A reporter for the *Denver Times* wrote lavishly of the hotel's comforts, claiming the aim of the owners was "to attract the attention of people of culture and refinement, who wish a quiet retreat from the hum, bustle, and worry of social and business cares." Regarding the hotel itself, the reporter declared:

> The mornings and evenings at any of the mountain resorts are as delightful as what we enjoy here at Perry Park; but there is not a hotel in the State of Colorado from which such a varied combination of attractive scenery greets the eye as from the broad piazzas of the Hotel Echo. The hotel is kept as neat as a pin, and the table is as gratifying as one can find at the oldest and most fashionable hotels in the West.[6]

Douglas County citizens were aware that the development at Perry Park would affect the way outsiders viewed their county and anxiously watched its progress. As noted in an 1890 issue of the *Castle Rock Journal*, transportation, namely railroad, topped the list of things the resort needed in order to succeed. The newspaper assured its readers that "[w]hen the improvements already commenced or contemplated are completed, and a railroad is laid into this beauty spot of nature, it will become more generally known that Douglas county can offer to the seekers of health, or pleasure, a retreat that is not only second to none but is superior to any."[7]

Although the Red Stone Town, Land & Mining Company agreed that railroad transportation to the resort was vital, more pressing financial problems kept the project from progressing beyond a potential route survey. Consequently, the line's charter expired unrealized in August 1892. The construction and maintenance of the Bear Creek Dam and Lake Wauconda were a substantial drain on the company's financial resources. The construction and operation of Nanichant House exacerbated the precarious financial predicament, as did an expensive excavation of a reservoir needed for a resort of this size.

Among the company's other problems was ambiguous legal title to the property. Upon examination of property deeds presented to the Red Stone company by John Perry, portions of the land, for reasons that were unknown, were found to be titled under Perry's son Charles, who died in 1876. John Perry could not establish legal heirship to the land. Secondly, missing deeds to other pieces of the property indicated that neither Perry nor his son owned the land. Rather, county records verified that title belonged to Native Americans, and no transfer was located. These legal tangles were not fully resolved until 1902, when a new company president, Colonel William E. Hughes, a banker, cattleman, and lawyer, took charge. The Perry Park property title received clarification during various court proceedings in which former residents of the area testified to John Perry's ownership of the ranch for twenty years, thus fulfilling the provisions of the Law of Limitations, which specified twenty years occupation of land for possession. Other court procedures established John Perry's legal heirship to property titled to Charles Perry.

Colonel William Hughes was at the right place at the right time. It is very likely that Hughes's keen business instinct recognized the Red Stone company's financial turmoil as personal opportunity. On March 2, 1900, Hughes had purchased one of two stone cottages constructed by the company and informed the *Denver Times* that "the property will be improved and put in shape, and is intended to make a fashionable resort."[8] Not long after his purchase, Hughes procured a large portion of stock in the development company and became its president. In 1903, he purchased the Perry family shares of Red Stone company and by October 1904 bought out the remaining shareholders, thus becoming sole owner of the property.

While Perry Park's legal status swirled in confusion, a whirlwind of a different variety wreaked havoc on the property itself. In August 1903, "a cyclone of terrific fury swept the valley . . . spreading devastation in its path and wrecking the summer resort." According to the *Denver Times*, a portion of the Nanichant House roof was ripped off, another cabin was demolished, and several trees were knocked down. The article described the damage to the hotel and a nearby approaching stage:

> In an instant a terrible whirlwind was dashed through the place, licking up everything within a radius of 200 yards. The hotel was almost in the center of the maelstrom, and the laundry, barns, tents and cabin were near the edges of the circle. Very nearly all the damage was done at the moment the wind struck the place. . . . The stage coach, bringing a party of three ladies . . . was but a few hundred feet from the hotel when the cyclone struck. It was raised completely from the ground and carried for a distance of twenty feet through the air at a height of more than four feet from the ground. It was then raised a few times and stamped heavily, the last time capsizing and throwing its occupants heavily upon the road.[9]

After the Nanichant House was repaired, Hughes renamed it Clifton Inn, most likely in remembrance of his daughter, Eliza Clifton, who died in 1904. He continued the traditional operations of both the hotel, which catered to the resort's guests, and the working ranch. Hughes's peculiarities charmed local resident Charles A. Nickson, who later remembered: "Although he drove his four-in-hand, dock-tailed horses with a Concord stage coach and a colored boy sitting up back to blow a bugle and open gates, the Colonel was very friendly."[10]

In 1912, Hughes sold the ranch to J. George Leyner for $37,500. One-eyed George Leyner was a successful inventor. A farmer's son from Georgetown, Colorado, he designed a compressed air-driven hammer drill that became an instant hit among miners and was particularly useful during the construction of Cheesman Dam on the South Platte River. Following this success, Leyner formed the Leyner Engineering and Manufacturing Company, which he eventually sold, along with the patents for his mining drill, in order to pursue a career in agriculture and ranching. He purchased Perry Park Ranch and began raising hogs as well as corn, beans, and potato crops. When the hogs fell victim to cholera in 1914, Leyner purchased some cattle and tried his hand at dairying.

During their ownership, the Leyner family ended the Perry Park hotel's long-standing service to paying customers. The building was still known as Clifton Inn, but it was now used only as a private guesthouse for acquaintances and visiting family members. It was never used commercially again and is believed to have burned down in the 1920s. Another loss during Leyner's ownership was the Bear Creek Dam, which formed Lake Wauconda. Repeatedly flood-damaged and neglected, the dam could no longer hold the lake water.

Leyner became obsessed with inventing a new form of tractor that operated with vertically lined steel crawlers that allowed for easier crop cultivation. With the drain of bringing this new invention to market, his financial situation deteriorated. He was forced to sell Perry Park Ranch in 1918. Three years later he was killed in a car accident on a Littleton road.

Perry Park's next owner, one-handed Robert Patterson Lamont Jr., was the son of Robert P. Lamont Sr., Chicago's American Steel Foundries president and Herbert Hoover's secretary of commerce in the late 1920s. During World War I, Lamont Jr. was discharged from military service with high honors from the French government after he received serious injuries, including the loss of his hand. An abiding interest in ranching prompted Lamont's purchase of Perry Park and later the adjoining 2,250-acre Benjamin Quick ranch. Lamont raised sheep and Hereford cattle quite successfully and was eventually named president of both the American Hereford Cattle Breeders Association and the National Western Stock Show Association. In *Around the World in Eleven Years* (a book written by three children, Patience, Richard, and John Abbe, who visited Perry Park in the 1930s), "Uncle Bob" Lamont's deep love for the cattle business was afforded a child's insight: "The cattle Uncle Bob thinks better of than any human being. He loves his cattle. These cattle are prize cattle and are very delicate like opera singers."

Throughout the 1920s, Perry Park flourished under Lamont's care. In addition to the restoration of Bear Creek Dam and Lake Wauconda, Lamont established a private game preserve on the property with turkeys, coyotes, eagles, deer, and other wild animals. Nevertheless, serious financial problems during the Great Depression forced Lamont to sell the Benjamin Quick portion of the ranch in 1936 to a neighbor, Reginald Sinclaire.

One year later, Lamont sold the remainder of his beloved ranch to Walter Paepcke, a fellow Chicagoan who owned the Container Corporation of America and later developed the silver mining town of Aspen, Colorado, into a thriving cultural hub. The Paepcke family used Perry Park as a summer residence and hired a foreman to raise cattle, hogs, turkeys, sheep, and horses year round on the ranch. In the 1930s, the Paepckes opened the ranch to the public and built a new guesthouse near Lake Wauconda. Rodeos and barn dances were popular events for guests and neighbors alike.

Eventually, Paepcke moved his Colorado headquarters and family from Perry Park to the snowy peaks of Aspen. He sold Perry Park in 1951 to Boyd E. Cousins, a Kansas City furniture retailer who maintained the property as a working ranch until ill health forced him to sell it to Lee Stubblefield in July 1967 for $2 million. Cousins retained approximately 1,000 acres, including the guesthouse built by the Paepckes in the late 1930s.

Stubblefield, a retired Air Force pilot and president of the newly created Colorado Western Development Company, was not quiet about his plans to develop the ranch into a country-club style residential development. Claiming "[o]ur Perry Park project involves the blending together of community development and conservation of natural resources," Stubblefield praised the development's "uniqueness" in *Panorama*, a newsletter published quarterly to inform residents and prospective buyers about the happenings at Perry Park.

> Developed entirely by private enterprise, the Perry Park community-conservation plan will result in people living and enjoying themselves within a 4,000 acre area of pine, spruce, cedar, lakes, streams, and rock formations that rival or surpass those in the Garden of the Gods.[11]

From the late 1960s through the mid-1970s, Colorado Western Development Company attempted to fulfill its grandiose plans. In addition to the proposed construction of a private airstrip, polo fields, pool, tennis courts, and 18-hole golf course, the company announced plans to remodel the Manor House, constructed in 1891 by the Red Stone company, for use as a country club. Stubblefield also announced that 40 percent of the property would be preserved as open space and recreational areas, while the remaining 60 percent would be subdivided into one-acre residential lots. Strict covenants and the formation of an architectural committee were intended to uphold the highest standards in home plans and improvements.

Because isolated, pristine Perry Park had never been home to more than a couple of families at one time, the construction of modern utilities and improvements was essential to the elaborate development plans of Colorado Western. Basic services such as water, sewage, electricity, gas, telephones, and roads topped the list of immediate needs. Intermountain Rural Electric Association provided the area with electricity, while Mountain States Telephone and Telegraph Company furnished telephone service. Homeowners used 500-gallon gas propane tanks for cooking and heating until late 1969, when Plateau Natural Gas Company of Colorado Springs laid approximately twenty-two miles of natural gas pipeline.

When Colorado Western completed a well capable of pumping 300 gallons of water a minute in October 1967, Stubblefield crowed, "There is absolutely no doubt that we will be able to obtain the water necessary to complete the Perry Park project in the scope and magnitude desired."[12] Nonetheless, Perry Park's water and sewage needs were not trivial matters, and management of the services passed from Colorado Western to the Perry Park Water and Sanitation District, formed in September 1969. The district constructed a waste treatment plant in 1971 and completed four miles of water and sewer lines each by early 1973.

Building roads in heavily timbered Perry Park was an enormous challenge. In June 1969, *Panorama* explained the problems:

> It involves more than simply moving dirt. Trees all must be downed, trimmed, and taken to the mill. Trimmings must be chipped up. Stumps are then pulled and hauled out for burial. Only then can the drainage be cut, culverts installed, dirt moved, and surface laid.[13]

By early 1973, Colorado Western had completed roads throughout nine residential centers and asphalted Red Rocks Drive from the entrance gate to the Manor House, allowing homeowners and visitors to "travel dustfree . . . all the way to the center of Perry Park."[14] Roads were also built into Perry Park East, a separate multipurpose residential development located east of Perry Park Village; Meribel Village, situated on the former Sinclaire and Vorenberg ranches; and Sageport Village, established on land in Perry Park East near the airstrip.

Asphalting continued up a winding, steep road that led to the Echo Hills Club, located about 500 feet above the Manor House on a sharply rising ridge known as Inspiration Point. The club, designed by James Johnson and Associates of Denver and completed in 1972, was a large social and business facility that included conference rooms, dining areas, lounges, and recreational facilities such as swimming pools and tennis courts. Members of the club were also promised free use of club facilities in developments planned for Marble, Colorado, and Manzanillo, Mexico, through the Echo Hills Club Internationale system.

In the mid-1970s, Colorado Western encountered financial and legal problems that prevented further development. In an effort to avert greater trouble during 1973, the company voluntarily curtailed sales of new home sites in order to focus on capital improvements to their existing projects. In 1975, the Perry Park Landowner's Association (PPLA) initiated a legal investigation of homeowners' complaints concerning failure by Colorado Western to fulfill promised improvements to the Perry Park property. The lengthy list of complaints included failure to lay utility lines underground, to complete road construction, to provide water and sewage lines, to sell lots no smaller than one acre, to set aside 40 percent of the property as a greenbelt, and to complete the Echo Hills Club, the Manor House country club, and the golf course. In 1976, the Colorado Real Estate Commission called a hearing in which Colorado Western was to show how it planned to honor its commitments. The hearing was postponed twice when the company failed to cooperate. When the commission set a June 1976 meeting to discuss terminating the company's license, Stubblefield met with the Perry Park Landowner's Association to discuss the planned resolution of various complaints, such as roads improvements, water access, and golf course improvement. Although one PPLA member pronounced after the meeting, "the fact that our developer is actively working with us to preserve the integrity of the development is cause of great satisfaction," the association still petitioned Douglas County commissioners to create a metropolitan district.[15] The request was granted and the district formed in early 1977.

Relations between Colorado Western and homeowners deteriorated throughout the remainder of the 1970s. In late 1977, the company failed once again to fulfill its promises, and landowners filed suit. The Castle Rock district court ruled on January 26, 1979, against Lee Stubblefield, who had acquired all of the company's assets for $2.8 million, and slapped him with a $1.3 million judgment for failure to complete the subdivision's roads and recreational amenities. Although the awarded amount was said to be the largest in Douglas County history, it was considerably less than the $12 million requested by the Metropolitan District, because the judge found that the Perry Park Water and Sanitation District, not Colorado Western, was responsible for the extension of water and sewer lines. The judge also determined that promises made in Perry Park brochures were not connected to purchase contracts and therefore could not be included in the judgment.

Stubblefield and attorneys Bruce and Eric Pringle immediately appealed the district court's judgment, and the issue went to the state court of appeals in January 1980. In an unusual turn of events, the court of appeals reversed the trial court decision. Burdened by the time and cost of appealing the decision to the state supreme court, the Metropolitan District board grudgingly decided to accept the ruling. Sally Maguire, former board president, recalled to the author the disappointment of determined Perry Park residents, who realized that completing the community and securing the lifestyle they desired was now in their own hands.

> We were very frustrated. We didn't have the money to fight the appeal. We couldn't fight it anymore because we

> were using taxpayer money and it's not something that you can just keep spending and spending money on. So we decided we had to draw back and bite the bullet and just do it ourselves. I mean, we did everything except get out there and rake the roads ourselves. . . . We worked extremely well as a community because we had to.

While the Metropolitan District board struggled to restore order to the chaos left in Colorado Western's wake, another hurdle obstructed their efforts. In 1977, inundated with legal problems, Stubblefield sold his Perry Park assets to Ramon Jarrell, a developer of industrial properties in Louisiana. Shortly after the sale, Jarrell began planning a community of 14,000 people called Douglas Park. Sally Maguire claimed that although residents initially likened Jarrell's presence to that of a savior's, reality quickly proved otherwise. Claiming he was unaware of the extensive problems in Perry Park when he purchased the property, Jarrell vehemently denied any obligation to correct the damage caused by Colorado Western, stating that he bought only Stubblefield's assets, not his liabilities or promises to further develop the area.

To make matters worse, in August 1979 he demanded the eviction of the Perry Park Country Club from the Manor House and golf maintenance building in the stable area, citing failure by the club to pay taxes, insurance, or rent. Outraged country club members, who argued that the two facilities were given to the people of Perry Park by Stubblefield, immediately filed suit against Jarrell, and the dispute was brought before the Douglas County District Court in late 1979. After the court ruled in favor of the country club, Jarrell responded with an appeal, and the issue remained in legal limbo until December 1982, when the two parties reached a private settlement. In the agreement, Jarrell, whose interest in developing the Perry Park area had waned, conceded and transferred the Manor House and golf maintenance facility deeds to country club members.

During and after the five years of tumultuous litigation, Perry Park residents labored to provide much-needed improvements to their community. The metro board's top concerns included the completion of the park's main and private roads, the preservation of greenbelts, mosquito abatement, and the elimination of the Mountain Pine Beetle and a parasitic growth known as the dwarf mistletoe, both of which posed serious threats to the area's trees. A Park Beautification program, created in 1981, and the Architectural Control Committee (ACC), first established by Colorado Western, tended to the area's aesthetic qualities.

The Perry Park Water and Sanitation District managed water and sewage improvements. Through the passage of water and sewer bonds, the district was able to construct the "Hog John" water tank in July 1980, expand the Wauconda Sewage Treatment Plant, and install a second community well in the early 1980s. Growth in Sageport and Perry Park East necessitated the installation of water and sewer lines in the mid-1980s.

In the 1990s, the ACC, one of the few organizations remaining from the Colorado Western days, received unprecedented focus. From 1991 to 1993, many residents, discouraged by ACC's tendency to enforce only those covenants that pertained to new home plans, attempted to revise and update the community's architectural regulations. The attempt floundered, however, when the issue failed to generate the 50.1 percent favorable response required for change, largely due to a lack of participation by absentee owners. For several years thereafter, a growing distrust and suspicion lingered among residents who questioned the ACC's policies and procedures, especially the lack of disclosure of the use of funds. This tide of doubt in the ACC culminated in *Jossi vs. Perry Park ACC Inc.* in 1995. The plaintiff, Perry Park resident Donald T. Jossi, sued on the basis of the ACC's lack of disclosure and accountability to residents for the fees levied to fund the committee. The end result of the litigation was a settlement that disbanded the ACC and turned over the $9,000 fund balance to the metro board. In a 1996 resignation letter, ACC members defended their performance to fellow Perry Park residents:

> We have acted in good faith in discharging the duties assigned to us as appointed members of the committee and have always attempted to maintain the best interests of Perry Park as our foremost goal.[16]

Efforts soon began to form a new ACC that better represented the entirety of Perry Park.

Ironically, the disbanding of the ACC directly benefited Perry Park. In 1997, the Perry Park Metropolitan District conducted an assessment of the open-space lands they owned within the community in order to best use the funds to purchase additional lands. Gordon Mickelson, a metro board member since 1994, claimed open-space acquisition was only one of the community's pressing needs for the future. Equally important, he felt, was an issue that virtually destroyed the Colorado Western developers and continued to nag 1990s Perry Park residents: road maintenance. The metro board spent years tackling the sensitive issue of funding options for bringing all roads up to county standards by paving them, thus ensuring county-funded maintenance. "We owe it to the residents living on these gravel roads to get them paved," Mickelson explained to the author in 1997. "But we also owe it to the rest of the Perry Park residents not to raise taxes." Consequently, the community issued municipal bonds to fund completion of the roads in 1999.

Residents of Perry Park are well acquainted with taxes. Among the most heavily taxed citizens in the county, these residents have come to realize that living in such natural beauty comes at a high price. Despite the stability and confidence inspired by institutions like the metro board, the area is governed not by humans but by nature. Today, after several decades of attempts by developers to tame the wild, residents understand that to coexist with nature they must first cooperate with one another. Although cohesiveness within the community was always strong, the threat of unfulfilled dreams after the abandonment by Colorado Western drew residents together in a common bond of astonishing strength and versatility. In this area, the beauty of Mother Nature seems to kindle cooperation among neighbors.

Perry Park Historic Sites

Benjamin Quick House (1885: Benjamin Quick), 6695 Perry Park Road. **Private residence.**

During the 1868 Cheyenne and Arapaho Indian raids, Benjamin Quick's property was transformed into a stockade known as Fort Washington. An eight-foot-high stockade fence enclosed the family home, ranch buildings, and a large well. When Indian trouble was at its worst, many families in the area moved into the fort. Others spent nights within the safety of the high walls and went out during the day to tend to their agricultural fields. On at least one occasion, the entire population of the valley moved into Fort Washington and spent more than two months there while their homes and ranches were raided. Priscilla Allafar Swinney, a child at the time of the raids, later remembered the horrifying night she and her family abandoned their home for the security of the fort:

> [A]ll the families on West Plum Creek came to the fort that night. Some of the men went to each house to warn them. The men at our house stood guard while mother packed our things, once [when] she had a small light a minute, one Indian whistled and another answered above the house, but they did not come nearer. I don't think I ever saw a darker night. . . . When we arrived at the fort Quick's house was crowded with people that had come from their homes. No one had gone to bed as no one knew where to make their beds or sleep. As we were the latest to arrive lots of questions were asked if we had seen any Indians. Mother said she had seen the campfires in what is now called Perry Park. . . . The men said they did not notice the fires. Mother told them she was afraid if she said anything brother and I would cry or make some noise that would attract the Indians, but if they went over there they could see where the fires had been. Sure enough 14 campfires had been built and for years the ashes and where the grass was killed showed where the fires had been.[17]

In 1885, Benjamin Quick built a new house from native rhyolite stone found on his land. A disagreement with his wife, Mary, concerning the desired texture of the stone ended in a compromise that is still evident in the house frame today: the north and east walls are rock faced, coarse cut, while the south and west walls are rusticated coarse-cut stone set in a common bond pattern. The two-story structure is topped by a shingle gable roof including a center gable with a wood frieze atop a small railed balcony. Four square native stone pillars capped with red stone support the balcony. Stone arch-shaped lintels top the tall main story double-hung sash windows with simulated keystones. The house and surrounding property were accepted into the National Register of Historic Places on October 1, 1974.

Glen Grove School (1910: Ben Saunders, builder), one-half mile south of 6695 Perry Park Road. **Private residence.**

Although replete with historical significance, the present-day Glen Grove School was not the first of its kind to serve the West Plum Creek Valley. Local resident George Nickson donated land for the first school and erected a foundation. Nickson's son Charles later related that a dissident, apparently unhappy with the school's location, "was given a bottle of whiskey to burn it down one night."[18] Benjamin Quick donated the next school site, and he and another local pioneer named Pete Brannan constructed a twelve-by-fifteen-foot, one-room, frame school building. Teachers were paid $25 for a three-month term, and local ranchers supplied their room and board. Fire destroyed the school in 1882, but it was immediately rebuilt. Teachers received a salary increase of $40 for April through December school terms.

Fire consumed the second building in 1909. Subsequently, Ben Saunders of Sedalia was paid $660 to construct the present-day school as an exact replica of its predecessor. As a former student of the school, Charles Nickson's memories are priceless:

> What a nice spot for a school! An irrigation ditch full of water ran through the yard all summer and afforded

> drinking water for the 5 or 6 horses the children rode or drove to school. . . . We were not permitted to leave the schoolyard without permission so it was quite a treat to be sent for drinking water. The spring was across the hill by Plum Creek. The original bucketfull [sic] usually arrived back at the school only half full necessitating more than one trip. . . . We used slates and sponges for our schoolwork, but some paper was furnished. There was a basin of water at the back of the room, sitting on a box, to wet the sponges to wash our slates—but sometimes we just spit on them. I still remember how shivers ran up my spine at the harsh grating.[19]

As an adult, Nickson kept a close correspondence with his second and third grade teacher, Mrs. Nell Billings Elting. In her letters, the former teacher reminisced about school days at Glen Grove and provided valuable recollections of the well-known pioneer Benjamin Quick:

> Mr. Quick did *not* approve of an organ. When I asked him to donate for it—he snorted—Hell's Bells! No! We hired you to teach those kids the three R's, not sing to them. I replied, "*I am* teaching them the three R's and I'm not going to sing *to* them but *with* them." After attending an entertainment—25 cent admission—he gave $10.00 toward the organ.[20]

The Glen Grove School, in use until the 1950s, features a high-pitched front-gable roof, common brick chimney, and double-hung sash windows on each side. As an example of the one-room schoolhouses commonly constructed during the early history of Douglas County and the state, the Glen Grove School was named to National Register of Historic Places on November 5, 1974.

Manor House (1891: architect and builder unknown),
7047 S. Perry Park Boulevard.

Located at the edge of Lake Wauconda, the elegant three-story Manor House is a noble reminder of Perry Park's past. Constructed in 1891 for Charles A. Roberts, the building was one of two similarly constructed stone cottages erected during the Red Stone Town, Land & Mining Company's ownership of Perry Park. While the other building, which originally belonged to company architect Herbert Jaques, burned in the 1930s, the Manor House—with its gabled roof, shed dormers, stone ridge chimney, and porch—survives today.

When legal problems starting in 1890 threatened to destroy the Red Stone company, General Bela Hughes resigned as the company's president and sold a portion of his stock to son-in-law Charles A. Roberts, who became the first owner of the Manor House. After Roberts's death in 1902, the company, plagued with financial problems, sold its remaining shares of stock to Colonel William E. Hughes. The purchase made Hughes the sole owner of the Perry Park property, including the Manor House. For several decades the successive owners of Perry Park held private title to the Manor House. Frances Kent Lamont added an art studio to the building when her husband, Robert P. Lamont Jr., owned the property, from 1918 to 1937.

Colorado Western Development Company purchased Perry Park in 1967 and immediately converted the Manor House into a country club for the private use of all residents. Renovation and expansion of the building, as well as the addition of a thirty-by-fifty-foot swimming pool, started in 1968. The Perry Park Country Club held its first annual meeting in the historic building on October 12, 1969, and elected a five-member board of directors to oversee club operations. Club members hailed the opening of the first nine holes of the golf course on July 4, 1971. Colorado Western completed one more hole of the course before abandoning the project; the remaining eight holes were financed by country club members.

In 1979, residents' possession of the beloved Manor House was placed in serious jeopardy. Ramon Jarrell, who had purchased Perry Park from Colorado Western Development Company President Lee Stubblefield in 1977, attempted to take control of the building from the country club, claiming that members had failed to pay rent, taxes, or insurance. The issue went to court, but in 1982 the parties reached an out-of-court settlement, and the deed to the Manor House went to the country club. It remains a vital part of club facilities today.

Reginald Sinclaire House (1931–1932: Reginald Sinclaire, architect), 6154 Perry Park Road. **Private residence.**

The Reginald Sinclaire House is Douglas County's only example of a Pueblo Revival home, a style common during the 1920s and 1930s throughout the nation. The building has several features typical of southwestern pueblo construction: the multilevel stepped appearance of the frame, a flat roof with rounded parapet edges, brown textured stucco walls, a portal, an enclosed courtyard, exposed interior vigas and latillas, and beehive corner fireplaces.

New York native Reginald Sinclaire, a French Foreign Legion member in World War I and U.S. Navy Gunnery Training School instructor during World War II, came to Douglas County in the 1930s and purchased 700 acres in West Plum Creek. After befriending an artist from Santa Fe, New Mexico, Sinclaire became enamored with the architecture of that region. He consulted several adobe construction specialists and began sketches for his unique ranch house in West Plum Creek. The house was built during 1931–1932, along with a split log gatehouse and barn, lean-to shed, and a large water tower that once held a 25,000-gallon copper tank.

Sinclaire eventually accumulated 4,500 acres of land surrounding the original ranch. Upon this land he raised cattle as well as polo and racehorses. One of these horses finished second in the 1946 Kentucky Derby. Sinclaire also enjoyed membership in the Arapahoe Hunt Club and the Broadmoor polo team.

Sinclaire and family lived in the house until 1965, when they moved to Colorado Springs. Five years later Colorado Western Development Company President Lee Stubblefield purchased the property, and it became part of the company's Perry Park landholdings. When Colorado Western abandoned its plans, the ranch was sold and remained vacant throughout most of the 1980s. In 1988, Edward and Beverly Statter purchased the ranch and restored the severely vandalized house to its original condition. The house was placed on the National Register of Historic Places on September 20, 1991.

Notes

1. Ardis Webb, *The Perry Park Story: Fulfillment of a Dream* (Denver, Colo.: Ardis and Olin Webb, 1974), p. 5.

2. Professor P. H. Van Diest, "Geology of Perry Park," *Transactions of the Denver Society of Civil Engineers*, vol. IV, July–December 1891, p. 66.

3. *Rocky Mountain News*, August 12, 1879, p. 1; July 21, 1881, p. 5.

4. *Castle Rock Journal*, July 12, 1882, p. 2.

5. Charles A. Nickson, *Just Reminiscing* (N.p.: Charles A. Nickson, 1964), p. 31.

6. *Denver Times*, July 20, 1889, p. 11; August 10, 1889, p. 2.

7. *Castle Rock Journal*, July 16, 1890, p. 4.

8. *Denver Times*, March 3, 1900, p. 2. Colonel William Hughes was not related to General Bela M. Hughes. For more information on William Hughes, see the Highlands Ranch chapter of this book.

9. Ibid., August 7, 1903, p. 1; *Denver Republican*, August 7, 1903, p. 1.

10. Nickson, *Just Reminiscing*, p. 32.

11. *Panorama: Perry Park*, September 1968, p. 4.

12. Ibid., p. 1.

13. Ibid., June 1969, p. 4.

14. Ibid., Spring 1972, p. 5; Winter 1972–73, p. 4.

15. *Rocky Mountain Journal*, June 9, 1976, p. 2.

16. Letter to Perry Park Residents of Filings 2, 3, 4, 5, 6, 7 from Perry Park Architectural Control Committee, August 7, 1996, printed in *The Sentinel*, September 1996.

17. "The Indian Raid in Douglas County of 1868," from the personal files of Kent Brandebery.

18. Nickson, *Just Reminiscing*, p. 33.

19. Ibid., pp. 35, 36.

20. Ibid.

ROXBOROUGH PARK

Should be owned by the city for the free use of the people.
—Robert W. Speer, writing in Henry S. Persse's guestbook, 1910

Rising two hundred feet above the valley floor, the vertical, slanted red rock formations of Roxborough State Park are indeed majestic. Geologists estimate that the layered sandstone monoliths formed nearly 150 million years ago, when dinosaurs roamed the land. Information gathered from nearby Lamb Spring Archaeological Site, where the remains of twenty-four prehistoric mammoths have been unearthed, indicates that humans may have used the area for hunting as early as 11,000 B.C. Today, developers and conservationists engage in heated debates in the struggle to direct the future of the rocky formations.

The Stephen H. Long Expedition of 1820 provided the first written description of Roxborough Park's unusual formations. In *Account of an Expedition from Pittsburgh to the Rocky Mountains*, Dr. Edwin James, botanist and geologist for the expedition, provided an early view of the rocks:

> The woodless plain is terminated by a range of naked and almost perpendicular rocks, visible at a distance of several miles, and resembling a vast wall, parallel to the base of the mountain. These rocks are sandstone. . . . They emerge at a great angle of inclination from beneath the alluvial of the plain, and rise abruptly to an elevation of one hundred and fifty, or two hundred feet. Passing within this first range, we found a narrow valley separating it from a second ridge of sandstone, of nearly equal elevation, and apparently resting against the base of a high primitive hill beyond. At the foot of the first range, the party encamped at noon, and were soon scattered in various directions, being eager to commence the examination of that interesting region.

The earliest inhabitants in the Roxborough Park area were the Plains Apache, Comanche, Ute, Cheyenne, and Arapaho tribes. The U.S. government forced the Cheyenne and Arapaho to move to reservations in Indian Territory in the 1870s, but the Utes, considered friendlier and more cooperative, remained in the area until the early 1880s when they too were moved to a reservation, in southwestern Colorado. Before their departure, the Utes conducted a three-day farewell ceremony to the land that had been their home.

White settlers began arriving in the area in the 1870s. These ambitious farmers and hopeful miners had German and English roots. Early pioneer Denis Cooper reportedly filed the area's first homestead in 1871. John Smiles followed in 1878, and Albert Epperson in 1887. As the natural beauty of the land attracted more and more attention, early settlers William E. Gray, Julius Carpenter, William R. Everett, Edward M. Griffith, and Henry S. Persse formed a partnership to oversee the development of the area, including the construction of reservoirs and irrigation ditches.

Henry Persse settled in the region in 1889 and eventually became its largest landholder. At the time of his arrival, Roxborough Park was known as Washington Park because of a striking resemblance to the profile of George Washington visible on one of the sandstone formations. However, that designation also belonged to a Denver park, creating confusion for mail carriers and tour agencies. Hence in 1902, Persse, who by then had acquired much of the land that would eventually fall within the boundaries of Roxborough State Park, suggested the name Roxborough Park, after the Persse family estate in Galway, Ireland.

Successful in land acquisition, Persse explored the park's commercial prospects. With two other settlers, John J. Weicher and William E. Gray, Persse formed the Roxborough Land Company, with plans to purchase land for residential, resort, and industrial purposes, to plot townsites, and to construct and operate transportation links to the park from other areas. A 1907 edition of the *Denver Republican* expressed high hopes for Persse's planned resort:

> By Aug. 1 of this year electric cars will be running from Denver to an all the year round resort in the mountains south of the city that promises to rival in attractiveness anything else the state can boast. A first-class, 200-room hotel, golf links, a club house, a well stocked lake, charming driveways, and comfortable cottages, all placed in surroundings said to be the most beautiful, these will form the attractions of Roxborough Park, a natural beauty spot.[1]

Despite the glowing media reports, the grandiose plans of the Roxborough Land Company were never fulfilled. The park did, however, become a favorite vacation spot and playground for the rich. Throughout the early 1900s, the scenic site offered relaxation and inspiration to an ever-growing number of visitors. Many picnickers traveled by horse and buggy or early automobile to enjoy a day among the red rocks. Most visitors to the park left feeling invigorated and revitalized, but one 1911 outing for a group of friends ended in tragedy:

> The party arrived at the Park about noon and were making preparations for dinner, when Mr. Elston arrived on the scene. He had apparently been hunting as he had his shot gun with him. He spoke very cordially to all and finally asked to have a few minutes private conversation with his wife. It is said he had previously tried to effect a reconcilliation [sic] with her. They were standing a little apart from the others and had been talking for some time, when Mrs. Elston turned to leave him and he raised his gun and shot her in the back of the head, killing her instantly. . . . At the time the first shot was fired, W.M. Daniels, son of Mrs. Elston by her first marriage, was a short distance away and saw his mother fall. He had with him a .32 calibre revolver with which he and the others had been shooting at targets. When he saw what had taken place, he started to run towards Elston and began shooting. . . . At least two of the bullets which were fired

by Daniels, took effect in Elston's body, one of which entering in the chest, was the cause of death.[2]

The park's beauty and popularity eventually prompted Denver Mayor Robert W. Speer to pen a message in Henry Persse's guest book that would reverberate for decades to come: "Should be owned by the city for the free use of the people." Many people shared Mayor Speer's sentiment. However, the battle waged by the state against various landowners and developers in order to acquire the Roxborough land for a public park proved long, controversial, and often heated.

The Colorado Mountain Club tried to persuade Denver city officials to include Roxborough in the new Denver Mountain Parks system being proposed as part of Denver's City Beautiful movement in 1915. The idea, which was the first move to secure the property as a public park, never received serious consideration from Denver officials and was dropped. In 1925, the city offered landowner Toney Helmer $21,000 for the heart of the park, where most of the vertical rock formations were found. This sum was $2,000 below Helmer's asking price, however, and the negotiations ended in a stalemate.

In 1957, the newly created Colorado State Parks and Recreation Board once again brought the issue of state purchase of Roxborough Park to the forefront. Hoping to make the area the first major park in a statewide system, the board ordered surveys and land appraisals and invited Governor Steve McNichols to tour the site in hopes of gaining his support. Although Helmer claimed he was anxious to see his longtime home established as a public park, he was reportedly coy about setting a firm price, leading some observers to question the strength of his commitment to preserve the property. Nevertheless, negotiations between state officials and Helmer continued until 1961, when disagreements between the state parks board and the state legislature's joint budget committee over funding ended efforts to acquire the property. Frustrated, Helmer turned to private buyers, and in 1967 sold a ten-year option on 3,200 acres, including the distinctive red sandstone formations, to the Eagle County Development Corporation (ECDC) for $2.5 million. Future public use and enjoyment of the park seemed unlikely.

However, other state agencies, namely the Colorado Game, Fish, and Parks Department, had a strong interest in preserving the land. The idea that Roxborough Park's beauty and character might be destroyed by development provided new momentum to secure it as a protected area. Department officials agreed with *Denver Post* columnist Dick Johnston, who warned, "This year may well be the last chance for preservation, in a public park, of probably the most spectacular of the four areas of colored rock pinnacles that dot the base of the foothills between Denver and Colorado Springs" and mounted a campaign to gain state funds to buy 1,600 acres of Roxborough Park's heartland.[3] The department prepared a slide presentation to show to state legislators that covered the history, ecology, and geology of Roxborough Park and how it could be developed for public use.

In February 1970, department officials cheered the decision of the joint budget committee to appropriate $1 million to buy the park, and made plans to apply to the U.S. Department of the Interior for matching funds. Their efforts were stopped short, however, when the joint budget committee informed them that the state had approved only $1 million for the entire purchase and that it would be illegal to spend $2 million without the further consent of the legislators. While park officials, conservationists, and state legislators engaged in an intense battle of accusations over the misunderstanding, an article in the local magazine *Colorful Colorado* expressed the apprehension felt by many interested observers:

> Sight-seers, hikers, camera bugs, geologists, students—it's hard to say who would benefit most from a public Roxborough Park. And it is even harder to say, at this date, what will become of the area—whether public initiative or private enterprise will prevail. Right now, only one thing is sure: until a decision is reached, Roxborough Park is firmly posted and closed to the general public. If this situation changes, whatever the cost, Denverites will surely consider it a true bargain.[4]

Hopes were high for state acquisition of the park, but events seemed to conspire against it. During their scramble to rectify the appropriation mistake, state conservationists and officials failed to notice that a competitor had moved into the ring. In July 1970, ECDC had quietly begun negotiations with representatives of Woodmoor Corporation, a Denver developer, for the latter's purchase of ECDC's ten-year option to purchase the park. Once again, state officials and conservationists watched the park slip through their fingers. "We publicized Roxborough Park so much trying to sell the legislature," a conservationist commented to the *Denver Post*, "that we sold it to a developer instead."[5]

Despite the apparent hopelessness of the situation, faith in possible state acquisition of the park remained. In 1971, Woodmoor Corporation, claimed it was sensitive to the need to preserve the park's most notable rock formations and offered the state 1,000 acres, including the park's heartland, for $2 million. The remaining 2,200 acres of the corporation's holdings would be used for residential and commercial sites, on which construction had already begun. When completed, the development would include a private golf course, a country club, and riding trails.

State parks department officials sought an additional $1 million in funds from the legislature for the purchase, but many legislators questioned the shrewdness of the deal. According to the negotiated agreement, approximately four hundred acres of the land offered to the state encompassed the tall red rock formations, but the remaining six hundred or so acres was comprised of unimpressive, steep hillside land near Pike National Forest. State Senator George F. Jackson, who had previously been a strong supporter of the state's purchase of the park, vowed to stop the deal, claiming that the four hundred-acre plot would not even allow visitors "enough flat land to get out of the car." The small amount of land was not worth the price, he said: "You should be able to do more than drive around [the rocks] and look at them for a million bucks."[6]

The joint budget committee agreed with Jackson and in May 1971 only approved the purchase of the park's four hundred most valuable acres for $800,000. While Woodmoor representatives considered the new offer, many interested citizens scoffed at the purchase of so little acreage, especially since it would be surrounded by houses that would detract from its natural beauty. Others felt that acquisition of the park had to start somewhere: "While 400 acres today is a depressing cutback, 10 years from now citizens may be even more resentful if that, too, has gotten away," claimed a *Denver Post* editorial.[7]

Woodmoor, disappointed by the monetary cut of the state's new offer, postponed a final decision, electing to focus instead on the company's housing and commercial plans at nearby Roxborough Park subdivision. In early1974, however, financial problems forced Woodmoor to accept the state's terms, and a contract between the two was nearly ready. When Woodmoor filed for bankruptcy, negotiations were tabled until the corporation could unravel itself from its financial troubles. Finally, in November 1975, after fourteen years of negotiation, the state of Colorado took possession of the original four hundred acres plus an additional one hundred acres in Roxborough Park's heartland for the price of $1 million. Susie Trumble, manager of Roxborough State Park, actively participated in the state's efforts to acquire the park. She remembers the relief and joy of those involved when the deal was at last finalized:

> There were a lot of people who had worked probably ten years before to try to put something together. . . [They] were just delighted that they were finally able to get something. They had worked so long and so hard.

As the state prepared plans for the development of the newly purchased park, Woodmoor Corporation's financial and legal problems deepened. The future of the Roxborough Park subdivision remained in limbo until 1979, when a new company called Roxborough Development Corporation, owned by Brad Wolff, stepped in. The new owner began planning much-needed community improvements, including revitalization of Arrowhead Golf Course, completion of streets, and the construction and sale of more than 1,000 homes.

Meanwhile, progress continued steadily at the state park next door. In 1976, the state approved a $350,000 purchase of 330 acres of land to the south and west of the park's boundaries. Additional acres were later purchased from developers and private landowners, bringing the total acreage of the park to 1,620.

In 1977, the Denver Chapter of the Colorado Archaeological Society began an extensive archaeological survey of Roxborough State Park. After a final visit in November 1978, the chapter reported the discovery of thirty-seven sites and ten isolated artifact scatters that encompassed the early Archaic through Historic periods. In its report on the archaeology, geology, and ecology of the park, the chapter concluded: "This office recommends that archaeological resources of Roxborough State Park be nominated to the National Register of Historic Places as an archaeological district." The designation was approved in 1983. Roxborough State Park also secured designation as a Colorado Natural Area in 1979 and as a National Natural Landmark in 1980.

The inevitable conflict between state park officials and new residents of Roxborough's burgeoning subdivision took place in 1981. Fearing violation of their property rights, many residents united to resist the transformation of their homes into "a tourist attraction." In an attempt to stall the much-anticipated opening of the park, homeowners erected "private road" and "no trespassing" signs along Douglas County Road No. 5 and Roxborough Drive, the park's only access roads. These efforts prompted a *Denver Post* reporter to mock that although the park belonged to the public, the only way to visit it was by helicopter. The state filed a lawsuit against the homeowners claiming the county road was public and therefore access could not be controlled by area residents. The feuding seemed ironic to a *Rocky Mountain News* reporter in 1984:

> It's the most spectacular vision to decorate the Front Range, a place for poets to find words that conjure feelings simple sentences cannot. It's a place to feel your soul stir, yet a place that mocks the failings and feuds of man. And the lawyers are *still* involved.[8]

In 1985, state officials and homeowners came to an agreement that allowed public access to the park via the roads in question. "Finally, after all these years, we're going to be able to share this beautiful place with the public," Colorado Division of Parks and Outdoor Recreation Director Ron Holliday optimistically told the *Rocky Mountain News*.[9] Although the path to the park's opening now appeared obstacle-free, officials chose to delay the start date until a visitor's center was complete. Roxborough State Park finally opened its gates to the public in 1987, seventy-seven years after Mayor Robert Speer made his prophetic pronouncement in Henry Persse's guest book. Nearly two hundred people attended a dedication celebration complete with Native American ceremonial dancing.

It wasn't long before more issues involving the area's future surfaced. In 1993, US Home announced plans to complete the long-postponed Southdowns subdivision. Located on the eastern border of Roxborough State Park, the undeveloped Southdowns land had for many years provided a buffer zone between the park and residential communities and was home to many species of wildlife. In early 1994, concerned citizens formed Friends of Roxborough State Park, a nonprofit organization committed to preventing development on the park's eastern edge. After announcing its plans to purchase the Southdowns land, the organization received widespread support in the form of financial contributions, including a $150,000 donation from Great Outdoors Colorado. Yet despite the fundraising success of the group, hopes for meeting US Home's $4 million asking price seemed unrealistic. Bill Wright, chairman of Friends of Roxborough State Park, campaigned heavily for the group and asked readers of the *Rocky Mountain News* to make a choice between a future of development and the preservation of nature:

> The Roxborough crisis presents us with an historic choice. Will we leave our children only row after row of cookie-cutter houses and a stack of 30-year mortgages? Or will we leave a legacy rich with beautiful open land inhabited by wild creatures?[10]

In May 1994, Friends of Roxborough State Park representatives guided Governor Roy Romer on a tour of the park grounds in hopes of gaining his support. Although Romer voiced his concern for the park's preservation, his support fell short of committing state funds to the cause. In 1995, the group began to make headway with US Home, which reduced the asking price for Southdowns to $2.35 million in exchange for a land swap with the state that gave the company two other desirable parcels. Finally, after months of legal squabbles and heated last-minute fundraising efforts, the Southdowns land was added to Roxborough State Park, to be preserved forever as open space. A festive group of conservationists, government officials, Native Americans, and developers celebrated the addition to the park in May 1996. The monetary contributions of the Great Outdoors Colorado Trust Fund, Douglas County, Colorado State Parks, the Friends of Roxborough State Park, and foundations such as the Gates Foundation, the Helen K. and Arthur E. Johnson Foundation, the Boettcher Foundation, the Denver Foundation, and the Bonfils-Stanton Foundation made the preservation of this open-space land buffer possible.

Park officials continue to carefully contemplate the future of the Southdowns property. In addition to updating the park's management plan, an extensive inventory of the property's cultural and natural resources was begun in 1997.

In a move less dramatic than the Southdowns acquisition, Douglas County and Colorado State Parks became partners once again in 1997 when they cooperated to purchase part of the Willow Creek Ranch South property. When added to other land secured that same year in Roxborough Park South and Rockett, the new properties amounted to more than 1,000 acres of additional open-space land for Roxborough State Park. Contemplating the pattern of land deals and acquisition of open space to preserve the serene surroundings of Roxborough State Park, Park Manager Susie Trumble stressed to the author that park officials need to continue to "keep a watchful eye on nearby development that would have an impact on the park. We can't go out and buy everything but we can keep an eye on it."

Roxborough Park's controversial history epitomizes the struggle between development and preservation that has been a source of conflict in all corners of the county and state. During nearly sixty years of bungled and ill-fated attempts by Denver and the state to purchase it, the park's integrity and stability were continually threatened by developers who focused on the area's potential for profit and ignored the importance of its preservation. Although many people celebrate the fact that state law now protects the park, others question whether this protection is enough, given the close proximity of residential and commercial development. Will the park's untamed beauty and natural wonders be less impressive if the rock formations are encircled by subdivisions or commercial centers? Certainly, visitors to Roxborough State Park deserve nothing short of unhindered vistas and open space to enjoy and appreciate the grandeur of the county's most spectacular geological formation.

Roxborough Park Historic Sites

Persse Stone House (1903: Henry S. Persse, builder), Roxborough State Park, at midway point on Fountain Valley trail.

Visitors to Roxborough State Park should plan on a 2½-mile round-trip walk if they want to see the Henry Persse house, one of the earliest structures constructed in the valley. The vernacular house consists of sandstone and mortar walls and a tin gabled roof. The two-story house is in very good condition compared to the buildings associated with it. Nearby stands a collapsed barn of hand-hewn logs, two log outbuildings (one of which is suspected to be a tool shed and the other a chicken coop), and the foundation of a bunkhouse. Various handwritten messages cover the walls of the building known as the tool shed. One message reads: "God helps those who try to help themselves, And damns the man who helps himself here."[11]

Henry Persse, a native of New York, came to Colorado in 1888 and purchased land in the Roxborough Park area one year later. At the time of his arrival, Roxborough Park was known as Washington Park because of the resemblance of one of the rock formations to George Washington. Persse is credited with changing the name to Roxborough Park after a family estate in Galway, Ireland. He constructed the stone house in 1903 and used it until 1915.

In 1918, Henry Persse died after being hit by a Denver Tramway streetcar, and the house passed to Persse family members. John Persse, a Denver policeman, found solace in the house until his death in 1937, at which point it was sold to the Anton Helmer family, which owned extensive land in the park. The house remained under Helmer family ownership until 1967, when it and several surrounding acres were sold to the Eagle County Development Corporation.

The house is now part of Roxborough State Park. Grants from the Colorado Historical Fund helped park officials conduct exterior and interior restoration work. The house, which can be seen today just off the state park's Fountain Valley trail, serves as an interesting rest stop for trail travelers.

Silicated Brick Company Kiln (1904–1918), Rampart Range Road, near Roxborough Fire Station.

This crumbling red brick kiln is the only remaining structure of a thriving turn-of-the-century brick business that spawned the small town of Silica. The company began construction of a brick manufacturing plant in 1904 after receiving a land and mineral lease from the Roxborough Land Company. The plant was built by a man known only as Mr. Gedges, who formed a partnership with the Western Feldspar Mining Company for production of bricks. Western Feldspar was known for its mineral extraction of feldspar deposits that contained calcium silicates, a component that gave the bricks a distinctive white color.

During the early 1900s, Silicated Brick Company became very successful, and the town of Silica, home to the brickworkers and miners, grew accordingly. In 1909, the Colorado & Southern Railroad constructed a spur to the town for export of bricks and feldspar deposits. Silica's success proved short-lived, however. The formula for manufacturing the unique bricks was known only by Mr. Gedges, so in 1910, when he died, he took the secret white brick formula with him, along with any hopes of further growth for the town of Silica. By 1918, the plant's brick production ceased and Silica became a ghost town. The tall, cylindrical brick kiln sits against a hillside near the entrance to the Arrowhead Golf Course, representing a grave reminder of the failures that resulted from one man's inability to share the secret of his success.

Notes

1. *Denver Republican*, January 21, 1907, p. 8.
2. *Record-Journal of Douglas County*, June 16, 1911, p. 1.
3. *Denver Post*, February 15, 1970, p. 30. The other three areas that the reporter was referring to were Red Rocks Park, Garden of the Gods, and Perry Park.
4. "A New Park for Denver?" *Colorful Colorado*, vol. 5, no. 6, May–June 1970, pp. 8D–9D.
5. *Denver Post*, June 6, 1971, p. 39.
6. *Rocky Mountain News*, February 15, 1971, p. 12.
7. *Denver Post*, June 6, 1971, p. 39.
8. *Rocky Mountain News*, September 20, 1984, p. 114.
9. Ibid.
10. Ibid., May 23, 1994, p. 20A.
11. Dale Cavanagh, *Roxborough State Park: Hogbacks and History* (Colorado Division of Parks and Outdoor Recreation, 1994), p. 12.

SEDALIA

Come and live here, either for business or pleasure, and you will not be sorry.
—Castle Rock Journal, June 12, 1889

The small town of Sedalia was founded at the intersection of roads that led county travelers elsewhere—to Denver, Castle Rock, Colorado City, or the mountain towns. When railroad tracks were extended to the town, Sedalia gained a new importance as a shipping center. Its strategic position within the county and its enterprising citizenry insured the town would thrive.

Like many Douglas County towns, the settlement that grew up at the junction of East and West Plum Creeks experienced several early name changes. First known as Round Corral, after a circular cattle corral built in 1865 by John H. Craig, the site served as an important meeting point for travelers on the First Territorial Road, which linked Denver to Colorado City. In 1869, Craig sold Round Corral to Jonathan House, who renamed it Plum or the Town of Plum, reportedly after plum trees that bordered the creek. In the early 1870s, the town underwent its final name change in honor of Henry Clay, a prominent local citizen who hailed from the famous cow town of Sedalia, Missouri.

After the Denver & Rio Grande Railroad established Plum Station on September 6, 1871, the town became a major shipping point for lumber cut in the Pike National Forest. The small town experienced the inevitable growth associated with a shipping center, prompting the railroad's subsidiary, the National Land and Improvement Company, to map and plot the streets that traversed the town. The company tagged the streets with the names of the settlement's founders, and the historical designations of Manhart Avenue, Clay Street, and Victor Street are still used today. The Atchison, Topeka & Santa Fe Railroad connected its tracks to Sedalia in 1887 and further contributed to the settlement's position as a leading transportation center for lumber, coal, wheat, cattle, and passengers.

With two railroads, stagecoach service, and a prime location along the heavily traveled First Territorial Road, Sedalia quickly attracted both settlers and businesses. A lively, gregarious Frenchman named Marquis Victor operated one of the town's earliest and most successful trades. Victor came to Sedalia in 1874 and, despite a scarcity of tools, opened a blacksmith shop that became quite profitable. The carefree nature of the Frenchman earned him the widespread respect of the county, as was noted by the *Castle Rock Journal*:

> M. Victor, the jovial and social blacksmith of Sedalia, we are glad to learn is constantly kept busy. He is a competent workman and always gives the best

satisfaction, and we are pleased to recommend him to the travelling public for promptness in all orders.[1]

In 1878, local citizen George Manhart and his father, Christian, opened the Manhart General Merchandise Store in two small rooms in the back of Marquis Victor's blacksmith shop. The father-and-son team remained partners until 1882, when Christian retired and George became the sole owner. The business flourished under George's management, and the *Castle Rock Journal* praised his success:

> It is no wonder that Sedalia can boast of such a great store business as is done by George Manhart. He started in business here ten years ago on a very small scale having nothing but his business tact to start with. How do you find him today? A rich man with his trade reaching as high as $3,500 a month and keeping the largest supply house in the county. George is a rustler and a great benefit to Sedalia.[2]

Manhart expanded his store in 1889 into a two-story, part-rhyolite stone structure that the *Castle Rock Journal* said is "the finest this side of the Queen City and is quite an addition to this thriving village."[3] Town citizens used the second floor of the store as a meeting place and dance hall for many years. In addition to a "privately owned electric plant" in the basement that provided light for the business and family home next door, Manhart also installed a unique water system that was admired by town and county residents alike.

> Mr. Geo. Manhart has the most complete water works we have seen in the county. The well is 710 feet deep. The water is pumped by a small engine into a tank which is placed on the top of his new stone store. The tank holds 250 gallons and is filled in about 30 minutes at a cost of 25 or 30 cents. Pipes are to carry the water to every part of the house as well as to the store. A hose is also attached to carry it to the yard for irrigating purposes. He has a neat stone engine house built over the well. In fact everything is as convenient as possible and has been made so at a cost of over $2,000.00. Most of the work is already completed but some of the pipes are yet to be arranged.[4]

Business was so good it even allowed for competition. John McDonald, Manhart's rival in the grocery trade, conducted a successful business, while E. Jacobs competed with Marquis Victor for the town's blacksmith patronage. John B. Karcher's 25-Mile House and Saloon, named after its distance from Denver, offered the customer, "Good Accomodations, [sic] Best Wines, Liquors, Cigars."[5] Karcher's good-natured humor also appealed to the *Castle Rock Journal*:

> J. B. Karcher, the jovial French "encyclopedia" and humorists' guide of Sedalia, was cracking his wit with friends in the Rock Monday. It is not often he comes into town, but when he does he makes Rome get up and howl.[6]

At one point, Sedalia supported three saloons, which discouraged citizens like Ethel Manhart, daughter of George Manhart, who reflected much later that "it was a very small community and for such a small locale the three saloons seemed more than enough."[7] Sedalia also did not lack for boarding facilities. In 1882, Erastus Weaver opened the Weaver House. The *Castle Rock Journal* noted:

> Erastus Weaver, of Sedalia, has his new hotel almost completed and ready to open to the public. He will have in connection a large stable, which is now being erected, and which, with the capacity of his present one, he will be amply prepared to accomodate [sic] the increasing demand.[8]

Other popular early Sedalia businesses included Frank J. Green's Meat Market, Adam Martz's lumberyard, Elmer Valentine Blunt's butcher shop, and shoe, jewelry, and barbershops run by Charles Abner Lowell. Edward Kreutzer enjoyed a position as Douglas County's only professional cigar manufacturer and sold 5,000 to 6,000 cigars per month in 1889. The *Castle Rock Journal* in June 1889 heralded the town's "Resources and Advantages:"

> We see many openings for business in Sedalia and would advise those wishing to try their luck to locate at this place. Business is prosperous here, and a person could not wish for a more healthy place. This is self-evident, from the healthy looks of its inhabitants.You will also find in Sedalia and surrounding country a friendly, jovial, people, who try to make it pleasant for all who come in contact with them. Come and live here, either for business or pleasure, and you will not be sorry.[9]

While businesses occupied the core of the town, the outskirts of Sedalia supported vast ranching and farming operations. In the early 1890s, town residents installed a separator to process milk from local ranchers. The Littleton Creamery, which opened a branch in the town, proved to be of significant assistance to ranchers who no longer had to haul their dairy products to outside markets; it contributed greatly to the sense of progress and self-sufficiency sought by many Sedalia residents. After processing the milk, the creamery shipped it north by rail to Denver and Littleton. The Sedalia creamery changed hands several times before its final purchase in 1922 by the Frink Creamery Company, based in Larkspur.

Although both the Denver & Rio Grande and the Atchison, Topeka & Santa Fe railroads contributed greatly to the growth of the town, they also posed dangers to its residents and farm animals. Residents occasionally misjudged their ability to cross the tracks as a train approached, resulting in tragedy and heavy newspaper coverage. One such incident involved Sedalia rancher Alexander McDonald in August 1899:

> He was approaching the main Sedalia crossing from the east when the fast California express, no. 2, came around the curve from under the Santa Fe overhead bridge. The engineer saw him and whistled repeatedly, but Mr. McDonald was evidently deeply engaged in thought as he drove nearer and nearer the crossing entirely unaware of the danger. Henry Manhart, Mr. McDonald's son-in-law, was standing on the depot platform and hearing the screeching of the engine he looked up, seeing the old gentleman's peril at once. He yelled, but Mr. McDonald apparently heard nothing until just as the train was upon him. Then he made an effort to get across the track in time, but the team was slow in responding and the pilot of the engine struck the wagon squarely. The man was thrown high into the air, striking the mail crane in his

decent. . . . Death was instantaneous, the skull being fractured.[10]

Another resident, who later admitted to being intoxicated, endured a similar experience, but escaped with only minor injuries:

> William Johnson attempted to cross the track and had just reached the center of it when the engine struck him, but strange to say instead of being thrown from the engine, he was caught on the "cow catcher," and with a death grip he held on for more than a mile before he was discovered, and when he was found in this position, the engineer thinking he was a tramp, asked him how he got there, and Johnson's reply was, I don't know. . . . Johnson may consider himself lucky under the circumstances; for his chances for life in this accident was one out of a hundred.[11]

As in many frontier towns, Sedalia's early days were not without violent confrontations. In 1899, a longstanding quarrel between cousins Thomas Campbell and William Hoffman led to a shootout. In an article titled "Shot Through the Heart," the *Castle Rock Journal* related the details. Campbell, a former Denver police officer, blamed his marital problems on Hoffman and often threatened his adversary's life. Known to be "quarrelsome when under the influence of liquor and . . . frequently engaged in brawls," Campbell pushed Hoffman to the edge one afternoon in May following a public event at the Manhart General Merchandise Store.

> About two o'clock as the crowd was preparing to go home, Campbell and Hoffman met at the door. John Lewis, Campbell's brother-in-law, noticed the meeting, and knowing of the bitter feeling between them hurried to overtake them in order to prevent trouble. He reached the foot of the stairs in time to see the two men facing each other, directly in front of the store. Campbell called Hoffman an offensive name. Instantly there was a shot and Campbell staggered backward. Hoffman fired again but the shot went wild. When Lewis reached Campbell's side, he had fallen to the ground. . . . Death had been instantaneous.[12]

At Hoffman's trial that November, witnesses confirmed Campbell's repeated threats to the defendant's life and revealed "that at the time of the killing he was about to attack him with a knife."[13] The jury convicted Hoffman of manslaughter but recommended the judge use mercy in sentencing. Consequently, Hoffman received the minimum sentence of one year in prison, but served only eight months before being pardoned by the governor and released.

All was not tragic in Sedalia, of course. Community social events and celebrations provided unity and camaraderie. Dances, sporting events, holiday celebrations, and picnics filled many joyful days in the town's early history. Sparring contests, described as "a scientific exhibition of the manly art of self defense," followed by grand balls were particular crowd-pleasers.[14] In 1883, the *Castle Rock Journal* commended the town for hosting a Fourth of July celebration unlike any other in the county:

> The people of Sedalia have determined to celebrate the Fourth of July with a grand basket picnic followed by good music and dancing. . . . All are invited to bring their

baskets, their sweet-hearts, their cousins and their aunts, and enjoy a jolly good time together. It seems as if this is the only place in the county where the energy has prompted activeness, so let us all accept the 'cordial welcome' and join the people of Sedalia, and make their efforts felt by the congregation of a large and cheerful crowd.[15]

Many residents took their socializing one step further with the establishment of various masonic lodges. In 1901, the Jasmine Rebekah Lodge, auxiliary to the Sedalia Odd Fellows, held its first meeting in an upper floor room of the Manhart store. A few years later they were joined by the Sunflower Grange, which heartily demonstrated its celebratory skills in 1913:

> About fifty "tripped the light fantastic toe" at the Grange meeting last Saturday at Sedalia. The music was lively, the hearts were light, and as the gentlemen were in the majority, the ladies did not get a chance to be wallflowers. The refreshment committee looked out for the poor fellows who had no partners and therefore no share of a basket. We believe everybody present enjoyed themselves and had a real good time and hope for more Grange dances in the near future.[16]

In 1921, the town rejoiced in the construction of its first church. Built largely from volunteer labor and funds, the Sedalia Community Presbyterian Church opened with high hopes and glorious visions for the future.

> This Sunday, October 23rd, 1921, will be a day long to be remembered in the history of Sedalia and her neighbors and they do well to extend their invitation to the county as a whole to witness and participate with them in the celebration of a work well done for the betterment of her citizens and town, the results of which will be as lasting as the hills which stand in the distance along the western horizon.[17]

With the approach of the 1930s, Sedalia businesses included two garages, two lumber mills, three general merchandise stores, a restaurant, a bakery, a billiards hall, and a hotel. The town also soon hosted a rejuvenated fire department. First organized in 1907, the Sedalia Volunteer Fire Department's membership had slowly diminished with time "when some of the more active ones passed to the Great Beyond."[18] In 1932, it was reorganized by a "live bunch of fellows who are determined to keep an active fire fighting crew ready for everyone at all times," and a cornerstone was laid for a new brick firehouse.[19] Because Sedalia lacked a water system, firefighters made arrangements with Santa Fe railroad officials to run pipelines from the company's water tank to the center of town for emergency use. In 1958, the railroad presented the tank, pipelines, and other water system equipment to the newly formed Sedalia Water and Sanitation District.

Sedalia made headlines in Denver newspapers in 1946 when the Brotherhood of the White Temple, a religious organization created by Dr. M. Doreal who borrowed from various aspects of ancient and modern religions, set up a retreat in the foothills southwest of town. In preparation for the nuclear war they were sure was coming, the group, led by Dr. Doreal, built what the *Rocky Mountain News* called an "atomic armageddon refuge."[20] For years the refuge, named Shamballa Ashrama, and the mystery surrounding its builders incited controversy and curiosity among Plum Creek and Jarre Canyon residents.

Suspicious county and state officials kept a close eye on the group and in 1973 confiscated 112 dynamite sticks. In contrast to its mysterious past, the church today is a quiet community of young and old families, many of whom participate in teaching metaphysics courses to students around the world by correspondence.

In April 1954, an article in the *Littleton Independent* screamed, "CURIOSITY VIEWED ON PLUM CREEK BEARS HUMAN AND ANIMAL TRAITS: Three Local Men Describe Antics of 'Ape-Like' Man With Green Face."[21] According to the story, three Colorado Springs bullfrog hunters witnessed what they described as a hairy "monster" with a green face and menacing jaws loitering along Plum Creek. As the horrified trio watched, the creature "went into an act like a voodoo ceremony; swinging [a] chicken around and wringing its neck like a gorilla."[22] The tale alarmed Plum Creek residents, many of whom demanded a posse be organized to find the strange invader. Within two days, two thousand people had swarmed to the Plum Creek area, hoping to catch a glimpse of the creature and the 13-inch footprints it left behind at the scene of its sacrificial rite. One woman penned a short poem entitled "The Legend of Plum Creek," offering an explanation for the creature's origins:

> Its body was covered with long black hair,
> The color of sage was its face,
> Its slobbering lips betrayed its rage,
> Was this creature from outer space?[23]

Days later, hysteria among residents reached new heights when a woman reportedly saw the creature in her headlights along Plum Creek Road. Rumors abounded that the green-faced monster was actually "an eccentric prisoner" recently released from a Littleton jail or the co-owner of a local radio station known to have rented a gorilla costume near the date of the creature's first appearance. The *Littleton Independent* received several anonymous letters claiming responsibility for the acts. Shortly thereafter, officials determined that the "Plum Creek Legend" was a hoax and dropped the case. Although the impersonator never surfaced, the anomaly was eventually forgotten, and Sedalia and Plum Creek residents settled back into normal, less-frightening routines.

Eleven years after residents put the green monster to rest, Plum Creek experienced a true nightmare: On June 16, 1965, East Plum Creek surged over its banks, sparking "the most destructive flood in the history of Sedalia."[24] The torrent washed away two bridges, two public buildings, and seven homes, and caused extensive damage to railroad tracks and electrical, telephone, and gas lines. Shocked residents watched as the rising river engulfed Sedalia's main streets and swallowed the Community Presbyterian Church and the cherished Sunflower Grange Hall. "All are grieved over the loss of the church and the Grange building which has taken years of hard work to build and maintain," a town resident reflected days later.[25] Despite the devastation, Sedalia demonstrated its resilience with reconstruction efforts the following spring. In September 1966, citizens reveled in the dedication of a newly erected Sedalia Community Presbyterian Church. The Sunflower Grange Hall was also resurrected when members acquired a used Air Force barracks. The first meeting was held in the renovated building in April 1969.

The 1980s saw new developments for Sedalia. In February 1980, an Arvada company called Western Sling, manufacturer of steel cable slings, chose Sedalia as its new plant site because company officials "wanted to get out of the hassle of Denver traffic, get away from the brown cloud and get to where there was affordable land."[26] That same year, the Peregrine's Perch became the town's first art gallery, and the Intermountain Rural Electric Association moved its headquarters from Littleton to Sedalia. The following year saw the beginning of Sedalia Days, an annual community celebration that featured chili contests, parades, tug-of-wars, and street dancing.

Gravel mining surfaced as one of Sedalia's most controversial issues during the 1980s. In June 1980, the Douglas County Board of County Commissioners denied an application by the Jarre Canyon Gravel Pit company to expand its mining operation after residents expressed concern over dangerous driving conditions posed by heavy truck traffic. Sedalia residents again opposed a gravel mining application, submitted in 1983 by the Cherokee Ranch Sand and Gravel Company. The Cherokee company formed after Tweet Kimball, one of the county's leading ranchers, entered into a partnership with Cooley Gravel Company to mine gravel from a parcel of Kimball's Cherokee Ranch, approximately two miles south of Sedalia. Residents listed noise pollution and incompatibility with the surrounding area as reasons to reject the project. Citing these protests and their own concerns over increased traffic along U.S. Highway 85, county commissioners denied the proposal.

Nonetheless, the determined mine owners resubmitted the application in April 1984, with the additional proposal that an onsite processing plant be constructed in order to decrease the amount of truck traffic on area roads. When the application was denied once again, the Cooley Gravel Company filed a lawsuit against the county commissioners that resulted in a 1985 settlement. The agreement secured the county commissioners' approval of the mining application as long as Cooley Gravel Company constructed acceleration and deceleration lanes leading into the project along U.S. Highway 85 and contributed $100,000 for improvements to the intersection of U.S. Highway 85 and State Highway 67. The processing plant opened in 1988 and gravel mining continued on the property until early 1998, when the operation closed due to a reduction in resources.

As growth issues enveloped many of the communities and areas surrounding Sedalia throughout the remainder of the 1980s, many residents expressed the need for a master plan that would allow them to retain control over the future of their village. In February 1990, the Douglas County Planning Commission appointed thirty residents to the Sedalia Subarea Planning Committee. One year later the group presented the "Sedalia Subarea Master Plan," intended as a supplement to the Douglas County Master Plan. The subarea plan proposed investigating improvements in water and sewage systems, preserving open space through parks and trails, and improving road paving. The document also outlined the varying interests and goals of the town and suggested a direction for its future.

> In general, Sedalia residents like the rural character of their community. They want to preserve historical structures, agricultural land uses, and both private and public open lands as an integral part of their rural lifestyle and as a link to their heritage. New growth must remain in scale and character with the current land uses in the Sedalia Subarea.

Sedalia was given a boost to those goals when, in December 1996, Tweet Kimball bestowed an extraordinary gift on the county—her home of forty-two years, Cherokee Ranch. Hoping to preserve the ranch as an open-space haven for wildlife and to ensure the protection of her fifteenth-century Scottish-style castle as a public museum, Kimball offered to sell the ranch's development rights to the county for a mere $2 million (the property had been appraised at roughly $20 million) with the proviso that the Cherokee Ranch and Castle Foundation manage the grounds and public education facilities. County officials immediately seized the offer and agreed to purchase the ranch as a conservation easement to prevent it from being developed.

Another spacious area was added near Sedalia in 1997. This land, however, was not set aside as a preserve for the general public. It consisted of a 7,100-yard, 18-hole private golf course owned by RE/MAX International chair and co-founder David Liniger. Known as The Sanctuary, the course was designed by Jim Engh, an internationally known golf course architect, who took considerable care to blend the greens and fairways into the site's natural terrain. The course received *Golf Digest*'s award for the best new private course in the nation. Although it is the personal domain of Liniger, the course is sometimes opened to business colleagues and select charities.

As some areas surrounding Sedalia secured permanent refuge from development, others were targeted for the blooming of modern communities. In late 1996, county planners received plans for a proposed luxury golf resort and residential community called Jackson Creek Ranch, located on approximately 1,300 acres southwest of town along State Highway 105. When the proposal met strong opposition from neighboring residents, mainly because it entailed acquisition of nearby Pine Cliff Ranch for its water rights, company officials went back to the drawing board and emerged a year later with a revised plan. The company proposed two instead of four golf courses and fifty-two rather than four hundred residential lots. Other plans included a private golf club, golf training facility, a 160-unit lodge, 325 guest cabins, a general store, a gas station, a water treatment and storage facility, stables, and a trail system. In response, neighboring residents formed the Western Douglas County Citizens Alliance (WDCCA), to convey their concerns over the intense pressure the development posed for already scarce water supplies. After more than a year of deliberation, a county water consultant gave a conditional approval to the plan in 1999, much to the chagrin of the WDCCA. Months later, the Douglas County Planning Commission refused to approve the project, claiming it did not comply with agricultural zoning requirements. WDCCA members, aware of the property's uncertain future, cautiously cheered the delays.

The little town that started out as a corral continues to serve as a crossroads between the metropolis of Denver and the ever expanding city of Castle Rock. In spite of changes unimaginable to those who settled here in the late 1860s, Sedalia retains some of the atmosphere of a small frontier settlement. The town's peaceful and prosperous history points the way to an equally bright future.

Sedalia Historic Sites

Cherokee Ranch (1924–1927: Burnham Hoyt, architect), 6113 N. Daniels Park Road. **Limited public access.**

This extravagant castle has the grandeur and elegance of a fifteenth-century Scottish castle. In the early 1920s, New England–born Charles Alfred Johnson, a real estate investor, and his wife, Alice Gifford Phillips, sought a rural weekend lodge away from their busy Denver household. They chose a hillside near Sedalia and bought the land from a sheep farmer. In 1924, the couple commissioned their friend, architect Burnham Hoyt, to build a summer retreat for them. Hoyt hired a group of

Cornish stonemasons to help him construct a typical Scottish castle, using native rhyolite stone quarried from the top of the mesa. Hoyt included various leaded and bottle-glassed windows, four towers, gargoyles, turrets, battlements, a walled courtyard, and several chimneys. Two and a half years later, the completed structure contained twenty-four rooms; the main room was 25 feet wide and 40 feet long.

The Johnsons named their new home "Charlford," a combination of the names of their two sons, Charles and Gifford. During their occupancy, from 1927 to 1949, the family entertained many socialites, politicians, and friends from all over the world.

In May 1954, an ambitious woman named Mildred Montague Genevieve "Tweet" Kimball became the new owner of the Charlford castle and property. A Tennessee native, Kimball was the daughter of a distinguished West Point graduate. After divorcing her first husband, Kimball looked toward the West to begin a new life. She settled into Charlford and embarked upon the male-dominated occupation of cattle ranching. After renaming the elegant home Cherokee Ranch, in honor of the Cherokee Indians of Tennessee, Kimball purchased several rare Santa Gertrudis cattle from Texas and became the first rancher to introduce the breed to the Rocky Mountain region. The Santa Gertrudis breed resulted from the accidental mating of a Brahma longhorn bull with a shorthorn cow on King Ranch in Kingsville, Texas, and was recognized in 1940 as the only breed solely of American origin.

Kimball established the Rocky Mountain Gertrudis Association in 1961 and conducted a breed improvement program sponsored by Santa Gertrudis Breeders International Association on her ranch. She was the first woman to become a member of the National Western Stock Show and won several stock show awards throughout the nation.

Kimball loved Cherokee Ranch and in December 1996, two years after its designation to the National Register of Historic Places, decided to ensure its preservation. She offered the ranch's development rights to Douglas County for $2 million, with the contingency that the Cherokee Ranch and Castle Foundation administer the property as an open-space wildlife sanctuary and maintain the castle as a public museum. County officials eagerly accepted the offer and agreed to purchase a conservation easement consisting of $200,000 payments for ten years to ensure that the property remained undeveloped. Kimball's generosity was honored with awards from the Southern Economic Development Council and Colorado Preservation, Inc. In March 1997, the Cherokee Ranch and Castle Foundation received a $24,000 grant from Great Outdoors Colorado to assist with construction of trail and road systems and a visitor's center, and with plans for open-space and wildlife preservation.

Kimball died of a heart attack in January 1999 at the age of eighty-four. Affectionately described as "Douglas County's venerable matriarch," her legacy of enormous contributions to the county will be as permanent as her beloved castle and ranchland.[27]

Church of St. Philip in the Field (1872: Newton S. Grout, original builder; William Curtis and John Harris, renovators), 5 miles south of Sedalia on Highway 105.

Visitors to this white Gothic Revival church pass through a black wrought iron gate and enter a peaceful graveyard graced by cedar trees and lilac bushes. A notable attraction of the church is its sharply peaked gable roof and six north- and south-facing double-hung windows framed by pointed arches. A small vestibule on the east side contains the main double doorway topped by a fanlight.

In 1872, trustees of the newly formed Bear Canon Methodist Congregation commissioned Newton S. Grout, a former drummer boy for the Union Army, to construct this first church of Douglas County. Grout chose to model it after his childhood memories of New England churches, particularly one he frequented in Maine. With volunteer labor and money, construction of the outside of the church was quickly achieved, but a lack of funds prevented completion of the inside. Nonetheless, the church opened that same year, furnished with pews of planks supported by boxes, and was used by various faiths.

In 1884, long-delayed plans for completion of the interior began, but these efforts were again thwarted when a man posing as a Methodist minister disappeared with most of the money fundraisers had collected. In 1886, Bishop Reverend William Spaulding of the Episcopalian Diocese of Colorado traded St. Mark's Church in Bergen Park for the unfinished church in Bear Canon. Funds were immediately raised for a complete renovation of the church, and William Curtis and John Harris were hired to supervise the construction. Curtis drew the plans, and Harris was employed as carpenter. When the work was completed, the remodeled interior included a sanctuary, vestibule, sacristy, pews, chancel, altar, communion rail, and brick chimney. Christened the Church of St. Philip in the Field, after an event in the life of St. Philip, the church held its opening services on December 23, 1888. It was further honored on April 11, 1973, by being entered on the National Register of Historic Places and is still in use as an Episcopal Church.

Indian Park Cemetery (1900), 10 miles west of Sedalia on State Highway 67.

The Indian Park Cemetery, also known as Jarre Canyon Cemetery, rests behind Indian Park School and holds the remains of several Sedalia and Jarre Canyon residents. William Smith, a sawmill operator, deeded the land for the schoolhouse to the school district in 1883. It was not intended to also serve as a cemetery, but when William died in the winter of 1900, he was buried behind the school because the snow was too deep to transport his body to Sedalia. His wife, Hannah, subsequently donated an acre of land surrounding her husband's grave to the school district to be reserved as a local cemetery. As years passed, more families chose the small cemetery as the final resting spot of their loved ones. Today, there are eight marked graves, six of which are the grandchildren of William and Hannah. The mother of the children, Margaret Smith Kirby, is also buried there.

The Indian Park Cemetery remains in excellent condition, a testimony to the care local residents devote to its upkeep. In the fall of 1963, Claude Smith, one of William and Hannah's grandsons, whose ashes were buried in the cemetery in 1977, constructed a fence around the graves, and Helen Pierce, Claude's niece, made "markers" from indigenous rocks. In 1972, the two acres that made up the schoolhouse and cemetery were sold to the Indian Park Schoolhouse Association, which was organized in 1972 by Jarre Canyon and Indian Park residents to protect and preserve the historical sites.

Indian Park School (1884: builder unknown), 10 miles west of Sedalia on State Highway 67.

This single-story, white wooden structure rises to a steep gable roof with overhanging eaves. The main entrance to the one-room schoolhouse is located on the south side of the building through an enclosed entry or cloakroom. Double-hung rectangular windows are set in a plain wooden frame.

The schoolhouse was constructed by local residents in 1884.

Twelve children, many of whom trekked over four miles a day to receive their education, were welcomed as its first students. Indian Park School operated from 1884 to 1958, during which time it was also used as a community meeting place. Social activities included picnics, holiday parties, pie socials, sledding parties, and dances. The school was abandoned until 1972, when it was purchased from the Douglas County School Board by the Indian Park Schoolhouse Association. The group sought to preserve the property as a historical site and community center. Members contributed much time and money to the renovation of the building. In 1974, the group organized a Fourth of July picnic, the first community event to be held at the school since its abandonment. Since then, the building has housed Christmas bazaars, community meetings, reunions, weddings, flea markets, square dancing, and many other events. On February 8, 1978, the schoolhouse was listed on the National Register of Historic Places.

Manhart Family Home (1908: builder unknown), 5450 W. State Highway 67.

This early nineteenth-century building is among the most beautiful in Sedalia. A regular-coursed red brick exterior dominates the first floor, while the second floor consists of alternating patterns of plain and fish-scale shingles. Vertically placed brick arches adorn each downstairs window and doorway. Bay windows, a full front and side facade porch, and several chimneys are among the building's most interesting features.

Built in 1908, the home belonged to two of Sedalia's most distinguished citizens, George and Bertha Manhart, and their thirteen children. In 1878, George and his father, Christian, started a mercantile business in two small rooms at the rear of Marquis Victor's blacksmith shop. Father and son remained partners until 1882, when Christian retired. George continued the business and in 1889 constructed a two-story, part rhyolite structure to house his store. He installed a heating and water system that supplied both the store and his grand residence next door. George's diligence and ambition made him one of the most successful merchants in Sedalia.

> As a merchant he is keen, painstaking, anxious to please, and content with small profit on each sale. His goods he sells at reasonable prices, which makes him popular among the people of the surrounding country. His entire time and thought are given to his business, and he has never mingled in public affairs, other than to cast a Republican ticket at elections.[28]

Although the Manhart store was torn down in 1987, the family home continues to grace the small town with unique charm. Starting in 1982, the building catered to hungry Sedalia residents and visitors as a gourmet restaurant called Mister K's. During the construction of additions to the building, the new owners—out of respect to its early quaintness and history—preserved many of the original architectural features, such as molding, detailed woodwork, and an elegant marble fireplace. Since 1986, the building has housed a popular restaurant called Gabriel's.

McDonald General Store/Jasmine Rebekah Lodge No. 83 (1886–1888: builder unknown), northeast corner of Manhart Street and Rio Grande Street.

This one-story, white clapboard structure features a front gabled roof with a stepped false front on its east side. A small porch and rear shed are connected to the building.

John McDonald, the original owner of the building, used it as a general merchandise store starting in the mid-1880s. McDonald, called "Peanut John" by town residents because of his penchant for sharing peanuts with customers, became one of Sedalia's most successful merchants. The *Castle Rock Journal* claimed he had "a snug little place well filled with goods, and he has the confidence of the public; he is nearly always busy with customers."[29]

In the 1920s the McDonald General Store closed and remained abandoned until the Independent Order of Odd Fellows purchased it in 1933. The organization converted the building into a Masonic hall by covering the storefront windows and door. In 1976 Jasmine Rebekah Lodge No. 83, whose members had used the hall as a meeting place since the 1930s, received title to the building from the Independent Order of Odd Fellows.

Victor House (1875–1876: Judge John Craig, builder), 5132 Plum Avenue. **Private residence.**

This two-story American Gothic home is believed to be the first brick house built in Sedalia. The bricks are set in common bond pattern and rise to a wood-shingled gabled roof with boxed cornices. A brick chimney straddles the rear peak of the roof, while stone lintels and sills frame the double-hung sash windows found on all sides of the house. A long, narrow, westward-facing balcony sits atop a veranda supported by four square wooden posts.

Marquis Victor, born in northern France on December 14, 1839, was the most notable resident of the house. As a young boy, Victor had a passion for adventure. He left home at the age of nine and sailed to various seaports throughout the world. During his travels, Victor learned the blacksmith trade and made use of the skill when he arrived in the United States in 1861. He settled in Sedalia in 1874 and bought "the finest brick house in the community" two years later from John H. Craig, one of Sedalia's founding fathers.[30] In June 1889 the *Castle Rock Journal* fondly noted:

> M. Victor, one of the old timers of Sedalia has done and is doing a large business in blacksmithing. He has made money at his trade, owning a large ranch and having one of the most beautiful residences here.[31]

A well-known blacksmith, livery owner, rancher, and school district director, Victor was described by Douglas County historian Josephine Marr as a "mythical figure of early day Sedalia."[32] Rumors and tall tales surrounded Victor. One anecdote claimed that the diminutive but strong Victor once lifted a fellow who pestered him and swung him in the air by his hair. Other tales had Victor cast as the hero of many Civil War battles in which bullets often tore at his clothing, yet he miraculously escaped unscathed.

During Victor's ownership, locals referred to the house as Victor Hall. The upstairs hosted town meetings and events such as weddings, funerals, grange meetings, and dances. Today known as the Victor House, it survives as a private residence.

Notes

1. *Castle Rock Journal*, October 18, 1881, p. 3.
2. Ibid., June 12, 1889, p. 1.
3. Ibid., June 19, 1889, p. 4; November 27, 1889, p. 1.
4. Ibid., September 11, 1889, p. 4.
5. Ibid., July 13, 1881, p. 1.
6. Ibid., July 15, 1885, p. 3.
7. *Douglas County Express*, October 18, 1978, p. 17.
8. *Castle Rock Journal*, October 12, 1881, p. 3.
9. Ibid., June 12, 1889, p. 1.
10. *West Creek Mining News and the Nighthawk Mountain Echo*, August 5, 1899, p. 2.
11. *Castle Rock Journal*, December 14, 1887, p. 3.
12. Ibid., May 12, 1899, p. 2.
13. Ibid., December 1, 1899, p. 2.
14. Ibid., April 28, 1899, p. 3.
15. Ibid., June 20, 1883, p. 3.
16. *Record-Journal of Douglas County*, November 28, 1913, p. 1.
17. Ibid., October 21, 1921, pp. 1, 4.
18. Ibid., November 24, 1933, p. 1.
19. Ibid.
20. *Rocky Mountain News*, August 30, 1946, p. 22.
21. *Littleton Independent*, April 30, 1954, Newspaper Clippings Notebook, Local History Collection, Philip S. Miller Library.
22. Ibid.
23. Newspaper and date unknown, Clippings Notebook, Local History Collection, Philip S. Miller Library.
24. *Douglas County News*, June 24, 1965, pp. 1, 5, 8.
25. Ibid.
26. *Douglas County News Press*, May 29, 1980, p. 3.
27. Ibid., January 20, 1999, pp. 1A, 6A, 16A; August 4, 1999, p. 1C; *Highlands Ranch Herald*, January 21, 1999, pp. 1, 17.
28. *Portrait and Biographical Record of Denver and Vicinity Colorado* (Chicago: Chapman Publishing, 1898), p. 1105.
29. *Castle Rock Journal*, quoted in Josephine Lowell Marr, *Douglas County: A Historical Journey* (Gunnison, Colo.: B & B Printers, 1983), p. 117.
30. Marr, *Douglas County: A Historical Journey*, p. 115; *Portrait and Biographical Record of Denver and Vicinity*, p. 1161.
31. *Castle Rock Journal*, June 12, 1889, p. 1.
32. *Douglas County News*, date unknown, Local History Collection, Philip S. Miller Library.

SPRING VALLEY-CHERRY VALLEY

This seems to be a place of many changes.
—Castle Rock Journal, April 23, 1884

Located in the southeastern sector of Douglas County, Spring Valley and Cherry Valley reflect the region's geography and history. The areas are located on the Platte-Arkansas Divide, a plateau that extends eastward from the Front Range giving way to many fingerlike creeks that flow into the South Platte River to the west and the Arkansas River to the southeast. The abundance of fertile land enticed farmers and ranchers to the area as early as the 1860s, and the remnants of these grand, productive homesteads are still found in the valley. The long distances between developing county towns and communities forged cooperation and harmony among valley residents. While shared goals and occupational similarities united the community for several decades, a surge of modern residential development has occasioned a precarious adjustment between old and new residents.

In July 1860, Englishman Joseph Gile and his wife, Annie, chose the lush, rolling hills of Spring Valley as their new home, and Joseph used the earth to harvest his dreams. Another resident wrote of Joseph:

> Mr. Gile, helped by Henry Daniels, plowed the first furrows ever plowed on that divide, and sowed the ground to turnips, which yielded well. But the antelopes began to eat the turnips out of the ground; so Mr. Gile dug them up while still small and sold them in Denver, getting 20 cents a pound for them.[1]

Gile constructed a log cabin on his property that, starting in 1863, doubled as a stage stop. Because the stage also brought the mail, Gile's ranch served as the area's post office until March 27, 1865, when an official post office was established for the Spring Valley area, with George Redman as postmaster. Later that year, Redman was killed in an Indian raid, and Joseph Gile took over the duties of postmaster.

Deadly clashes between settlers and Native Americans such as the Arapaho and Cheyenne peaked during the 1860s throughout much of the Colorado plains. The tribes distrusted the incursions of newcomers on land that their ancestors had lived upon for centuries, and the sound of the natives' war cries struck terror among settlers. For protection from native uprisings, Spring Valley residents constructed a log fort with high walls and portholes from which guns could be fired. While most of the settlers eagerly moved into the fort during times of crisis and avoided all contact with local tribes, Jonathon Lincoln, one of the area's farmers, reportedly showed no fear even when faced with certain death.

> Lincoln and a Mexican were out in the harvest-field binding oats when they saw the Indians approaching. The Mexican saved himself by flight, but Lincoln folded his arms and calmly awaited the coming of the savages. Without hesitation they killed him, took his scalp, and departed again into the recesses of the adjacent pinery.[2]

Despite the danger posed by local tribes, the fertile land of Spring Valley persuaded many western pioneers to grab a shovel and establish a homestead. Among these early settlers were brothers John and Jacob Geiger, who passed through the area in 1864 while convoying Confederate prisoners to Fort Bent, Colorado. They were so enthralled with the valley that they returned in 1867 to live within the small settlement. The two became active members of the Divide Grange, which established a chapter in the area in 1874. Jacob Geiger managed a general store owned and operated by grange members. Geiger conducted his duties as store manager with an alacrity that overflowed into his store advertisements.

THE GRANGE STORE
AT
SPRING VALLEY
Is now in full blast and the ranchmen can get their
Groceries, Supplies, Garden Seeds, Farm Implements, etc.,
as cheap as the cheapest.
Call on the Wild Dutchman AND SEE FOR YOURSELF
Bring your Ranche Produce
JACOB GEIGER, manager[3]

In April 1884, in a letter to the *Castle Rock Journal*, the Divide Grange Co-operative Association, organized by grange members to run their mercantile and supply operation, announced that it had "sold its entire interest in Divide Grange store to Jacob Geiger, who will continue the store at the old stand."[4] The store occupied one end of the building that also housed the area's post office. Adjacent to the store was a one-room schoolhouse built by John Geiger and resident Harrison Bucks sometime before 1874. A nearby livery stable sheltered the horses for the stage that supplied goods for the store.

Among the stage drivers was Lorenzo Leppart, a well-regarded member of the grange who performed odd jobs for Jacob Geiger in return for board in the back of the grange store. In April 1884, the Spring Valley correspondent for the *Castle Rock Journal* revealed that Leppart had more than his career on his mind: "Mm. Leppart and Jim Baker are baching together this spring, but rumor says they are trying to secure partners of the female persuasion so as to quit baching."[5] Indeed, love came to Leppart in the person of Louisa "Janie" Richey, an eighteen-year-old who worked for John Geiger. After a brief courtship, the two announced their engagement; unfortunately, both soon fell victim to one of the worst smallpox epidemics in Douglas County's history.

> L. Leppart . . . is little better at present and his complaint has developed into a genuine case of small pox. When the disease was pronounced genuine he was in the Postoffice here, and the school children were all exposed. As soon as the fact was made known school was dismissed, and precautious methods have been employed to keep the children and those who have been exposed from association with others. Intense excitement prevails

> in the vicinity. Leppart is Postmaster and no one now goes to the office. The inconvenience necessitates the leaving of our mail matters at Greenland. It is not known from what source the contagion was contracted. However, he was in Denver about fourteen days prior to the time of taking sick.[6]

During Leppart's illness, Janie Richey faithfully tended to her fiancée and reportedly never left his side until he passed away on January 27, 1885. Leppart's fellow grange members honored his memory with a touching tribute:

> It becomes our sad duty to pay a mournful and sorrowful tribute of respect to an honored brother; and to his memory we would gladly do fitting honors of fraternal love and friendship, but that we know his true and exemplary life has already written his worth in imperishable words, and in terms far more eloquent than any pen can command. . . . In the death of Lorenzo Leppert his father has lost an affectionate son, the community a respectable citizen, and the Grange a valued member whose watchword was, 'ever where duty calls.' In his Grange and neighborhood he will be sadly missed and his loss keenly felt; but in this, as in all things else, we bow submissively to the Hand that doeth all things well. We believe our loss to be his gain, and that the gate of death is but the door that opens to eternal life, the harbinger of the morn that precedes the day of eternal sunshine and rest.[7]

Shortly thereafter, the "gate of death" opened to admit Janie Richey. She and Leppart were laid to rest in the Spring Valley Cemetery, dressed in their unused wedding garments. In an expression of mourning for the losses, the grange draped its charter for thirty days.

Although the *Castle Rock Journal* reported that both Jacob and Annie Geiger also contracted the deadly disease, Leppart and Richey were the only fatalities. Because the afflicted spent a great deal of time in the grange store and post office, many residents shunned the building for fear of infection. Paranoia apparently overcame some unknown party in the community, who set fire to the structure in April 1885. The *Castle Rock Journal* reported a mixture of good and bad news for the community:

> The Spring Valley post office has burned down, the building and goods being a total loss. The building and store were insured for $2400, which will not cover the loss. It is not known how the fire originated. Mr. Cnowles [sic], John Pollock, and Phillip Crawshaw were soon on the ground, and to them we are under obligation for saving the school house, as large pieces of burning wood were blown to it from the burning building.[8]

With one strike of a match, the building that had become the center of community business and social gatherings was destroyed. More than a year later, the simple comment of a Spring Valley columnist reflected an enduring sense of loss among area residents: "We are lonesome now, we have no corner grocery."[9]

As more settlers moved into the divide country, isolation among valley residents decreased. New ranches and farms speckled the areas north and east of Spring Valley and eventually became small communities named after early homesteaders, homes back East, or features unique to the valley landscape. In some of these settlements residents repeatedly changed the names of these communities to honor popular citizens or ranches.

One of these early settlements, located six miles northeast of Spring Valley, was first known as Virginia Ranch. It served as an important stage stop and post office along the Cherokee Trail in the 1860s. In February 1871, the name was changed to Frost's Ranch, and one year later it became Rock Ridge. In May 1885, the Rock Ridge post office was moved to the house of Jonathan Case, manager of the general merchandise store, but the town's name was not officially changed to Case until 1897. A final switch from Case to Irving, after W. Irving Whittier—a local schoolteacher, clergyman, *Castle Rock Journal* editor, and Case post office manager—took place in 1913. Despite the many name changes, the settlement retained a solid community identity with the establishment of a school, cemetery, grange, and community hall that featured dances, church services, and literary society meetings.

In May 1900, the Case Cheese and Butter Company began operation and later offered stock in the business at five dollars a share. With the enormous popularity of dairy farming among divide ranchers, creameries were not only needed but were a guaranteed success. The small factories processed fresh milk into cheese and then shipped the finished product to outside retailers, creating convenient markets for locally produced milk. In addition to Case Cheese and Butter, the Spring Valley Cheese Company also catered to ranchers beginning in 1894, when Jesse Knowles and Newton Alderman initiated an ambitious partnership. Despite the importance of the two factories, neither could match the success of the Williams Cheese Factory, developed by David Rice Williams on his West Cherry Creek ranch during the 1880s. After gold fever prompted a move from their cozy Massachusetts home to the West, Williams and his wife, Elvira, ran a shoe store in Denver before moving to the valley in 1873. Always on the lookout for opportunity, Williams saw the need for a local creamery and built a two-story building on his ranch to house the operation in 1889. Preparations included buying a tall steam boiler and several 5,000-gallon storage vats, employing a New York cheesemaker named John Rupert, and procuring milk from local ranchers. In 1895, the *Castle Rock Journal* reported that the factory accepted "thirteen hundred pounds of milk every other day," and shipped more than 200 cheeses by rail from Greenland in one week.[10]

Anchored by the prospering Williams Cheese Factory, a small settlement called Williamsville emerged. The name was changed to Cherry after the postal department, which established an office in the settlement in 1900, rejected the name Williamsville as too long.

Early settlers of the divide area did not allow the miles separating ranches to thwart their desire for socialization. Neighborly dances, picnics, holiday celebrations, dinners, spelling bees, and weddings at local schools, churches, and homes were popular events. The gatherings unified these early settlers, and their celebrations were conducted in grand style.

> The Fourth passed off very pleasantly at [Rock] Ridge. A good number were present and all seem to enjoy the exercises. No report of the winners of prizes has been sent us but we did receive a report on the dinner which is said to be entitled to first prize. Of course. That is what we expected.[11]

After the Spring Valley cheese factory (constructed in 1894) was abandoned, the building was converted into a dance center.

It was named "Tipperary Hall," after a fondness among dancers for the Irish tune "It's a Long, Long Way to Tipperary." Two-steppers also attended celebrations in the homes and on the landscaped grounds of settlers throughout the valley. Outdoor picnics and dances in tree groves belonging to Jonathan Case near Rock Ridge and to David Tintle along East Cherry Creek were popular Fourth of July and Memorial Day activities.

Gatherings with a more intellectual focus took place among members of the Case Enterprise Literary Society. The group met weekly to debate important nineteenth-century issues such as the influence of the press upon society. The society symbolized yet another means of unification among valley residents and contributed to what the Divide Valley Board of Trade felt were unique traits of the area's residents:

> The character of the present residents of the Divide is the best, being composed of intelligent, progressive, orderly men and women. Our schools and churches, farmer's club unions, social gatherings, and societies, all are supported by old and young. A more hospitable, kind-hearted, healthy and intelligent people it would be difficult to find.[12]

The ranches and farms that peppered Cherry Valley and Spring Valley during the late nineteenth-century were important family businesses, and the local newspapers chronicled their successes and failures. "The crops in Spring Valley never looked better than at present," the *Castle Rock Journal* beamed in 1882. "There has been considerable small grain and potatoes put in this spring and the ranchmen are feeling encouraged."[13] In 1888, editors marveled at the size of a Rock Ridge farmer's corn, which was reportedly "so tall it has to bow its head to stand up in the office."[14] Successful harvests required days of hard work and determination. "One of the Divide farmers says he is now working under the eight-hour law," reported one local paper. "He works an eight-hour shift before noon and another one in the afternoon."[15]

Although farmers enjoyed much success from the cultivation of corn, beans, sugar beets, wheat, and other crops, it was the valley's potato crops that gained national recognition. In 1889, the Divide Valley Board of Trade heralded the advent of prosperous potato farming:

> Potato culture on the Divide is rapidly being reduced to a science. The best machinery for the rapid and cheap planting, digging, sorting and sacking of the crop has been largely introduced. The natural adaptability of the soil for the complete growth of the tuber, added to our situation as regards the best potato markets of the west, gives the Divide a great advantage over the other potato districts of Colorado. We are on a direct line to markets in every direction. Potatoes from the Divide take a high position on the markets wherever shipped. We think it safe to say that potato culture on the Divide pays a greater net profit to the acre than in any other country east or west.[16]

By the mid-1890s, approximately 20,000 acres of divide country were devoted to potato cultivation, and nearly 2,000 freight carloads were shipped out of nearby towns every year. Annual Potato Bakes in nearby Monument often featured the prized Arkansas Divide potatoes.

Interestingly, potato cultivation on the divide, albeit successful, was short-lived. From the late 1890s through the turn of the century, a serious onset of blight crippled potato harvests and reduced the potatoes to the size of a walnut or even a pea. The disease signaled the end of an era for divide farmers, as the grand expanse of potato fields was forever razed from the valley landscape.

Ranching was another important occupation among residents. Pigs, sheep, chickens, and especially cattle and horses were highly valued by local ranchers, who gave the animals scrupulous care. Methodist circuit rider John L. Dyer, whose faithful service to the valley began in 1870, was particularly struck by this close relationship between man and beast:

> The settlers were ranchmen. Stock was ranging far away, and the loss of a cow was more seriously felt than that of a human being. If a man were killed, it was looked over, and the murderer allowed to escape justice. But if a man stole cattle, he was almost sure, if caught, to be hung. Trial by court was too slow and uncertain.[17]

Injuries or deaths to Spring Valley and Cherry Valley ranch animals received newspaper coverage that rivaled that given to human sicknesses or accidents. In 1885, the Rock Ridge correspondent for the *Castle Rock Journal* chronicled the death of Mr. Hugo John's "fine mare" in the same column in which the "sudden and unexpected" death of the rancher's wife was also announced.[18] In the mid-1880s, when newly invented barbed wire fencing arrived in the valley, many columnists quickly objected to its use and the threat of injury it posed to ranch animals. Details of the gruesome injury of assessor Gideon Pratt's mare, Donna, by the "barb wire nuisance" elicited sympathy among newspaper readers. Some of them no doubt agreed with the sentiments of a Rock Ridge columnist who wrote, "Fencing is the present mania, if you can call tacking a couple of wires on posts several rods apart 'fencing.' Some of the people think that 'horse-killer' is a more appropriate name than 'fence.' "[19] Others demanded the outlawing of the wiring, "as that kind of fence is a nuisance, and ought not to be allowed."[20] Annoying and unjust as it may have seemed to some, barbed wire became a permanent fixture in the divide valley and concluded the era of open-range ranching that still inspires romantic visions of early western frontier life today.

In their often-hurried quest to transform wild frontier lands into productive agricultural fields, early pioneers frequently met with serious injuries or death. Spring Valley and Cherry Valley settlers were no exception. "John Wedden hit his head with a post which slightly turned his brain," the Williamsville correspondent for the *Castle Rock Journal* commented in May 1895.[21] Other accidents to divide residents took place while tending to ranch duties:

> A few days ago Mr. Chris Schreiber, of Rock Ridge, was in Franktown. While there he roped a cow, tied her to the saddle on his horse and attempted to lead the horse. The cow became fractious and in some way wound the rope around Mr. Schreiber and the horse. Mr. S was very severely injured.[22]

Sadly, many of the fatalities and injuries on divide farms and ranches involved children. Elliott West explains in *Growing Up with the Country: Childhood on the Far Western Frontier*, that disease was the greatest threat to frontier children, with diphtheria topping the list. Spring Valley farmer Joseph Gile and his wife experienced the horrifying ailment firsthand in 1880, when all six of their children passed away within days of one another. Another deadly disease, scarlet fever, claimed the lives of three Gwillim family children, Mary, Trevor, and Edgar, in Spring Valley in the mid-1880s. Cholera infantum took a two-year-old son of the George McCracken family in 1890.

In 1895, another young McCracken son "was severely hurt . . . by being hit on the head by a falling crowbar."[23] Like adults, children were vulnerable to farm and ranch accidents. The youngsters' budding curiosity or eagerness to help their parents with everyday duties often placed them in hazardous situations with devastating results.

> Dave Tindel who lives on Cherry creek 8 miles west of Elbert ran over his little five-year old son with a wagon load of posts, breaking his neck. While loading the wagon he told the little one to go off and lie down in the shade and it seems he crawled under the wagon, laying down in front of the hind wheel. When Mr. Tindel started the team it resulted in the heart rendering accident.[24]

Another accident involved a six-month-old child of the Harry Bucks family, who "fell into the fire, seriously burning its head, face, and breast. The unfortunate child was taken from the flames by its excited mother, but not until it was too late so as to seriously endanger its life."[25]

Undoubtedly the most publicized death took place in January 1887. A Spring Valley rancher named Mott Crawford shot Oscar Pratt, the young son of Gideon C. Pratt, one of the county's most respected citizens. Called the "most dastardly, heartless and unprovoked murder ever recorded in the annals of crime in Douglas county," the shooting occurred after the elder Pratt challenged Crawford's accusation that the young boy stole a gun from him.[26] Reportedly, Crawford's violent reaction to the challenge culminated in the shooting of the boy. The *Castle Rock Journal* reported the incident with considerable passion:

> Upon reaching the yard Crawford struck Mr. Pratt several times in the face. At last, Mr. Pratt, who was stepping backward and endeavoring to pacify his antagonist, stumbled over a stick, falling prone upon the ground; whereupon the now furious human hyena SET HIS DOG UPON HIM. Seeing his father in danger of being seriously injured by the blood thirsty brute, Oscar picked up a stick and struck the dog. . . . In a moment [Crawford] reappeared at the door with a DOUBLE BARREL SHOT GUN in his hands asserting that he would shoot [Gideon Pratt] . . . the blood-seeking vampire took deliberate aim at him, but Mr. Pratt stepped a little to one side and out of range, when he turned his gun on Oscar who was standing directly in front of the house, and fired, the charge striking him in the left side just ABOVE THE HIP.[27]

Young Oscar died shortly thereafter, and one year later Crawford was found guilty of second-degree murder. Sentenced to jail, Crawford's real punishment was the shunning from the divide settlers he once called friends and a lifelong notoriety as one of the most hated men in Douglas County.

Amid the toils and struggles of everyday life, the divide valley slowly began to modernize. Like many rural areas throughout the western United States, the great distances to more modern towns presented challenges for Spring Valley and Cherry Valley residents, who often realized that progress and technological advancements would reach their area only through their own determination. Before the turn of the century, many foresighted valley residents strung telephone wire along fence posts and formed the Divide Mutual Telephone Company. The service consisted of one party line with a series of rings assigned to each household. Finicky and unreliable, the quality of the service allegedly could be affected by opening or closing neighborhood gates. In the mid-1940s, local residents erected telephone poles and called the new connection the Farmer's Line. Shortly thereafter, the Mountain Bell Telephone Company took over the service.

The 1940s heralded the advent of another major technological advancement for the area. During a 1939 meeting at the nearby town of Black Forest, many local residents listened intently to the alluring concept of introducing electricity to their area, made possible by President Franklin D. Roosevelt's Rural Electrification Administration. Divide valley residents formed the cooperative association required to receive the utility, but a wire shortage during World War II delayed its completion until the late 1940s.

Progress of the divide road systems transpired at a laggardly pace. Early roads consisted of nothing more than the wagon ruts of travelers, and frequent stops to remove large obstacles from the path plagued most drivers. Among these early roads was the Frankstown & Gile Station Wagon Road, constructed in the mid-1860s, which began at California Ranche in Frankstown, went through George Engl's ranch near the future Castlewood Dam, then down to Spring Valley, where Joseph Gile's stage station was located. Before the turn of the century, Spring Valley and Cherry Valley residents could reach Castle Rock by way of a labyrinthine route that snaked through Upper and Lower Lake Gulch and then hooked up with Ridge Road (today's Douglas County Highway 35). The circuitous route prompted many valley residents to conduct their business at more easily accessible locations in Elbert County, a prospect that troubled the *Castle Rock Journal*:

> The road leading from Castle Rock to Lake Gulch and Rock Ridge should be straightened. It is no wonder that the people living in those places complain at being obliged to go around over the sand hills to get to the county seat, and it is but justice to them that the matter be attended to. Again, from a business point of view, the business men of this town should encourage the straightening of the road, as it would draw trade from Rock Ridge that now goes to Elizabeth and Elbert because it is a better road.[28]

In the 1870s, construction of Post Road 32, also known as the Cherry Creek Road—which followed the quirks and bends of Cherry Creek from just south of Denver through Pine Grove (later Parker), Frankstown, Rock Ridge, and into Elbert County—made travel somewhat easier. In a controversial 1913 decision, Douglas County commissioners, after receiving a road improvement grant from the state highway commission, declined to upgrade the Cherry Creek route, instead choosing to improve the road between Sedalia and Palmer Lake. Disgruntled property owners along Cherry Creek road coalesced into the Cherry Creek Valley Good Roads Association to lobby for state highway designation, and thus state funds, for the road.

> Every farmer and all others who are interested in the Cherry Creek road being made a State Highway at once, should see that their names are on the Cherry Creek Valley Good Roads Association. . . . Now is the time to

be progressive and enterprising. Jump into the band wagon and we'll try the road out.[29]

Perseverance paid off, and in the 1920s sections of the Cherry Creek road became State Highway 83, which by then had been extended to Colorado Springs. A 1950s alteration diverted highway travelers away from the original path through Russellville and along the rim of Castlewood Canyon south of Franktown.

In the late 1960s, workers began grading and stabilizing the gravel highway, and by August 1968, thirteen miles of the highway's Cherry Valley section had been transformed into a smooth, paved surface. A ribbon-cutting ceremony sponsored by the Cherry Homemakers' Extension Club, which had joined the effort to petition county and state officials for the improvements, marked completion of the work. Governor John A. Love's dramatic helicopter entrance and subsequent dedication address highlighted the ceremony. One club member wrote:

> It was quite a thrill to see the helicopter set down on the highway and see the governor and Mr. Charles Shumate step out. . . . It's something we will never forget. . . . After the ribbon had been cut everyone drove down the road to Bruce Younger's residence where Deane Younger and Helen Arfsten had coffee, rolls and cookies waiting. It was really something to have the governor and the other gentlemen take time to sip coffee, eat rolls and chat with all of us. I enjoyed this more than seeing all the movie stars in Las Vegas.[30]

Ever willing to lend support to such community improvement projects, the homemakers' club—a branch of the Douglas County Home Demonstration Council and later the El Paso County Extension Homemakers Council—provided valley women with a collective voice to articulate their concerns, desires, and ideas. Active from 1925 through 1994, the group focused on topics such as sewing, cooking, health, safety, child care, and education. The club also made regular donations to charitable organizations such as the El Paso County 4-H Foundation, the Safehouse Program of the Domestic Violence Prevention Center, the Colorado Heart Association, the Society for Crippled Children and Adults, and the American Cancer Society. In addition to such noble charity work, the Cherry Homemakers hosted social events such as dances, luncheons, and holiday parties. Their club song (sung to the tune "Lazy Mary, Will You Get Up?") was full of fun and gaiety:

> We belong to the Cherry Club
> A fairy club, a merry club
> We are very proud of our club
> We're boosters, every one.
> We learn to cook and sew and patch
> Our chickens hatch, our colors match
> We teach our husbands how to batch
> When we are at the club.
> Sometimes we have a picnic day-
> That's when we're gay, in bright array
> Club's not all work and never play
> On watermelon day.
> Oh won't you come and join our club
> And learn to scrub, and eat our grub
> We'll let you ride the Billy Goat
> If you will join our club.[31]

The Mountain View Social Club, in existence since the 1960s, also offered opportunities for valley women to escape the loneliness that could be part of rural life. According to co-founder Lois Dahlberg, the group began as an extension club, very similar to that of the Cherry Homemakers, but a few women later branched off to start their own organization. Members participated in community improvement and charity work, as well as social luncheons and holiday parties. At the 1968 Valentine's Day gathering, the scheduled topic of conversation was "How I Met My Husband."

During the mid-1970s, divide residents focused their energies on needs other than socializing. The great distance between their valley and the nearest fire and emergency centers prompted many residents to call for the construction of a fire station. Land was donated by rancher Emil Anderson, and residents funded and built the Cherry Valley Fire Station—exemplifying the unity, cooperation, and collective spirit so prevalent among residents. The firehouse today is a substation of the Franktown Fire Department staffed by local volunteers who serve and protect a ninety-eight-square-mile area. Annual pig roasts are a major source of funding for the station's equipment.

Several residents formed the Cherry Valley-Spring Valley Historical Society in 1993 to consider the area's historical preservation needs. In the spring of 1994, the group received a grant from the Colorado Historical Society to gather and duplicate an estimated 200 to 300 old photos of the divide valley and its early pioneers. Completed in early 1996, the exhibit traveled to various localities throughout the county for public viewing. At this writing, the group is collecting photos of past Cherry Valley School students for display at the school's fiftieth anniversary celebration in 2002.

The fellowship so clearly exhibited by Cherry Valley and Spring Valley residents during social gatherings and community projects also prevailed when the valley's agrarian lifestyle was threatened. In May 1981, area residents coalesced into a property owners association, in order to contest a proposal made by the Douglas County commissioners to build a county landfill near Lake Gulch Road. In addition to voicing concerns over the impact of increased traffic, decreased property values, and possible hazardous waste drainage into Cherry Creek, the association challenged the actions of commissioners, who negotiated a lease agreement for the land from the state without first holding a public hearing. Commissioner Carl Winkler retorted that the alleged lease was nothing more than an agreement with the state, and approval of the landfill would depend on the consent of both the Colorado State Board of Land Commissioners and the Douglas County Planning Commission. Despite reassurance by Winkler that the commissioners never intended to deceive the public, the *Douglas County News Press* expressed outrage over their actions:

> There are three things that will enrage Douglas County citizens—location of gravel mines, location of water tanks and location of landfills. But what enrages county residents even more . . . is failure to make decisions to locate those facilities publicly. . . . If this is indeed the way the commissioners wish to conduct their business they deserve all the petitions, angry residents storming their offices and calling them all hours of the day and night, and court suits they get . . . all of the possible advantages of the Lake Gulch Road site went out the window because of the manner in which the commissioners chose to accomplish the needed task.

> It will be very difficult to convince residents in that area that the site is the best one around—even if it is.[32]

After the land commissioners refused to sign the lease agreement until a public hearing was held, Douglas County commissioners shied away from the location, citing the distance from the northern section of the county, which generated most of the trash. Eventually, officials dropped their search for a county landfill site, and county waste was transported to a landfill on Lowry Air Force Base in Denver County.

Residential development, so prevalent in other parts of Douglas County, made a clear but less conspicuous mark on the Spring Valley and Cherry Valley area. The valley continued to be dominated by sprawling farms and ranches, but several subdivisions, most located west of Spring Valley, were constructed beginning in the 1960s. Bald Mountain Estates and Assembly Estates received plat approval in the early 1960s, and Eldorado Acres, adjacent to the Douglas County–El Paso County line east of State Highway 83, was approved in 1969. The late 1970s witnessed the beginnings of large communities such as Mesa Grande and True Mountain Estates; much smaller ones such as Olen, Spring Valley West, and Sandi Acres dominated the early 1980s.

Apprehensive nearby residents often challenged these developments. In 1973, a rezoning request submitted by owners of a proposed 530-acre development called Antelope Springs, located southeast of Greenland, sparked a heated debate over high-density residential growth in the area. Residents complained that the high-density zoning proposed for Antelope Springs was contrary to the area's existing land use, which was primarily ranches and residential homes on large acreage. The Douglas County Planning Commission took the residents' concerns under advisement, but later recommended approval of the rezoning request, with the condition that a 100-foot open-space buffer be created on three of the subdivision's boundaries. On February 14, 1973, Douglas County commissioners approved Antelope Springs's final plat, but financial problems prevented the controversial development's blueprints from ever becoming reality.

Spring Valley West, located immediately south of the Spring Valley School, also raised concern among residents. During a May 19, 1981, public hearing before the Douglas County commissioners, residents objected to the builder's request for fifteen-acre lots on the property, claiming incompatibility with surrounding residences, and suggested a twenty-acre minimum lot size. After commissioners countered that five-acre residential sites in adjoining El Paso County contradicted this claim, Spring Valley West's final plat passed, and construction began soon after.

Subdivision of thirty-five-acre lots dominated 1990s residential development in the divide vicinity. Remington Ranch Estates and Shadow Mountain Ranch sprouted west of State Highway 83, while Rossi Investments, Country Estates, Cherry Valley Ranchettes, A-Bar Ranches, and Knight's Creek Ranch arose east of the road. The Tomac and Gilliand developments were located along Russellville Road, and the Ehmann and Fox Glen properties developed along Lake Gulch Road.

Longtime farmers and ranchers in the valley struggle to make sense of the increasing number of rural fields replaced by modern homes. While the typical side effects of growth, such as traffic congestion and pressure on local water sources, present major hurdles for the quiet valley, many established residents view threats to their lifestyles as the most unjust consequence of the development. In an interview with the author, one Cherry

Valley rancher claimed it is the new residents' misunderstanding of country living that is carving a division between valley neighbors:

> These [newcomers] are building in alfalfa fields and then wonder why the hay grows so high in their yards. They don't have a clue what country living is about. There are a lot more problems down here now. It's not a rural community anymore. Most people out here, especially the ones who have been here the longest, are devastated by it. To see all the land torn up with huge houses. . . . It used to be a beautiful place to live. . . . The land around me could someday be sold to developers. That would really disturb me. I know people would move in from the city and say, "I don't like your sheep. They make too much noise." They don't understand that the country has its own sounds, its own natural sounds. If they don't like country living, they shouldn't move out to the country.

Richard Geiger, grandson of Spring Valley pioneer John Geiger, and his wife, Iola, reside on the original family homestead and claim the area's growth has caused them both financial and emotional difficulties. Problems previously found in the city have migrated to their backyard, including vandalism, out-of-control pets, trespassers, and the erosion of land due to nearby construction. With a golf course planned across their street and large residential homes looming upon the nearby hillsides, Iola prophesized a dismal future for the ranch that played such a vital role in the valley's history:

> Our children cannot maintain our way of life. There is no way. We've made a good living. We haven't always had everything we wanted, but we had clothes on our back, food in our stomachs, and our bills paid. But our children will never be able to maintain our way of life. As the residential developments are coming in, they're cleaning everything out. . . . We're going to stay here until we die, but then what will the children do with the place? I'm sure they'll have to sell it. . . . I hate to see it, but I know it's coming. The kids won't be able to afford to keep it. This would be an Uncle Tom's Cabin in the middle of town if they tried to maintain it the way it is. I'm not going to be here to see it happen, but I know it's coming. It's terribly sad. There's a way of life that's passing.

Despite the division between the valley's old and new residents, in 1998 the two groups encountered a common threat. The U.S. Army Corps of Engineers announced that it was considering Cherry Valley as the site of one or more dry dams as part of a plan to address safety concerns at Cherry Creek Dam in Denver. If constructed, the dams had the potential to inundate more than 2,000 acres of land and displace dozens of residents. United as Citizens Against Dry Dams, opponents of the plan mounted an exhaustive campaign aimed at discrediting the corps' statistics on possible rainfall levels for the area and emphasizing other alternatives to the proposal. The citizens' efforts were rewarded when the corps announced in mid-1999 that it was abandoning its dry dam plans in Douglas County. A Cherry Valley resident congratulated those who challenged the threat: "This is a triumph for the residents of southeastern Douglas County. . . . Each of you are to be honored as citizens who care enough to fight for your rights."[33]

Rural both in distance and thought, the longtime residents of Spring Valley and Cherry Valley now struggle with the reality that the city is coming to them. Throughout its history, commonality of occupation and purpose among valley farmers and ranchers fostered unity and cooperation. With the introduction of newcomers with disparate interests and goals, many wonder if the area's neighborly relations, displayed so powerfully during the defeat of the dry dam proposal, will last.

Spring Valley-Cherry Valley Historic Sites

Cherry/Pratt School (1877, first building; construction date of existing building unknown; builder unknown), 11201 State Highway 83. **Private residence.**

The pride of early pioneers in the Williamsville vicinity, the Pratt School was reportedly constructed in 1877 on land donated by popular West Cherry Creek resident Gideon C. Pratt. Pratt, who served as the district's school director, was credited with bringing many improvements to the small schoolhouse, including twelve new double seats in 1895. As with many of the small divide schoolhouses, the Pratt building became a center for community affairs as well. "The children's day exercises at the Pratt school house was a nice affair and a credit to those getting it up," reported the Spring Valley correspondent for the *Castle Rock Journal* in 1895.[34] The facility also featured a popular Sunday school and services led by the inspirational Reverend B. F. Todd.

Fire engulfed the cherished building in 1899, ending its service to the community. Shortly thereafter, the *Castle Rock Journal* reported, "The Pratt school house, a mile south of Williamsville, which was destroyed by fire a couple weeks ago, will be rebuilt at once."[35] Six months later, the newspaper reported, "The new schoolhouse in the Pratt district is to cost $650."[36] Although it is unclear whether these plans were carried through immediately, local residents did eventually see the resurrection of their schoolhouse and affectionately named the new facility after the surrounding community of Cherry.

The Cherry School accommodated the local citizenry in much the same way as its predecessor. Community celebrations, meetings, dances, church services, weddings, funerals, and school events transpired within its welcoming walls. At Christmas, schoolchildren performed programs before a curtain suspended in the classroom, and Halloween parties featured games, dancing, and costumes. A pot-bellied stove warmed the cold students and attendees, while laughter and companionship warmed their hearts.

In December 1913, a blizzard that reportedly dumped six to ten feet of snow on Douglas County stranded six students at Cherry School overnight. Their worried fathers joined the children the next day, but the inclement weather necessitated another night's stay before the hungry, tired group could return home. Looming snowdrifts made travel throughout the area extremely difficult and forced a six-week closure of Cherry School.

The classic one-room, front-gabled, clapboard Cherry School fostered the educational needs of local children until the early 1950s, when regional schools were consolidated into one school district known as Cherry Valley. Since then, the building has been a private residence.

Irving School (1932: builder unknown), 9244 State Highway 83.

Among the best-preserved and functional historic sites in the Spring Valley and Cherry Valley area is the former Irving School building. The construction is typical of small, one-room schoolhouses found throughout the Douglas County area. A gabled, normal-pitched roof tops clapboard, wood siding with several double-hung windows, and three doors.

Named after the community of Irving, the archetypal schoolhouse was originally constructed in 1932 along Russellville Road as a replacement for the much smaller Case/Rock Ridge School. At this location, the Irving School boasted a full-length basement, the first for an educational institution in the area. As the largest schoolhouse in the area, Irving School quickly became a hub for community social events and hosted many church services, weddings, and parties.

Following an early 1950s vote in which local schools were combined into one school district called Cherry Valley, the Irving building was moved to its present location adjacent to the Cherry Valley School, where it served as a teacherage and rental unit. Presently used as a classroom by the Douglas County School District, the prim building quietly accepts a return to its roots and continues to ensure that the community children learn their three Rs.

Prairie Canyon Ranch (1860s: Frederick Bartruff, builder?), 4620 State Highway 83. **Private residence.**

Archaeologists agree that the land known today as Prairie Canyon Ranch has sustained 8,000 to 9,000 years of human occupation. Plains Indians such as the Cheyenne, Arapaho, Kiowa, and Comanche are thought to have used the area in the 1800s. Between 1859 and the early 1860s, the Colorado City Road, a stage and postal trail from Denver to Colorado City, passed through the property, leaving tracks visible today.

In 1867, Frederick Bartruff, a German immigrant who came to the United States in 1862, filed for a homestead on part of the land. He constructed a 14-by-18-foot log house, fenced sixty acres of land, and cultivated thirty acres. In 1875, Bartruff and two of his daughters died of diphtheria and were buried in a small graveyard on the property. One year later, Bartruff's wife, Barbara, married John Bihlmeyer, who owned property adjacent to the ranch. The couple combined their properties and lived together until Barbara's death in 1903. Although John returned to his home country of Germany in 1910, the ranch remained with his descendants until the late 1930s, when it was purchased by Ralph and Walter Clugy.

In 1980, Robert Schultz bought the property, and he and his son, Randy, raised Texas Longhorns and Plains Buffalo. Father and son hosted a variety of tours during summers and were involved in water and soil conservation practices on their historic ranch.

Several buildings dot the Prairie Canyon Ranch, so named by Schultz because prairies and canyons meet on the property. The most notable of these buildings are an immense two-story 1880s barn and a two-story, gabled clapboard house constructed in the 1870s.

In 1996, the Douglas County Open Space Advisory Committee recommended that the county purchase Prairie Canyon Ranch as an open-space preserve. Douglas County commissioners heeded the advice and agreed to purchase an initial 240 acres for $600,000, with options to acquire the remaining four parcels. The county closed on the final parcel of Prairie Canyon Ranch in March 2000.

Rock Ridge Barn (1874: Peter Dumont), 7054 State Highway 83. **Private residence.**

Perched conspicuously along State Highway 83, the Rock Ridge Barn represents a vestige of the settlement once known by the names Rock Ridge, Case, and Irving. The barn's builder, homesteader Peter Dumont, used the structure to shelter farm animals and store hay. In 1899, Asher Hilyen purchased the barn and surrounding property and, after a series of other land purchases, increased his holdings to 1,000 acres. He named the spread Rock Ridge Ranch and raised cattle and cultivated hay, corn, and various grains. After the cows were milked, the cream was separated and sold to local creameries such as the Case Cheese and Butter Company and the Frink Creamery Company in Larkspur, then transported by train to nearby towns.

Ownership of Rock Ridge Ranch remained in the Hilyen family until 1970, when Max Stern purchased twenty acres of the land, including the original barn. Stern owned the property for five years before selling it to sheep ranchers Charles and Janet Herman. Devout preservationists, the Hermans conducted extensive restoration of the barn and aided its nomination to the State Register of Historic Properties on November 9, 1994. The barn received the designation based on the fact that it is one of Colorado's few remaining examples of hand-hewn post and beam construction. In this popular nineteenth-century building method, also known as timber framing, mortise and tenon joints are held together with wooden pegs as opposed to wire nails. Three additions by previous owners increased the barn's original 625 square feet to an expansive 2,500 square feet. In March 1997, the Hermans received a State Historic Funds grant to aid their restoration efforts, and replaced the barn's broad sloping roof, stabilized some interior stalls, and painted the exterior.

Spring Valley Cemetery (1870), Spring Valley Road, north of Lorraine Road.

Hidden beneath lofty pine trees, the Spring Valley Cemetery is the final resting place for the toils, tragedies, and spirit of Spring Valley's history. Many of the community's pioneers are buried there, offering tales for visitors. The oldest readable grave is dated 1870 and belongs to the auburn-bearded Methodist circuit rider Horace Reynolds. Nearby stand the headstones of Joseph Gile's six children, all of whom were victims of a diphtheria epidemic that ripped through the region in 1880. Three of G. R. Gwillim's children, taken by scarlet fever in the 1880s, are also interred in the cemetery. Love-smitten smallpox victims Lorenzo Leppart and Janie Richey spend eternity together in the solace of the roadside cemetery.

In 1877, Daniel Holden, a wealthy landowner and rancher, deeded the cemetery's eastern half to the Spring Valley community for one dollar, and Newton B. Alderman, an early East Cherry Creek rancher, sold the western half in 1913 for fifty dollars. Efforts by early pioneers to maintain the yard were later taken over by Henry Gandy, who attempted to identify the occupants of all gravesites and marked all unknowns with a "G." In 1945, Gandy retired and the community formed a cemetery board to oversee care and maintenance of the property. Appointed to the board in 1961, Richard and Iola Geiger initiated annual cemetery cleanup days, in which community volunteers performed needed improvements. Annual Memorial Day fundraising dinners, organized by Iola starting in 1969, financed many other improvements, including the construction of an encircling wooden fence. In an interview with the author, Iola fondly remembered her thirty-five years as a dedicated caretaker of the cemetery as a labor of love:

> We worked in the cemetery a lot of times while other people took their vacations elsewhere. During Sunday afternoons we would take a couple of hours to go down there with a wheelbarrow and shovel and fill in a little here and cut weeds there. The cemetery was our thing. I had a ball doing it. I always tried to help people any way I could.

A small chapel added in 1966 provided the most extravagant modification to the cemetery's appearance. In his will, J. Louis Killin left these instructions for the chapel:

> Said Trustee shall as soon as possible after my death cause to be constructed a chapel in Spring Valley Cemetery, Douglas County, Colorado, at which place my father and mother are buried. . . . Said chapel shall be constructed at a cost of between $50,000 and $60,000 and shall be dedicated as a memorial to my deceased father and mother.[37]

The James and Olive Killin Chapel now stands sentinel before the small cemetery. The building features arched wood beams, wood paneling, and a large central window with a cross in the center. All Christian denominations are allowed use of the chapel, but burial in the cemetery is limited to those with Spring Valley ties.

Spring Valley School (prior to 1874: Harrison Bucks and John Geiger, builders), corner of Spring Valley and Lorraine Roads. **Private residence.**

This small, single-story white schoolhouse is the last remaining structure of the early Spring Valley settlement, which once included a general store, post office, fort, stage stop, creamery, and sawmill. Constructed sometime prior to 1874 by two of the community's pioneers, Harrison Bucks and John Geiger, the Spring Valley School fulfilled more than the scholastic needs of young residents. It also served as a center for the political and social life of the area and hosted weddings, funerals, dances, religious services, spelling bees, school plays, holiday parties, and even court trials. Local organizations such as the grange, the Good Templars, and the Grand Army of the Republic also held meetings in the building.

The schoolhouse originally featured a south-facing porch that was later enclosed to form an anteroom used by the teacher for living space. The balloon-framed clapboard exterior rests on a stone foundation that is now covered with cement. Shingles adorn the gable roof, and a single red brick chimney straddles its northern end.

As the hub of community essence and activity, the Spring Valley School embodied the pride of the tiny settlement it served. When funds allowed, area residents made repairs or additions to the building. Donations in 1884 financed a new organ, and the schoolhouse received a new roof in 1897. An 1885 school election granted more improvements for the cherished building:

> The school election passed off quietly at this place. Jesse Knowles was elected President of the Board. A tax of three mills was voted for the teachers' fund, one mill for incidental fund, and one half mill to procure maps and a globe. Our school will be well equipped with modern appliances and will be the banner school of the county.[38]

In use until 1946, the schoolhouse was later donated to the Douglas County Historical Society with the hope it could be moved to Castle Rock for use as a museum. When it was determined that the move could jeopardize the structural integrity and stability of the building, the society abandoned those plans and in 1974 sold it to Mr. and Mrs. Robert Beadles. The Beadles restored the old schoolhouse into a summer residence and aided its nomination to the National Register of Historic Places on December 18, 1978.

Notes

1. Francis W. Cragin, *Early Far West Notebook* (Colorado Springs, Colo.: Pioneers Museum, n.d.), XIV, p. 19.

2. Irving Howbert, *The Indians of the Pike's Peak Region* (New York: Knickerbocker Press, 1914), p. 220.

3. *Castle Rock Journal*, June 14, 1882, p. 2.

4. Ibid., April 9, 1884, p. 3; April 23, 1884, p. 3.

5. Ibid., April 23, 1884, p. 3.

6. Ibid., January 28, 1885, p. 3.

7. Ibid., May 6, 1885, p. 2.

8. Ibid., February 4, 1885, p. 2; April 15, 1885, p. 3.

9. Ibid., June 16, 1886, p. 3.

10. Ibid., February 27, 1895, p. 4; July 10, 1895, p. 1.

11. Ibid., July 10, 1895, p. 4.

12. Ibid., June 26, 1889, p. 1.

13. Ibid., June 14, 1882, p. 3.

14. Ibid., September 19, 1888, p. 4.

15. *West Creek Mining News and the Nighthawk Mountain Echo*, February 3, 1900, p. 1.

16. *Castle Rock Journal*, June 26, 1889, p. 1.

17. John L. Dyer, *The Snow-Shoe Itinerant, An Autobiography* (Cincinnati, Ohio: Cranston & Stowe, 1890; rpt. Father Dyer Methodist Church, 1975,), pp. 261–262.

18. *Castle Rock Journal*, May 20, 1885, p. 3.

19. Ibid., May 13, 1885, p. 3; May 20, 1885, p. 3.

20. Ibid., May 27, 1885, p. 3.

21. Ibid., May 22, 1895, p. 4.

22. Ibid., June 13, 1888, p. 4.

23. Ibid., July 10, 1895, p. 4.

24. Ibid., August 6, 1890, p. 4.

25. Ibid., January 18, 1888, p. 4.

26. Ibid., January 26, 1887, p. 2.

27. Ibid.

28. Ibid., December 12, 1888, p. 1.

29. *Record-Journal of Douglas County*, May 2, 1913, p. 1.

30. "Scrapbook, Research Copy, 1957–1985," *Records of Cherry Homemakers Club, 1924–1994*, MSS-005, File #6, Box 2, Local History Collection, Philip S. Miller Library.

31. "Membership Lists, Dues Paid, Ephemera, n.d., 1933–1991," *Records of Cherry Homemakers Club, 1924–1994*, MSS-005, File #15, Box 1, Local History Collection, Philip S. Miller Library.

32. *Douglas County News Press*, May 12, 1981, p. 4.

33. Ibid., June 30, 1999, p. 6A.

34. *Castle Rock Journal*, July 10, 1895, p. 4.

35. Ibid., November 10, 1899, p. 4.

36. Ibid., May 18, 1900, p. 3.

37. Last Will and Testament of J. Louis Killin, February 15, 1965, pp. 1–2, Local History Collection, Philip S. Miller Library.

38. *Castle Rock Journal*, May 20, 1885, p. 3.

Resources

NEWSPAPERS

Castle Rock Journal
Colorado Springs Gazette
Denver Commonwealth
Denver Post
Denver Republican
Denver Times
Denver Tribune
Douglas County Express
Douglas County News
Douglas County News Press
Douglas County Town and Country Squire
Douglas County Trail
Englewood Herald
George's Weekly
Highlands Ranch Herald
Highlands Ranch Reporter
Highlands Register
Las Animas Leader
Littleton Independent
The Mountain Echo
Panorama: Perry Park
Parker Press
Pioneer
Record-Journal of Douglas County
Rocky Mountain Journal
Rocky Mountain News
The Sentinel
Trail
Weekly News Chronicle
West Creek Mining News and the Nighthawk Mountain Echo
Western Progress

PERIODICALS

The Chronicle
Colorado Heritage
Colorado Magazine
Colorado Business Directory
Colorado Business Magazine
Colorful Colorado
Denver Magazine
Denver Westerners Roundup
Douglas County Community Connection
HRCA News
Indian Park Schoolhouse Newsletter
The Newsletter

Quarterly of the Colorado School of Mines
Parker Country
Time

INTERVIEWS/ORAL HISTORIES

(All interviews conducted by the author except as noted.)

Allen, Betty. January 26, 1998.
Anderson, Gladys. Video interview. May 23, 1997. Douglas County Television. Castle Rock, Colorado.
Anonymous Cherry Valley Rancher. February 20, 1998.
Been, Myrna. May 5, 1998.
Benn, Mary Stewart. Oral History Tape. August 9, 1993. Local History Collection. Philip S. Miller Library. Castle Rock, Colorado.
Brandebery, Kent. March 24, 1995.
Brandebery, Kent. June 1, 1998.
Burch, Florence. May 6, 1998.
Burch, Lester. May 6, 1998.
Clark, Micki. May 12, 1998.
Dahlberg, Lois. February 1, 1998.
"Franktown Panel." Oral History Tape. September 29, 1987. Local History Collection. Philip S. Miller Library. Castle Rock, Colorado.
Geiger, Iola. February 28, 1998.
Geiger, Richard. February 28, 1998.
Glasier, Loyd. January 3, 1994.
Glasier, Loyd. April 25, 1995.
Harden, Johanna. May 5, 1998.
Hatfield, Bill. February 1, 1998.
Hoover, George. August 8, 1995.
Jones, Clyde. January 8, 1994.
Jones, Clyde. June 25, 1995.
Jones, Clyde. March 31, 1998.
Jones, Clyde. May 4, 1998.
Lowenberg, Bob. January 15, 1994.
Lowenberg, Bob. April 2, 1994.
Maguire, Sally. May 6, 1997.
Maguire, Sally. June 11, 1997.
Mickelson, Gordon. July 7, 1997.
Oberlin, Starr. April 6, 1994.
Pinamount, Joan. January 26, 1998.
Higginson, Amy Stewart. Oral History Tape. August 9, 1993. Local History Collection. Philip S. Miller Library. Castle Rock, Colorado.
Roerig, Dorothy. Oral History Tape. March 17, 1992. Local History Collection. Philip S. Miller Library. Castle Rock, Colorado.
Rood, Donna. June 25, 1995.
Simeth, Jane. Oral History Tape. March 23, 1992. Local History Collection. Philip S. Miller Library. Castle Rock, Colorado.
Snyder, Fran. June 26, 1995.
Stone, Joanna. April 14, 1994.
Tennal, Arlene. October 1, 1994.
Theriault, Peggy. August 7, 1995.
Thomas, Marlene. December 17, 1999.
Trompeter, James. August 5, 1998.
Trumble, Susie. June 14, 1995.
Whiton, Barbara. June 26, 1995.
Willis, Lee. July 30, 1998.

MONOGRAPHS

Abbe, Patience, Richard Abbe, and John Abbe. *Around the World in Eleven Years*. New York: Frederick A. Stokes, 1936.
Abbott, Carl, Stephen J. Leonard, and David McComb, *Colorado: A History of the Centennial State*. Niwot, Colorado: University Press of Colorado, 1982.
Bauer, William H., James L. Ozment, and John H. Willard. *Colorado Postal History: The Post Offices*. Golden, Colorado: J-B Publishing, 1971.
Bauer, William H., James L. Ozment, and John H. Willard. *Colorado*

Post Offices, 1859-1989. Golden, Colorado: Colorado Railroad Museum, 1990.
Bird, Isabella. *A Lady's Life in the Rocky Mountains*. New edition. Norman, Oklahoma: University of Oklahoma Press, 1960.
The Book Committee, ed. *Our Heritage: People of Douglas County*. Shawnee Mission, Kansas: Inter-Collegiate Press, 1981.
Bull, James C. *A Short History of Frankstown, Colorado: A Douglas County Cross Roads*. N.p.: Kwik Kopy Printing, 1994.
Carrillo, Richard F., and Daniel A. Jepsen. *Exploring the Colorado Frontier: A Study in Historical Archaeology at the Tremont Hotel, Lower Downtown Denver*. Denver, Colorado: Colorado Department of Transportation and Federal Highway Administration, U.S. Department of Transportation, 1995.
Cavanagh, Dale. *Roxborough State Park: Hogbacks and History*. Colorado Division of Parks and Outdoor Recreation, 1994.
Chamblin, Thomas S., ed. *The Historical Encyclopedia of Colorado*. Denver, Colorado: Colorado Historical Association, 1975.
Cragin, Francis W. *Early Far West Notebook*. vol. XIV. Colorado Springs, Colorado: Pioneers Museum, n.d.
Crofutt, George A. *Grip Sack Guide to Colorado*. Denver, Colorado: Overland Publishing, 1881.
Davis, Kenneth C. *Don't Know Much About History*. New York: Avon Books, 1980.
Douglas County, Colorado, Yearbook-Directory. Seibert, Colorado: National Directory, 1935.
Dyer, John L. *The Snow-Shoe Itinerant, An Autobiography*. Cincinnati: Cranston & Stowe, 1890; rpt. Father Dyer Methodist Church, 1975.
Grant, William W. *A Quarter Century of the Arapahoe Hunt Club*. 1954?
Hafen, Leroy, ed. *Pike's Peak Gold Rush Guidebooks of 1859*. Glendale: Arthur Clark, 1941.
Hafen, Leroy, and Ann Hafen, eds. *Colorado*. Denver, Colorado: Out West Printing, 1943.
Hall, Frank. *History of the State of Colorado*. Chicago: Blakely Printing, 1891.
Harris, Cyril, ed. *Illustrated Dictionary of Historic Architecture*. New York: Dover Publications, 1977.
Howbert, Irving. *The Indians of the Pike's Peak Region*. New York: Knickerbocker Press, 1914.
James, Edwin, ed. *Account of an Expedition from Pittsburgh to the Rocky Mountains 1819-20*. Philadelphia: H. C. Carey and I. Lea, 1823.
Lavelett, Lucille. *Monument's Faded Neighboring Communities and Its Folklore*. Colorado Springs, Colorado: ABC Printing, 1979.
Leonard, Stephen J., and Thomas J. Noel. *Denver: Mining Camp to Metropolis*. Niwot, Colorado: University Press of Colorado, 1990.
Long, Margaret. *The Smoky Hill Trail*. Denver, Colorado: W. H. Kistler Stationery, 1947.
Lowenberg, Robert L. *Castle Rock: A Grassroots History*. Castle Rock, Colorado: Lowenberg, 1980.
Machann, Barbara Belfield. *Sedalia: 1882-1982*. Publishing information unavailable.
Marr, Josephine Lowell. *Douglas County: A Historical Journey*. Gunnison, Colorado: B&B Printers, 1983.
Mathews, Carl F. *Early Days Around the Divide*. St. Louis, Missouri: Sign Book, 1969.
McAlester, Virginia, and Lee McAlester. *A Field Guide to American Houses*. New York: Knopf, 1984.
McLaughlin, F.B. *A Guidebook to Historic Sites in the Parker Area*. Parker, Colorado: Parker Area Historical Society, 1994.
Merrill, Kay R. *Colorado Cemetery Directory*. Denver, Colorado: Colorado Council of Genealogical Societies, 1985.
Mumey, Nolie. *Wigwam: The Oldest Fishing Club in the State of Colorado*. Boulder, Colorado: Johnson Publishing, 1969.
Nickson, Charles A. *Just Reminiscing*. N.p.: Charles A. Nickson, 1964.
Noel, Thomas J. *Growing Through History with Colorado: The Colorado National Banks, The First 125 Years, 1862-1987*. Denver, Colorado:

Colorado National Banks and Colorado Studies Center, University of Colorado at Denver, 1987.

Noel, Thomas J., and Barbara S. Norgren. *Denver: The City Beautiful.* Denver, Colorado: Historic Denver, 1987.

Noel, Thomas J., Paul F. Mahoney, and Richard E. Stevens. *Historical Atlas of Colorado.* Norman, Oklahoma: University of Oklahoma Press, 1994.

Ormes, Robert M. *Tracking Ghost Railroads.* Colorado Springs, Colorado: Century One Press, 1980.

Perry Park, Colorado. Denver, Colorado: Chain, Hardy, 1890.

Poor, M. C. *Denver South Park and Pacific.* Denver, Colorado: Rocky Mountain Railroad Club, 1976.

Portrait and Biographical Record of Denver and Vicinity Colorado. Chicago: Chapman Publishing, 1898.

Rifkind, Carole. *A Field Guide to American Architecture.* New York: New American Library, 1980.

Schuyler, James Dix. *Reservoirs: For Irrigation, Water-Power, and Domestic Water-Supply.* New York: John Wiley, 1908.

Scott, Glenn R. *Historic Trail Map of the Denver 1° x 2° Quadrangle, Central Colorado.* Denver, Colo.: USGS, 1999.

Stone, Wilbur Fiske, ed. *The History of Colorado.* Vol. IV. Chicago: SJ Clark Publishing, 1913.

Townshend, Richard B. *A Tenderfoot in Colorado.* Norman, Oklahoma: University of Oklahoma Press, 1968.

Webb, Ardis. *The Perry Park Story: Fulfillment of a Dream.* Denver, Colorado: Ardis & Olin Webb, 1974.

West, Elliott. *Growing Up with the Country: Childhood on the Far Western Frontier.* Albuquerque, New Mexico: University of New Mexico Press, 1989.

Whelchel, Sandra. *Parker, Colorado: A Folk History.* Parker, Colorado: Parker Distributing, 1990.

Wilkins, Tivis E. *Colorado Railroads: Chronological Development.* Boulder, Colorado: Pruett Publishing, 1974.

Wolle, Muriel Sibell. *Stampede to Timberline.* Denver, Colorado: Artcraft Press, 1949.

PAMPHLETS

"American Co-Masonry." The American Federation of Human Rights. Larkspur, Colorado.

"A Brief History of Highlands Ranch." Highlands Ranch Historical Society. Highlands Ranch, Colorado.

"Cheesman Dam Designation as a National Historic Civil Engineering Landmark." 1973. Local History Collection. Philip S. Miller Library. Castle Rock, Colorado.

"Cherry Valley / Spring Valley Historical Society." Local History Collection. Philip S. Miller Library. Castle Rock, Colorado.

Decker's Mineral Springs and Resort. Denver, Colorado: J. M. Rhoads, The Printer. Colorado Historical Society. Denver, Colorado.

"First National Bank of Parker, 1983-1993." First National Bank of Parker. Parker, Colorado.

Franktown Chamber of Commerce. 1994. Local History Collection. Philip S. Miller Library. Castle Rock, Colorado.

"The Gifted Land." Roxborough Development Corporation. Local History Collection. Philip S. Miller Library. Castle Rock, Colorado.

"Highlands Ranch: The Guide to Great Living." 1996. Mission Viejo Company. Highlands Ranch, Colorado.

"Historic Castle Rock Structures: A Walking Tour." Town of Castle Rock and the Centennial Committee. Castle Rock, Colorado.

"Historical Facts." Dorothy Roerig. Local History Collection. Philip S. Miller Library. Castle Rock, Colorado.

"How It All Began." 1990. Parker Area Historical Society. Parker, Colorado.

"Model Home Directory." Highlands Ranch Community Association. Highlands Ranch, Colorado.

"Perry Park Ranch's First Century." A. L. Schafer. Pamphlet in the possession of Kent Brandebery.
"Revive '75." 1988. Parker United Methodist Church. Parker, Colorado.
"Roxborough Park at Arrowhead: Update." Roxborough Park Foundation. January 1992. Local History Collection. Philip S. Miller Library. Castle Rock, Colorado.
"75th Anniversary." Christ Episcopal Church. 1982. Local History Collection. Philip S. Miller Library. Castle Rock, Colorado.

GOVERNMENT DOCUMENTS

"Annexation History for the Town of Parker." Town of Parker. Parker, Colorado.
Bylaws. Douglas County Historic Preservation Board. Copy in possession of author.
"Castle Rock Community Letter." Castle Rock Town Board. 1984. Local History Collection. Philip S. Miller Library. Castle Rock, Colorado.
Census Records from 1870 through 1990 for various communities in Douglas County. United States Census Bureau.
Colorado Historical Society. National Register of Historic Places Files for: Benjamin Hammar House, Benjamin Quick Ranch and Fort, Castle Rock Elementary School, Castle Rock Depot, Cherokee Ranch, Church of St. Philip's in the Field, Daniels Park, Douglas County Courthouse, Glen Grove School, Highlands Ranch Headquarters, Indian Park School, Pike's Peak Grange Hall No. 163, Reginald Sinclaire House, Roxborough State Park Archaeological District, Ruth Memorial Chapel, Spring Valley School, Victor House.
"Comprehensive Plan." Update, March 1987. Town of Larkspur. Larkspur, Colorado.
Constructed Highway Plan Sets. Colorado Department of Transportation.
"A Cultural Resource Inventory of Roxborough State Park." Marcia Tate. 1979. Office of the State Archaeologist. Colorado Historical Society. Denver, Colorado.
Deeds and Grantee-Grantor Books. Douglas County Clerk and Recorder's Office. Castle Rock, Colorado.
"Douglas County, Colorado Subdivisions." Map. December 1996. Douglas County Assessor's Office. Castle Rock, Colorado.
Douglas County Historic Resources, Map Appendix. Douglas County Parks and Recreation Department. Castle Rock, Colorado.
"Douglas County Planning & Community Development Interoffice Memorandum." November 6, 1989. File USR 84-5 Cherokee Ranch Sand and Gravel. Douglas County Planning Department. Castle Rock, Colorado.
Douglas County Planning Department. Files for: Antelope Springs; Assembly Estates, # MI62-200; Bald Mountain Estates; Eldorado Acres, # SB69-100; Mesa Grande, # SB73-101; Olen, # MI78-165; Sandi Acres, # MI81-087; Spring Valley West, # MI80-185; True Mountain Estates, # SB68-101; Whispering Pines North.
"Douglas County Population and Development Report, Appendix." Douglas County Planning Department. Castle Rock, Colorado.
"Douglas County Population and Development Report, Master Plan Area Summaries, 35 Acre Developments." Douglas County Planning Department. Castle Rock, Colorado.
"Downtown Urban Design Plan for the Town of Castle Rock." RNL Design. July 7, 1994. Town of Castle Rock. Castle Rock, Colorado.
"Franktown Subarea Master Plan." February 6, 1989. Douglas County Planning Commission. Castle Rock, Colorado.
"Historic Preservation Handbook." May 5, 1994. Town of Castle Rock. Castle Rock, Colorado.
Homestead Papers of Frederick Bartruff. In possession of Bob Shultz.
Homestead Papers of George Engl. In possession of Joe Winkler.
Letter to Perry Park Property Owners. June 1983. Perry Park Metro District Board of Directors. In possession of Sally Maguire.

Letter to Perry Park Residents of Filings 2,3,4,5,6,7. Perry Park Architectural Control Committee. In possession of Sally Maguire.

Meeting Notes. Douglas County Historic Preservation Board. March 18, 1993. Copy in possession of author.

Meeting Notes. Douglas County Historic Preservation Board. September 19, 1996. In possession of author.

Memo. Castle Rock Historic Preservation Board. January 28, 1995. Copy in possession of author.

Memo. Castle Rock Historic Preservation Board. February 11, 1995. Copy in possession of author.

Minutes. Castle Rock Historic Preservation Board. February 1, 1995. Copy in possession of author.

Minutes. Douglas County Commissioners Meeting. July 2, 1984. Douglas County Planning Department. Castle Rock, Colorado.

Minutes. Douglas County Historic Preservation Board. October 21, 1993. Copy in possession of author.

Minutes. Executive Committee of the Colorado Review Board Under the National Preservation Act. May 29, 1981. Colorado Historical Society. Denver, Colorado.

Pemberton File. WPA Files. Colorado Historical Society. Denver, Colorado.

"Perry Park Water and Sanitation District Bond Sale Progress Report." Perry Park Water and Sanitation District President, Glen Reitz, and Perry Park Metro Board President, Sally Maguire. May 22, 1981. In possession of Sally Maguire.

Preemption Papers of Frederick Bartruff. In possession of Bob Schultz.

Rock Ridge Ranch Barn. State Register of Historic Properties File. Colorado Historical Society. Denver, Colorado.

"Sedalia Subarea Master Plan." Sedalia Subarea Planning Committee. Douglas County Planning Department. Castle Rock, Colorado.

"Stipulation for Settlement and Entry of Consent Decree." Civil Action No. 84CV217, District Court, County of Douglas , State of Colorado. Douglas County Planning Department. Castle Rock, Colorado.

"Town of Parker Master Plan." November 1994. Town of Parker. Parker, Colorado.

Warranty Deed from James Kelly to Douglas County Commissioners. February 13, 1884. Local History Collection. Philip S. Miller Library. Castle Rock, Colorado.

MANUSCRIPTS AND ARCHIVAL SOURCES

"A Brief Larkspur Community History." Town of Larkspur. Larkspur, Colorado.

"Cantril School." Kent Brandebery. Copy in possession of author.

Capital Stock Sales Receipt for the Case Cheese and Butter Company. Cherry Valley/Spring Valley Notebook. Local History Collection. Philip S. Miller Library. Castle Rock, Colorado.

Castle Rock Historic Buildings Inventory Forms for: City Hotel, Cantril Courthouse, The Doctor's House, Keystone Hotel, Owens House, St. Francis of Assisi Church. All located at the Philip S. Miller Library, Castle Rock, Colorado.

"Cedar Hill Cemetery." *Douglas County Cemetery Records*. Philip S. Miller Library. Castle Rock, Colorado.

"Christmas Star Lighting Ceremony." Time Schedule and Music Lists. November 28, 1965. Scrapbook of Anne McConnell. Local History Collection. Philip S. Miller Library. Castle Rock, Colorado.

Colorado Cemetery Inscriptions for Douglas County, Kiowa County, Larimer County, Lincoln County, and Prowers County. Denver Public Library. Denver, Colorado.

Dawson Scrapbooks. Transportation Book 1, vol. 46. Colorado Historical Society. Denver, Colorado.

"Determination of Eligibility Notification." Heritage Conservation and Recreation Service. September 17, 1979. National Register of Historic Places. Colorado Historical Society. Denver, Colorado.

Douglas County Historical Society Papers. Local History Collection. Philip S. Miller Library. Castle Rock, Colorado.

Douglas County Historic Preservation Board Files. Historic Buildings Inventory Forms for: Betts Barn, Greenland Ranch, Indian Park Cemetery, Lone Tree School, Newlin Cemetery-Tallman-Newlin Ranch, Spring Valley Cemetery, Toluca-Louviers Depot, Twenty-Mile House Barn, Victor House. All located at Local History Collection. Philip S. Miller Library. Castle Rock, Colorado.

"Douglas County's First Courthouse." Kent Brandebery. Draft. March 28, 1995. Copy in possession of author.

"Drawn Plans for Castle Rock Depot." Castle Rock Historical Society. Copy in possession of author.

Drawn plans for Stone Church Restaurant Addition. Handout. Castle Rock Historic Preservation Board. Copy in possession of author.

"Greenland History." Douglas County Historic Preservation Board Files. Town of Greenland and Greenland Ranch Notebook. Local History Collection. Philip S. Miller Library. Castle Rock, Colorado.

"Highlands Ranch Chronology, AKA Sunland Ranch, Chronology of Hughes and Springer Families." Local History Collection. Philip S. Miller Library. Castle Rock, Colorado.

"Highlands Ranch Facts At A Glance." Mission Viejo Company. Highlands Ranch, Colorado.

"Highlands Ranch Historic Park Master Plan." Draft. HOH Associates, Inc. Revised July 1993. Highlands Ranch Metropolitan District. Highlands Ranch, Colorado.

"The Highlands Ranch: An Historical Survey for the Mission Viejo Company." Alan Culpin. Copy in possession of author.

"Highlands Ranch Mansion Fact Sheet." Mission Viejo Company. Highlands Ranch, Colorado.

"An Historical, Architectural, and Archaeological Study of the Big Dry Creek Cheese Ranch (5DA221) At Highlands Ranch, Douglas County, Colorado." Richard Carrillo. 1986. Copy in possession of author.

"The History of Highlands Ranch: A TimeLine." Mission Viejo Company. Highlands Ranch, Colorado.

"History of Jarre Canyon Cemetery." Douglas County Historic Preservation Board Files. Local History Collection. Philip S. Miller Library. Castle Rock, Colorado.

"History of Jasmine Rebekah Lodge #83." Douglas County Historic Preservation Board Files. Local History Collection. Philip S. Miller Library. Castle Rock, Colorado.

"History of Sedalia." Tom Hier. Local History Collection. Philip S. Miller Library. Castle Rock, Colorado.

"History of Sedalia and Jarre Canyon." Nina Roudebush. October 29, 1981. Local History Collection. Philip S. Miller Library. Castle Rock, Colorado.

"The Indian Raid in Douglas County of 1868." Personal Files of Kent Brandebery.

"Jarre Canyon." Indian Park Association. Newspaper Clippings Notebook. Local History Collection. Philip S. Miller Library. Castle Rock, Colorado.

"John Williams Higby." Louis R. Higby, Jr. Town of Greenland and Greenland Ranch Notebook. Douglas County Historic Preservation Board Files. Local History Collection. Philip S. Miller Library. Castle Rock, Colorado.

Last Will and Testament of J. Louis Killin. February 15, 1965. Local History Collection. Philip S. Miller Library. Castle Rock, Colorado.

Letter. Grace McMurdo Berry. Local History Collection. Philip S. Miller Library. Castle Rock, Colorado.

Letter. Jean Sinclaire Paulk. Research Folder. National Register of Historic Places Files. Reginald Sinclaire House. Colorado Historical Society. Denver, Colorado.

Letter. Susan Anderson. Local History Collection. Philip S. Miller Library. Castle Rock, Colorado.

Letter. William Holmes. Newspaper Clippings Notebook. Local History Collection. Philip S. Miller Library. Castle Rock, Colorado.

Letter to Barbara Norgren, National Register Coordinator, from Edward and Beverly Statter. August 7, 1989. Research Folder.

National Register of Historic Places Files. Reginald Sinclaire House File. Colorado Historical Society. Denver, Colorado.

Letter to Bishop Edwin B. Thayer from Alan Fisher, Acting Colorado State Liaison Officer. April 27, 1973. Colorado Historical Society. Denver, Colorado.

Letter to Brenda Helton from Arthur C. Townshend, State Historic Preservation Officer. March 14, 1978. Colorado Historical Society. Denver, Colorado.

Letter to Castle Rock Historical Society from James E. Hartmann, Colorado State Preservation Officer. May 12, 1993. Copy in possession of author.

Letter to Dr. William J. Murtagh, Keeper of the National Register of Historic Places from Robert Beadles. Spring Valley Cemetery and School. Douglas County Historic Preservation Board Files. Local History Collection. Philip S. Miller Library. Castle Rock, Colorado.

Letter to J.P. Cochran from John Carlson. Castle Rock Historic Preservation Board. August 11, 1994. Copy in possession of author.

Letter to Joseph Blake, Senior Vice President of Mission Viejo Company from Clyde Jones, Chair of the Douglas County Historic Preservation Board. April 12, 1992. Copy in possession of author.

Letter to Julia Stokes at the Colorado Historical Society, from F.E. Jacquot, Manager of Louviers DuPont Plant. February 21, 1935. CWA Files. Colorado Historical Society. Denver, Colorado.

Letter to Mike Davenport, Castle Rock Town Planner from Lane Ittelson, Deputy State Historic Preservation Officer. January 19, 1995. Copy in possession of author.

Letter to M/M Harlan Doud from Gwendolin Ammons McLaughlin. Typescript. Local History Collection. Philip S. Miller Library. Castle Rock, Colorado.

Letter to M/M William Murray from D.H. Hammar. Local History Collection. Philip S. Miller Library. Castle Rock, Colorado.

Letter to Parker Mayor Ann Waterman from Clyde Jones. April 25, 1991. Copy in possession of author.

Letter to Perry Park Country Club members from president Ralph L Reed. June 1, 1981. In possession of Sally Maguire. Perry Park, Colorado.

"Louviers History." Newspaper Clippings Notebook. Local History Collection. Philip S. Miller Library. Castle Rock, Colorado.

"The Manhart Family Book." Local History Collection. Philip S. Miller Library. Castle Rock, Colorado.

"Map of Douglas County, Colorado, Compiled from Official Records by H. H. Curtis." September 1937. Local History Collection. Philip S. Miller Library. Castle Rock, Colorado.

"McMurdo Cemetery." Report by Smoky Hill Trail Chapter of the Daughters of the American Revolution. May 10, 1890. Local History Collection. Philip S. Miller Library. Castle Rock, Colorado.

Minutes of a Meeting Called by W. E. Converse. April 5, 1889. Local History Collection. Philip S. Miller Library. Castle Rock, Colorado.

My Father's Belgium FONDER Roots And Their American Family Descendants. Kathy Wait Fonder. 1991. Local History Collection. Philip S. Miller Library. Castle Rock, Colorado.

Note to author from Arlene Tennal. October 1994.

Notes to author from Karen Kievit. November 1996.

Notes to author from Kent Brandebery. December 1997.

Personal Files of Kent Brandebery.

Prospectus of the Greenland Stock Farm. The Union Real Estate, Live Stock and Investment Company. 1893. Douglas County Historic Preservation Board Files. Local History Collection. Philip S. Miller Library. Castle Rock, Colorado.

Records of Cherry Homemakers Club, 1924-1994. "Correspondence-Business, n.d., 1952-1990," MSS-005, File #7, Box 1. Local History Collection. Philip S. Miller Library. Castle Rock, Colorado.

Records of Cherry Homemakers Club, 1924-1994. "History, El Paso County Extension Homemakers Council." MSS-005, File #14, Box 1. Local History Collection. Philip S. Miller Library. Castle Rock, Colorado.

Records of Cherry Homemakers Club, 1924-1994. "Membership Lists,

Dues Paid, Emphmera, n.d., 1933-1991." File #15, Box 1. Local History Collection. Philip S. Miller Library. Castle Rock, Colorado.

Records of Cherry Homemakers Club, 1924-1994. "Scrapbook, Research Copy, 1957-1985." MSS-005, File #6, Box 2. Local History Collection. Philip S. Miller Library. Castle Rock, Colorado.

Records of Cherry Homemakers Club, 1924-1994. "Secretary's Report, Adult Extension Homemakers Club," in "Secretary's Report, 1966-69." MSS-005, File #42, Box 1. Local History Collection. Philip S. Miller Library. Castle Rock, Colorado.

Registered Survey Notes of Franktown Cemetery. June 20, 1982. Local History Collection. Philip S. Miller Library. Castle Rock, Colorado.

Rock Ridge, Case, Irving, Pine Grove, Spring Valley, Cherry-Pratt, East Cherry Notebook. Douglas County Historic Preservation Board Files. Local History Collection. Philip S. Miller Library. Castle Rock, Colorado.

"Rock Ridge Ranch Barn Grant Application." Handout. Douglas County Historic Preservation Board. Copy in possession of author.

"Roots and Memories." Cora Eddelman Kuykendall. Local History Collection. Philip S. Miller Library. Castle Rock, Colorado.

"Roxborough: A History Etched in Stone." Paula S. Ehresman. October 12, 1993. Local History Collection. Philip S. Miller Library. Castle Rock, Colorado.

"Roxborough State Park Fact Sheet." Roxborough Park File. Colorado Historical Society. Denver, Colorado.

"School Notes and Research." Research Collection of Mary E. Cornish. Local History Collection. Philip S. Miller Library. Castle Rock, Colorado.

"S.M. Dyer House." Dyer House File. Local History Collection. Philip S. Miller Library. Castle Rock, Colorado.

"The South Platte District." James Sullivan. Newspaper Clippings Notebook, Local History Collection. Philip S. Miller Library. Castle Rock, Colorado.

Spring Valley School and Cemetery Notebook. Douglas County Historic Preservation Board Files. Local History Collection. Philip S. Miller Library. Castle Rock, Colorado.

"Survey of Cheese Ranch Farmhouse at Highlands Ranch." Alan Culpin. Inventory Form. Copy in possession of author.

Typewritten Speech of Elizabeth Tallman given at the 40th Anniversary Celebration of Ruth Memorial Chapel. May 24, 1953. Local History Collection. Philip S. Miller Library. Castle Rock, Colorado.

"Victoria's House: Plans of Restoration and Addition of Castle Rock Chamber of Commerce." Michael Collins, architect. January 25, 1995. Copy in possession of author.

"A Window of Opportunity: Cantril School County Museum." Douglas County Historic Preservation Board. April 5, 1994. Copy in possession of author.

"75th Anniversary: Louviers Works, 1908-1983." duPont, E.I. de Nemours & Company. Local History Collection. Philip S. Miller Library. Castle Rock, Colorado.

MISCELLANEOUS

Gravestone of Jonathan H. Tallman. Parker Cemetery. Parker, Colorado.

Gravestone of Victoria Christensen. Cedar Hill Cemetery. Castle Rock, Colorado.

Index